# With
# These Hands

**Women Working on the Land**

**WOMEN'S LIVES WOMEN'S WORK**

## Project Staff

SUE DAVIDSON, *Editor*

MERLE FROSCHL, *Field-Testing Coordinator*

FLORENCE HOWE, *Director*

ELIZABETH PHILLIPS, *Editor*

SUSAN TROWBRIDGE, *Design and Production Director*

ALEXANDRA WEINBAUM, *Teaching Guide Editor*

# With These Hands

## Women Working on the Land

**Joan M. Jensen**

NEW MEXICO STATE UNIVERSITY / LAS CRUCES

**The Feminist Press**

OLD WESTBURY, NEW YORK

**The McGraw-Hill Book Company**

NEW YORK, ST. LOUIS, SAN FRANCISCO

**Library of Congress Cataloging in Publication Data**

Jensen, Joan M
    With these hands.

    (Women's lives/women's work)
    Includes bibliographical references and index.
    1. Rural women—United States—History. 2. Women farmers—United States—History.
3. Women in agriculture—United States—History. 4. Rural women in literature—History.
5. Minority women—United States—History. I. Title.    II. Series.
HQ1419.J39    305.4'3    80-13944
ISBN 0-912670-90-8 (Feminist Press)
ISBN 0-912670-71-1 pbk. (Feminist Press)
ISBN 0-07-020441-1 pbk. (McGraw-Hill)

The findings and conclusions of this volume do not necessarily represent the views of the National Endowment for the Humanities.

**Acknowledgments**

Grateful acknowledgment is made for permission to reprint the following material:
    Anonymous, "Speech of the Cherokee Women." From Archives of the American Board of Commissioners for Foreign Missions. By permission of the Houghton Library, Harvard University.
    Joyce Antler, ed., "I Am Quarlsome When Tired and Fatigued." Originally appeared in "Letters on Maternity" in *Women & Health*. Copyright © 1977 by SUNY/College at Old Westbury. Reprinted by permission of *Women & Health*.
    Harriette Arnow, "Gertie." Reprinted with permission of Macmillan Publishing Co., Inc. from *The Dollmaker* by Harriette Simpson Arnow. Copyright © 1954 by Harriette Simpson Arnow.
    Theresa Banfield, interviewer, "A Woman Works Everywhere." Used by permission of the Dearfield Oral History Project, Boulder, Colorado.
    Katharine Bartlett, "Pueblo Grinding Tools." Excerpted from *Pueblo Milling Stones of the Flagstaff Region and Their Relation to Others in the Southwest: A Study in Progressive Efficiency* by Katharine Bartlett. Copyright © 1933 by Katharine Bartlett. Reprinted by permission of the Museum of Northern Arizona.
    John F. Bayliss, ed., "Farm Women Refugees." Reprinted with permission of Macmillan Publishing Co., Inc. from *Black Slave Narratives* edited and with Introduction by John F. Bayliss. Copyright © 1970 by John F. Bayliss.
    James C. Bonner, ed., "A North Carolina Plantation." From "Plantation Experiences of a New York Woman" edited by James C. Bonner. Originally published in *North Carolina Historical Review*, copyright © 1956 by James C. Bonner. Reprinted by permission of James C. Bonner and *North Carolina Historical Review*.
    Linda Brent, "The Slaves' New Year's Day." From *Incidents in the Life of a Slave Girl* by Linda Brent, copyright © 1973 by Walter Magnes Teller. Reprinted by permission of Harcourt Brace Jovanovich, Inc.
    Josephine C. Brown, "The Rural Social Worker." Reprinted from *The Rural Community and Social Case Work*, by Josephine C. Brown, by permission of the publisher, The Family Service Association of America, New York.

*(acknowledgments continued on page 294)*

# Table of Contents

248 **A Photo Essay**

**Documentary Photography
During the Depression**

# Publisher's Acknowledgments

EARLY IN 1973, Mariam Chamberlain and Terry Saario of the Ford Foundation spent one day visiting The Feminist Press on the campus of the State University of New York, College at Old Westbury. They heard staff members describe the early history of The Feminist Press and its goal—to change the sexist education of girls and boys, women and men, through publishing and other projects. They also heard about those books and projects then in progress; they felt our sense of frustration about how little we were able to do directly for the classroom teacher. Advising us about funding, Terry Saario was provocative. "You need to think of yourselves," she said, "in the manner of language labs, testing and developing new texts for students and new instructional materials for teachers." Our "language" was feminism, our intent to provide alternatives to the sexist texts used in schools. The conception was, in fact, precisely the one on which the Press had been founded.

Out of that 1973 meeting came the idea for the *Women's Lives / Women's Work* project. This project, which would not officially begin for more than two years, has allowed us to extend the original concept of The Feminist Press to a broader audience.

We spent the years from 1973 to 1975 assessing the needs for a publication project, writing a major funding proposal, steering it through two foundations, negotiating with the Webster Division of McGraw-Hill, our co-publisher. We could not have begun this process without the advice and encouragement of Marilyn Levy of the Rockefeller Family Fund, from which we received a planning grant in 1973. For one year, Phyllis Arlow, Marj Britt, Merle Froschl, and Florence Howe surveyed the needs of teachers for books about women, reviewed the sexist bias of widely used history and literature texts, and interviewed editorial staffs of major educational publishers about their intentions to publish material on women. The research accumulated provided a strong case for the grant proposal first submitted to the Ford Foundation in the summer of 1974.

During the winter of 1974–75, Merle Froschl, Florence Howe, Corrine Lucido, and attorney Janice Goodman (for The Feminist Press) negotiated a co-publishing contract with McGraw-Hill. We could not have proceeded without the strong interest of John Rothermich of McGraw-Hill's Webster Division. Our co-publishing agreement gives control over editorial content and design to The Feminist Press; McGraw-Hill is responsible for distribution of the series to the high

school audience, while The Feminist Press is responsible for distribution to colleges, bookstores, libraries, and the general public.

In the summer of 1975, the final proposal—to produce for co-
publication a series of twelve supplementary books and their accompanying teaching guides—was funded by the Ford Foundation and
the Carnegie Corporation. Project officers Terry Saario and Vivien
Stewart were supportive and helpful throughout the life of the project.
In 1978, The Feminist Press received funds from the National
Endowment for the Humanities to help complete the project. Additional funds also were received from the Edward W. Hazen Foundation
and from the Rockefeller Family Fund.

Once initial funding was obtained, The Feminist Press began its
search for additional staff to work on the project. The small nucleus of
existing staff working on the project was expanded as The Feminist
Press hired new employees. The *Women's Lives / Women's Work*
project staff ultimately included six people who remained for the
duration of the project: Sue Davidson, Merle Froschl, Florence Howe,
Elizabeth Phillips, Susan Trowbridge, and Alexandra Weinbaum. Mary
Mulrooney, a member of the project staff through 1979, thereafter
continued her work as a free-lance production associate for the duration
of the project. We also wish to acknowledge the contributions of Dora
Janeway Odarenko and Michele Russell, who were on the project staff
through 1977; and Shirley Frank, a Feminist Press staff member who was
a member of the project staff through 1979. Helen Schrader, also a
Feminist Press staff member, participated on the project during its first
year and kept financial records and wrote financial reports throughout
the duration of the project.

The *Women's Lives / Women's Work* project staff adopted the
methods of work and the decision-making structure developed by The
Feminist Press staff as a whole. As a Press "work committee," the project
met weekly to make decisions, review progress, discuss problems. The
project staff refined the editorial direction of the project, conceptualized
and devised guidelines for the books and teaching guides, and identified
prospective authors. When proposals came in, the project staff read and
evaluated the submissions and made decisions regarding them.
Similarly, when manuscripts arrived, the project staff read and
commented on them. Project staff members took turns drafting
memoranda, reports, and other documents. And the design of the series
grew out of the discussions and the ideas generated at the project
meetings. The books, teaching guides, and other informational
materials had the advantage, at significant stages of development, of the
committee's collective direction. All major project policy decisions

about such matters as finance and personnel were made by The Feminist Press Board at its monthly meetings.

Throughout the life of the project, The Feminist Press itself continued to function and grow. Individuals on staff who were not part of the *Women's Lives / Women's Work* project provided support and advice to the project: Jeanne Bracken, Brenda Carter, Ranice Crosby, Shirley Frank, Brett Harvey, Frances Kelley, Emily Lane, Carol Levin, Kam Murrin, Karen Raphael, Marilyn Rosenthal, Helen Schrader, Nancy Shea, Nivia Shearer, Anita Steinberg, Sharon Wigutoff, and Sophie Zimmerman.

The process of evaluation by teachers and students before final publication was as important as the process for developing ideas into books. To this end, we produced testing editions of the books. Field-testing networks were set up throughout the United States in a variety of schools—public, private, inner-city, small town, suburban, and rural—to reach as diverse a student population as possible. We field tested in the following cities, regions, and states: Boston, Massachusetts; Tampa, Florida; Greensboro, North Carolina; Tucson, Arizona; Los Angeles, California; Eugene, Oregon; Seattle, Washington; Shawnee Mission, Kansas; Martha's Vineyard, Massachusetts; New York City; Long Island; New Jersey; Rhode Island; Michigan; Minnesota. We also had an extensive network of educators—350 teachers across the country—who reviewed the books in the series often using sections of books in classrooms. From teachers' comments, from students' questionnaires, and from tapes of teachers' discussions, we gained valuable information both for revising the books and for developing the teaching guides.

Although there is no easy way to acknowlege the devotion and enthusiasm of hundreds of teachers who willingly volunteered their time and energies, we would like to thank the following teachers—and their students—with whom we worked directly in the testing of *With These Hands: Women Working on the Land.* In Kansas, David Wolfe, District Social Studies Supervisor, helped to contact the following teachers in the Shawnee Mission school district: Vicki Arndt-Helgesen, Jerry Hollembeak, Warren Knutson, Mike Ruggles, John Seevers, Pat Spillman, Marjorie Webb. In Michigan, Jo Jacobs, Coordinator, Office for Sex Equity in Education—with the assistance of Karla Atkinson and Karen Cottledge—helped to contact the following teachers in schools throughout the state: Jo Ann Burns, Mary Ellen Clery, Frances Deckard, Suzanne du Bois, Karen Fenske, Del Gerhardt, Pat Geyer, Shirley Harkless, Sylvia Lawhorn, Susan McFarland, Lenore Morkam, Bert Montiegel, Florence Pangborn, Rose Riopelle, Judy Rogers, Ruth Valdes,

Joan Von Holten. In Minnesota, Don Hadfield, Specialist, Equal
Educational Opportunities Section, State Department of Education,
helped to contact the following teachers: Sonja Anderson, Edward
Bauman, Barbara Braham, Colleen Clymer, Katharine Dumas, Judie
Hanson, Sandy Johnson, Maya Jones, Gary Olsen, Kathryn Palmer,
Dorothy Rock.

Three times during the life of the *Women's Lives / Women's Work*
project, an Advisory Board composed of feminist educators and scholars
met for a full day to discuss the books and teaching guides. The valuable
criticisms and suggestions of the following people who participated in
these meetings were essential to the project: Mildred Alpern, Rosalynn
Baxandall, Peggy Brick, Ellen Cantarow, Elizabeth Ewen, Barbara Gates,
Clarisse Gillcrist, Elaine Hedges, Nancy Hoffman, Susan Klaw, Alice
Kessler-Harris, Roberta Kronberger, Merle Levine, Eleanor Newirth,
Judith Oksner, Naomi Rosenthal, Judith Schwartz, Judy Scott, Carroll
Smith-Rosenberg, Adria Steinberg, Barbara Sussman, Amy Swerdlow.
We also want to express our gratitude to Shirley McCune and Nida
Thomas, who acted in a general advisory capacity and made many
useful suggestions; and to Kathryn Girard and Kathy Salisbury who
helped to develop the teacher and student field-testing questionnaires.

Others whom we want to acknowledge for their work on *With These
Hands* are Ruth Adam for restoration of the historical photographs;
Charles Carmony, who prepared the index; Angela Kardovich of
McGraw-Hill for administrative assistance; Miriam Weintraub and Les
Glass of Weinglas Typography Company for the text composition; and
Irwin Rabinowitz for the music engraving on pages 18–19.

The work of the many people mentioned in these acknowledgments
has been invaluable to us. We would also like to thank all of you who
read this book—because you helped to create the demand that made the
*Women's Lives / Women's Work* project possible.

THE FEMINIST PRESS

# Author's Acknowledgments

WHILE WRITING IS A SOLITARY OCCUPATION, a writer quickly becomes aware of her dependence on others. Over the almost three years that this book has been in process, I have leaned heavily on some friends for support and have not been able to give other friends the support I wanted to give to them. Many psychic and material gifts and debts, therefore, have made this book possible. Among those to whom I am especially indebted are the women of The Feminist Press. Their original enthusiasm for the project, their careful criticism, their capacity for hard work, and their attention to detail have truly amazed me. Sue Davidson, who worked with me as editor, seemed tireless as she flew back and forth between New York and Seattle, and wrote long letters of encouragement, comment, and query. More than anyone, she has nurtured both me and this book as it took form. Her work has been a model of feminist editing.

JOAN M. JENSEN
*Las Cruces, New Mexico*

# Introduction

THE TASK OF FINDING MATERIAL to document a history of women working on the land is a difficult one—more difficult than I had at first expected. The problem, certainly, is not that farm women have been few in number: since a majority of women lived on farms during most of North America's history, millions of our foremothers were farm women. They grew up as farm daughters; learned the necessary skills to survive in a rural, often primitive, environment; worked most of their lives on the land to which they returned at their deaths. My main goals, as I began to assemble this anthology, were to reveal that these numerous farm women included many races, ethnic groups, and classes, and to make clear both the diversity and the likenesses of the work experiences of women in different cultures, and at different times. In short, I wanted to bring to light a new, culturally pluralistic concept of who those farm foremothers were and how they lived.

Because so many farm women crowd our past, I thought my primary job would be one of selection. I wanted documents that would explain what was most significant about the relationship of women to the land—how women felt about their work, how they learned the necessary skills to survive on the land, how their work affected those among whom they lived and labored, and the ways in which they looked at their own lives as women. And I wanted the documents to be as close as possible to the first-hand thoughts and feelings of the women themselves. I hoped to find their own words, and where I could not, to find the words of people who understood the circumstances of their lives and who were skilled in conveying a real feeling for the experiences of farm women.

I soon became aware of some serious difficulties in documenting this large part of women's past. These difficulties need to be discussed, because they help explain why rural women have been neglected by history.

Perhaps the most important factor in this neglect is that historians have relatively few written records from which to derive the rural women's past. Most rural women left no written records of their own lives because they lacked the tools: they were not literate. Among Native American women, most had no written language of their own, and little motivation for utilizing English until contemporary times. Afro-Americans in the South, under slavery, were forbidden by law to learn to read or write, and in practice were denied literacy long after slavery was abolished. Until the late nineteenth century, few Hispanic women had the opportunity to become literate in either Spanish or English, and only in recent times have they begun to explore their family and community experiences in prose and poetry. Deprived of written communication to a severe extent, each of these groups maintained strong oral traditions for the preservation of their culture and heritage. In this process, women were important contributors; but few were able to leave any records written down by themselves.

Even among Euro-American women (as I will refer to women whose ancestors came from Europe), access to literacy was limited until the early nineteenth century; and the literacy of rural women lagged behind that of urban women. Some upper-class women of the eighteenth century wrote letters and diaries which have survived. But diary accounts by rural women outside of New England were rare before the 1830's. By 1850, literacy rates for women in the educationally advanced areas of New England were over 95 percent, but only 75 percent for white women in the South. Even literacy, usually measured by the ability to write one's name, did not in itself mean that rural women would leave written records.[1]

Although some accounts written by rural women before the mid-nineteenth century have undoubtedly been lost, it is not likely that a great many such accounts ever existed. Not only were most farm women unable to communicate in written form, but they had little time or energy to spare for it. The work of most farm women—perhaps with the exception of the Native American women of some tribes—was so demanding and so fully occupied them that either diary or letter writing would have been a luxury hard to accommodate. Moreover, their time was seldom their own; they could be and were interrupted at any pursuit, particularly at such a private leisure activity as reading or writing. Needlework or visiting probably occupied those moments when, at the end of a long day or during winter months, farm women might have jotted down a few words about their lives.

Finally, it is unlikely that most early farm women felt a pressing need for written communication. Among all rural women, the oral tradition predominated. Skills were learned not from books, or in school, but from other persons. Practical experiment tested and expanded these skills. Kin lived close enough for the exchanging of family news and the recounting of experiences. Even the need for poetic expression might be satisfied, in part, through the re-telling of folk tales and the embellishment of ballads. It was not until the disruption of settled farming communities in the early nineteenth century, and with it, the more frequent and more distant moves West, that women in any numbers found the occasion for utilizing the literacy they had so recently attained. Letters home kept women in touch with their families.

These factors, then—illiteracy, long and exhausting work hours, scarcity of uninterrupted leisure, and the absence of a practical need for written communication—all affected the amount of written material that has come down to us.

Nevertheless, because so many women worked on the land over so many years of American history, the number of documents describing the work of farm women is astounding. Tracking down documents, letters, and diaries mentioned fleetingly by various authors—usually in passing, in a few words; more often in a brief footnote—I discovered that women had left far more records than their treatment by historians has led us to believe. For example, it was in an obscure footnote that I found a reference to the 1818 speech of Cherokee women reproduced in this anthology. Yet it provides us with an indication of the way in which Native American women made early protests against demands that their people move West.

By looking through the collections of state archives, university libraries, and local historical associations, I found other accounts, both in manuscript form and published in limited editions. Susan B. Anthony's speech to the farmers of Wayne County turned up in a list of her papers. The Federal Writers'

Project interviews, which were collected in the 1930s and remain scattered throughout the country in state collections, proved to be another rich source of documents.[2] The collection at the University of North Carolina at Chapel Hill, from which the accounts of the Black women Aunt Nellie and Aunt Alice Kee are taken, is only one of many state collections.

A search of old magazines and state historical journals brought to light accounts like Mary Poor's New England diary of the 1830s and Iron Teeth's account of growing up among the Montana Cheyennes during the early nineteenth century. Friends in different parts of the country sent me suggestions of where to look, copies of their favorite accounts, and enthusiastic encouragement for the project. The process of searching produced the selection of writings printed here.[3]

Letters and journals are perhaps the most common types of surviving documents, and a large number are included in this collection. Letters became a regular form of communication between frontier women and their friends and relatives in the East and in Europe. Letters told everyday details of life and contrasted frontier life with life in the more settled areas. Journals were more intimate than letters. They might consist of no more than brief notes about the common chores performed daily. On the other hand, they were often kept as a deliberate record of memorable events in the life of a women, which could be passed on to children and kin. The tradition of journal-keeping was particularly strong among women inheriting the Puritan practice of recording life's events, to be reflected upon by writer or reader.

This anthology also expands the range of farm women's experience through novels and poetry, forms more often looked upon as literature than as history. But women's literature is a valuable key to social and emotional experiences which most historians have yet to tap. Because women in the past were seldom historians, their own accounts of public and private experience were most often cast in the forms of writing allowed to them: novels, poetry, and the kind of journalism that, for the most part, did not require straying very far from home. The literary selections in this anthology show us the ways in which history becomes part of the fabric of women's lives, as women authors explore their own and other's lives through the experiences of farm women. The recording of autobiographical experiences like those of Anne Moody's growing up on a Mississippi farm can convey the social impact of historical conditions, the emotional reaction to rural life as historians have yet to convey them. And even third person accounts, like Willa Cather's Nebraska story of the struggles of Bohemian farm daughters, and Susan Glaspell's description of an Iowa farm woman driven to violence by the isolation of her life, offer us dimensions not yet available through other historical material.

No less important than literary materials for filling in historic gaps are the accounts of farm women who did not write but who told their stories to interested listeners. Through these oral accounts of farm women, written down by others, we gain access to the oral tradition through which these women learned about life and work in their own cultures, and can better understand the lives they led. Anthropologists, historians, relatives, and others interested in preserving the heritage of particular cultures have all used the method of collaboration between the interviewer and the woman recalling her experiences. It is an approach that has made possible the recording of memories of rural farm women who have been too busy and burdened, too unfamiliar with traditional styles of written narrative, or too uncomfortable with autobiographical expression to give voice, alone, to their thoughts and recollections. Thus, among the most valuable sources on the lives of rural women of all cultures are oral accounts of the kind included here, such as that of ex-slave Annie Coley, and the memoirs of the Hispanic woman Eulalia Perez, dictated at the age of ninety-nine.

But if so much material on rural women exists, as this collection indicates, readers will wnat to know why historians have not used this material more extensively. That the materials are widely scattered and that much labor is required to dig them out and bring them together is only a partial answer to this question. To engage in that labor, the historian must consider it a worthwhile undertaking; and women and their work, whether rural or urban, have in the past not been subjects historians have valued. This bias was not altogether due to the fact that historians were predominately male. It also reflected a devaluation of the lives of the poor and minorities by historians of both sexes, who have been primarily concerned with the history of the white males who have held and exercised power in our society. In the value system underlying this bias, people who worked with their hands—women especially— were considered to be performing acts unworthy of the attention of historians. Indeed, for most historians, history *is* the history of white, male, ruling groups.

The documents brought together in this book, then, represent a view of history which takes into major account the lives and contributions of those whom history has passed over, its particular focus being one of the most disregarded groups, the women who have worked on the land. Because the history of their work in North America is so diverse, I have chosen for each section an organizing theme, rather than a strict chronological progression. Sections 1 through 3 contrast ways of life in the early nineteenth century. The first section, "In the Beginning: Native American Women," portrays the work of the women more closely in touch with the land, as a group, than any other: Native Americans. Selections show a culture in which women held spiritual power, which they expressed in terms of their links to the land; controlled the land; took responsibility for its cultivation; developed an attitude toward the land which emphasixed self-sufficiency and independence; and resisted being alienated from it. This section ends with the protest of the Cherokee women against attempts of white people to push them west of the Mississippi.

The second section, "Staying Put, Moving On: Women East and West," concentrates mainly on the type of farm work which Euro-American women performed in the early nineteenth century. Whether on Northeastern farms or the frontier, in nuclear families, extended families, or communal living experiments, women engaged in a wide variety of farm work, including domestic production of yarn and cloth, care of animals and dairies, and processing of all types of food. From these cultures, too, a type of self-sufficiency developed, in which farm families, although dependent upon the market for some material goods, aspired to produce as much food and manufacture as many needed items as possible.[4]

The ways in which the lives of Black women and white women were intertwined in the cotton plantation economy forms the theme of third section, "In Bondage to Cotton: Women of the South." Here the interests, concerns, and experiences of Southern rural women, most of them working at producing cotton, are explored. Self-sufficiency was achieved within the plantation economy, but at the cost of isolating white women and enslaving Black women. Independence of the market was not the goal of this system of farming; and even after slavery ended, Black women remained trapped as sharecroppers in the rural poverty of the South, as were many poor whites.

Section 4, "On the Last Frontier: Women Together, Women Divided," focuses on the experiences of farm women in the area west of the Mississippi, between 1865 and 1910. On this last frontier, women of Native American, Black, and Euro-American cultures (including the Hispanic and Mormon) encountered hard conditions. The search for a farm product to sell on the market, for ways to avoid expending scarce dollars on store bought items, for education, for female companionship, and for ways to build or maintain cultural traditions occur and reoccur in the selections here. In this period, the vision of rural self-sufficiency was fading before the economic realitys of farming in a developing industrial economy. Meanwhile, Native American, Balck, and Hispanic farm women often struggled against systematic efforts to destroy their lives and cultures.

Section 5, "Less Corn, More Hell! Women and Rural Reform," documents the part women played in agrarian reform from 1870 to 1940. Whether as critics of American economic and political institutions in the late nineteenth century grange, alliance, and populist movements, or as early twentieth century creators of progressive techniques to reform rural schools, health facilities, and farm households, women engaged in vigorous collective protest. For those whose lives were not reached by public reform movements, individual action was still possible, to protest and change conditions of personal oppression. The selections reflect both these individual actions and the long-standing involvement of rural women in organized political activity.

The last section, "The Uncertain Harvest: Women Who Don't Give Up," contrasts the movement of women off the land in the great exodus to the cities since the 1930s with the struggles of a small minority of women to remain on the land. The selections document the migration of Black and white farm women to the cities, the activity of Chicanas in organizing farm workers, the efforts of Native American women to resist corporate encroachment on their land. This last section also documents the ways in which generations of farm women of all races have attempted to recreate links to their past, to change or adapt to rural conditions, and to return to the land as a source of political and spiritual power.

Taken together, the documents in this anthology reveal women as active participants in every stage of agricultural production and in every period of agricultural history. They are the dieties who bring seeds and who teach agricultural practices to Native American communities. They are the farmers who control agriculture and land in these communities. They are field workers who labor in the hot sun. They are the administrators of small and large holdings. They are the processors of food. They are the shapers of social customs which define and order the relationships of those who live on the land. From the writings collected here emerge images of women who give to and derive from their work on the land great energy and strength.

The selections in this anthology barely touch the rich historical tradition of women working on the land. They are but small pictures in a vast landscape. These documents are part of the raw materials out of which, some day, the full history of women working on the land can be written.

# With
# These Hands

## Women Working on the Land

*For my mother, who at sixteen*
*ran away from the farm to the city,*

*and for all women who struggle*
*to remain on the land.*

# ONE:
# In the Beginning

## Native American Women

BEFORE EUROPEANS ARRIVED in North America, and for centuries after, Native American women dominated agricultural production in the eastern half of what is now the United States. In other parts of North America, they shared in farming and food

gathering; everywhere they processed food from the land.[1] This collection begins with material which shows the heritage left to us by Native American women working on the land: female deities, women's rites, work methods, protest. The struggle of Native American women to remain on the land will reappear in ensuing sections. No group of American women has struggled longer or harder to maintain their right to the land. The resistance of Native American women to violent displacement has been nourished by their ancient traditions of kinship with the land. This section reflects their feelings of pride and self-sufficiency as early agricultural guardians and workers.

Native American women and men traditionally divided their work in the community. Before the domestication of corn, men hunted and women collected wild seeds and roots. Because of this sexual division of labor, many anthropologists believe that women were the first to domesticate corn in Mexico, about five thousand years ago. By the fifteenth century, women were at work in corn fields as far north as the Great Lakes and as far east as the Atlantic. Seldom were the communities in this area willing to risk relying solely upon the meat of animals hunted by the men. Almost always, the corn harvest, combined with gathered seeds and plants, were the staples for the winter months.[2]

Along the river bottoms in the areas of corn domestication, men and women cleared the land together, then women hoed and planted the corn—each year improving the crop by carefully selecting the best seeds. Often women accompanied the men of the tribe on hunts during the early growing season, then returned to tend their crops, to harvest, and to store the produce for winter. The women joined together in work groups to plant, harvest, and grind the corn. The account by Buffalo Bird Woman included in this section describes this women's work among the Hidatsa. In other parts of the land, men began to join with women in the planting of corn; but much of the responsibility for food growing and collecting remained with women, as Anna Moore Shaw, a Pima, later recalled. Both the accounts by Buffalo Bird Woman and Anna Moore Shaw were written down in the early twentieth century, but they described traditional agricultural practices developed much earlier.

After harvest, women ground the corn in two ways—in the Northeast in large hollowed-out logs, using a long rounded pounder; and in the Southwest, on a stone slab, by rubbing a smaller stone over the surface. In the Southwest, women improved their grinding techniques and grinding implements during these centuries of hand milling. Grinding songs were still being sung by Zuni women when anthropologists visited New Mexico to record their songs in the early twentieth century. Because of their responsibility for the storage of food, and their skill in fashioning woven baskets and clay storage pots, women also took a large part in building shelters. In the Southwest,

Pueblo women erected the walls of large adobe apartment houses; in the Northeast, women wove mats to cover wood frames for shelter.

This division of labor among women and men also affected the social relations in most of the tribes that practiced agriculture. As the tribes settled down to a less migratory life based on agricultural production, women took a prominent part in organizing the social life of their communities. In some tribes, men lived separately in hunting societies, which young boys joined at seven or eight, while women lived in their own groups with the young children. By the time Europeans arrived, households were mixed in some areas, with men and women living together in families. Sometimes fifty or sixty people lived in these households. Regardless of which of the two types of households predominated, the people divided themselves into clan groups. In many of these clan groups, the special responsibilities of the women for managing households led to a matrilineal type of kinship system: groups of related women, their husbands and children lived together; and family descent was often traced through the female line, with children belonging to the mother's clan.[3]

This household arrangement did not mean that women dominated the men, but rather that the two sexes had separate sources of power—the woman in her production of food, and the man in hunting. Women were sometimes chiefs and warriors, but men usually provided the diplomatic and military skills necessary for the communities. The female agricultural and the male hunting groups tended to take care of their own domestic affairs. The women were responsible for the land that each clan cultivated. They formed female work groups and shared child care. The men were responsible for maintaining hunting rights in the areas controlled by their clan, for training male youths, and for the protection of the agricultural villages, which sometimes were quite large. A few of the early Seneca villages, for example, contained 100 to 150 clan households.

Because women had so much responsibility for the crops, many tribes developed stories like that of Sky Woman to explain how important female deities had influenced the development of plants. Other oral traditions, similar to the Corn Woman story, depicted corn as the gift of special women who visited the earth and the communities of particular tribes. Each of these stories, in turn, became a source of additional power for the women in the community because women participated in special rituals dedicated to these female deities, thus adding spiritual power to their economic power. The Seneca women developed an elaborate ritual in which their control over the supply of corn was symbolized in dance and song and in the distribution of specially prepared food to the rest of the tribe. In the early nineteenth century, a visitor to a Northeast village of the Iroquois (the linguistic group to which the Seneca belonged) recorded the following song of thanksgiving dedicated to the three sisters: corn, beans and squash.

On the planted fields I walked,
Throughout the fields I went,
Fair fields of corn I saw there. . . .
I have thanked the sustainers of life.[4]

Into these settled, close-knit agricultural villages came the European invaders. Bringing with them disease and warfare, followed by an economy which drastically changed the living patterns of each community, these Europeans eventually proved an irresistible force moving the Native Americans from their lands. In the Southwest, the Spanish government maintained some Native American communities. Instead of doing only their own work, however, Native American women were forced by missionaries and officials to labor in the fields, build churches, process food, and manufacture clothing for the needs of Europeans as well as for the needs of the community. From its formation in the late eighteenth century, the American government also attempted to replace communal ownership of land, controlled by Native American women, with individual family farms owned by men.

Despite the cultural conflict resulting from different attitudes toward the use of land, there were frequently friendly contacts between European women and Native American women in areas newly settled. Sometimes by choice, sometimes by force, Native American women visited European communities and taught new settlers how to gather herbs and seeds, how to plant, fertilize, and cultivate corn, and how to manufacture items from New World materials. Euro-American women were sometimes captured and held as hostages in Native American villages where they learned the work patterns of Native American women. While for some this was a harrowing experience, for others such as Mary Jemison, whose account is reproduced in the selections that follow, the experience was a pleasant one. In numerous cases, white women refused to return to their old way of life because in their new homes they had more freedom and less work.

Under the pressure of constant warfare, the Native American communities steadily retreated before the wave of aggressive immigrants, and contact grew more strained. Because of their heritage of control of the land, however, Native American women remained active in negotiations involving transfer of land and movement of the tribe. In both the Seneca and the Cherokee tribes, records remain of women intervening in the negotiations of Native American and Euro-American males. While in these cases the women were represented by male speakers, because men and women had divided political councils and men negotiated foreign affairs, there was no doubt that the women influenced the men regarding land settlements and in opposing early removal of tribes westward. The women did not go willingly, but in the East, Native American agricultural communities gradually disappeared, as Europeans pushed forward on the frontier. By 1850, most Native American tribes had moved voluntarily or been forcibly removed to regions beyond the Mississippi River, where the United States government promised they could maintain their nations and live in peace.[5]

# Sky Woman

*For the Iroquois and the Huron, tribes once living in Western New York and Michigan, this story about Sky Woman explained how the first people and crops were created.*

*Children learned this story from the elders of the tribe in the
evening around the fire. Through stories such as these, the
children learned to listen carefully and began their training in
the traditions which bound them together as a people.*

In the beginning, there was nothing but water—nothing but a
wide, wide sea. The only people in the world were the animals
that live in and on water.

Then down from the sky world a woman fell, a divine person.
Two loons flying over the water happened to look up and see her
falling. Quickly they placed themselves beneath her and joined
their bodies to make a cushion for her to rest upon. Thus they
saved her from drowning.

While they held her, they cried with a loud voice to the other
animals, asking their help. Now the cry of the loon can be heard
at a great distance over water, and so the other creatures
gathered quickly.

As soon as Great Turtle learned the reason for the call, he
stepped forth from the council.

"Give her to me," he said to the loons. "Put her on my back.
My back is broad."

And so the loons were relieved of their burden. Then the
council, discussing what they should do to save the life of the
woman, decided that she must have earth to live on. So Great
Turtle sent the creatures, one by one, to dive to the bottom of the
sea and bring up some earth. Beaver, Muskrat, Diver, and others
made the attempt. Some remained below so long that when they
rose they were dead. Great Turtle looked at the mouth of each
one, but could find no trace of earth. At last Toad dived. After a
long time he arose, almost dead from weariness. Searching Toad's
mouth, Great Turtle found some earth. This he gave to the
woman.

She took the earth and placed it carefully around the edge of
Great Turtle's shell. There it became the beginning of dry land.
On all sides, the land grew larger and larger, until at last it formed
a great country, one where trees and other plants could live and
grow. All this country was borne on the back of Great Turtle, and
it is yet today. Great Turtle still bears the earth on his back.

After a while, the woman gave birth to twins, who had very different dispositions. Even before they were born, they struggled and disputed. The mother heard one of them say that he was willing to be born in the usual manner; the other angrily refused to be born in that way. So he broke through his mother's side and killed her.

She was buried in the earth, and from her body grew the plants that the new earth needed for the people who were to be created. From her head grew the pumpkin vine, from her breasts the corn, and from her limbs the bean.

## Corn Woman

*Stories varied from tribe to tribe but agriculturally based communities like the Seminole, the Cherokee, the Seneca, and the Pueblo all had a similar story that explained the origin of corn. The Kikasuki group of Seminoles in Florida told Alice Marriott this twentieth century version, in which Native Americans had already obtained guns from the European invaders.*

**T**wo brothers lived with their grandmother in a chickee in the Big Cypress Swamp.* The old lady kept the house and did the cooking, and the two grandsons went out hunting every day. They were fine hunters. They brought in birds and rabbits, fish and eels; they brought in big game, too—deer and wild turkeys.

They lived in a fine chickee. The uprights were made of cypress poles, and the roof was thatched with palmetto. Every spring the young men gathered fresh palmetto fans and the old lady braided them into the old ones to make the roof thicker and tighter. The floor of the chickee was raised as high above the ground as a flea can jump, and the rafters were set close together

*Chickee:* a type of shelter.

so there was plenty of room above them to store whatever the family had. Off to one side was another storehouse, for dried food, and the old lady had her grandsons build that with solid paling walls so no one could see into it.

One morning the old lady looked out of the door, and saw her grandsons sitting in the dooryard, cleaning their guns. The hibiscus were in bloom, and in the deep heart of every other blossom sat a little frog, greener than any leaves. The humming-birds were lighting up the trumpet flowers like sparks dancing above a fire. It was a beautiful morning, but the twin grandsons sat there, cleaning their guns, and looking as if they didn't have a friend in the world.

"What's the matter with you boys?" their grandmother asked them. "It's a beautiful morning, and all the world's alive and singing. Why do you look so sorry?"

"We're tired of always eating meat," Older Brother said. "Why can't we have something else to go with it, for a change?"

"Meat is God's food that he has given you," the old lady replied.

"God is great," said Younger Brother. "If he can give us all the different kinds of meat, perhaps he can give us other foods, too. Then we won't kill so many of His animals, and we won't get so tired of eating them."

"That's an idea," said the grandmother. She stood and watched the boys while they finished cleaning their guns, and then she asked, "What kind of meat do you plan to kill today?"

"Deer," said Older Brother.

"When you come home with the meat, part of the dinner will already be cooked," Grandmother promised. "It will be the most delicious food you ever ate, and we will cook the deer meat to go with it."

All day, while they hunted, the brothers thought and wondered about what their grandmother had told them.

"Do you think she can do it?" Younger Brother asked.

"She's very strong," Older Brother reminded him. "She has a lot of power. I believe maybe she can."

Late in the evening, when the first mists were rising from the bayous, and one little star was trying to show itself off in the west, the brothers came home. As they came near the chickee, they smelled a food-smell that was like perfume.

"Grandmother! Grandmother!" Older Brother called out. "What are you cooking that smells so good?"

"Clean and butcher your deer, and when the meat is cut up, bring it to me," Grandmother instructed them." "Then you will soon taste the most delicious food in the world."

So the boys hurried with their butchering, and when they had the meat cut fine and small, they took it into the house and gave it to their grandmother.

"Thank you! Thank you!" Grandmother said. She lifted the lid of her cooking pot and dropped in the meat, and the smell of the food was so good the boys' mouths watered.

It was a young deer and the meat was tender, so it was quickly cooked. Then Grandmother put the wooden bowls of food on the platform of the chickee, with a wooden spoon for each one, and called to her grandsons, "Come and eat."

The food in the bowls tasted like nothing the boys had ever known before. It was sweet and delicate; it melted on their tongues. "What is it, Grandmother?" they asked her.

"It is called corn," the Grandmother answered, and that was all that she would tell them about it that night. When the boys had eaten all that they could hold of the wonderful corn, they went to bed and slept deeply.

In the morning, the grandmother again looked out, and again she saw the boys cleaning their guns. This time their faces were broad with smiles, and they looked as if they loved the whole world.

"What are you going to hunt today?" Grandmother asked.

"Wild turkeys," Older Brother replied. "We thought they would taste good if they were cooked with corn."

"Wild turkeys are always good," his grandmother agreed. "Tonight, though, I will have another new food for you, in case you get tired of eating corn."

"What do you think that new food will be?" Younger Brother asked, as the two boys entered the woods.

"I don't know," Older Brother replied, "but I don't think I will like it as well as corn, whatever it is."

But all the same the boys were in such a hurry to taste their new surprise dinner that they drew and plucked the wild turkeys they had shot as they walked along the path on their way home. When they got to the chickee, the twins smelled the new food cooking. It smelled like corn, but at the same time, it smelled different, with a perfume of its own.

"I see that I won't have to wait long for you to cut up the meat," was all their grandmother said. She took the wild turkeys over to the cooking fire and plopped them into the pot, and soon the meal smelled better than ever.

"Come and eat," Grandmother called to the twins, and when they had washed their hands and faces at the water jar, they came in under the thatched roof, filled their bowls from the cooking pot, and began to eat.

"What is this food called?" Older Brother asked his grandmother, when he and Younger Brother had eaten all that they could hold.

"It is called grits," Grandmother said. "It is another of the gifts of corn."

The next day the boys killed muskrats, and as they came near their home a new delicious smell met them.

"Where does Grandmother get all these foods?" Younger Brother asked of Older Brother.

"I don't know," Older Brother answered, "but maybe we can find out. Tomorrow, when I go hunting, you hide in the clump of trees behind the house. Watch and see what Grandmother does. Then perhaps we will know where these corn foods come from."

That night Grandmother had a pot of dried cracked corn simmering on the fire. She cut the muskrats into it, and when the meat had cooked the brothers ate their fill.

"Oh, that was good, Grandmother," they told her. "That was delicious. How many ways are there to cook this corn food?"

"No one person will ever know how many," Grandmother answered. "No one person can ever live long enough to take all the good gifts that corn has for humankind."

The next morning the brothers left home together, but when they reached a wild orange grove a little way from their home the Younger Brother dropped back and hid, and Older Brother went on alone.

It seemed to Younger Brother that he waited a long, long time, hidden in that orange grove. It was mid-June and the trees were loaded with blossoms. They were as perfumed as cooking corn, and Younger Brother grew hungry, waiting there.

At last he saw his grandmother come out from the chickee, and go to the storehouse. The sun was high in the sky, so Younger Brother knew that it must be midday, the time when Grandmother usually started to cook their evening meal. He slipped through the grove without a sound, and at length he reached a place where he could peek through the open door into the darkness of the storehouse.

Younger Brother saw Grandmother spread a dried deer skin on the floor, and place a wooden bowl beside it. Then she stood on the hide, and rubbed her open palms down her sides. Wherever Grandmother's hands passed, grits tumbled from her body onto the deer skin. When she had enough grits for their evening meal, Grandmother gathered the edges of the deer skin together, and went back to the chickee.

Younger Brother turned away, and walked quickly along the hunters' path to meet Older Brother. When they came face to face, Older Brother asked, "Did you find out where our grandmother gets the corn?"

"Yes," Younger Brother replied, "it is part of herself. She rubs her hands against her sides, and the corn falls on the earth for her to gather up."

"That's impossible!" Older Brother exclaimed. "Why would she want to do that? Why does she think we want to eat our own grandmother? Only Caddos and Tonkawas are cannibals! Mikasukis would never eat anybody."

They hurried home, and dinner was waiting for them. Grandmother had added dried turkeys from the storehouse to the grits. Even though the food looked tempting and smelled delicious, the brothers could hardly swallow it.

"What's the matter?" Grandmother asked them. "Aren't you hungry? Don't you like my cooking, all of a sudden?"

"The food's as good as always," Older Brother said. "We're just too tired from hunting to eat much, that's all."

"Aieee!" Grandmother cried, and she fell to the floor, almost without life. The brothers picked her up and laid her on her pallet in the chickee.

"What can we do to help you?" Younger Brother cried. "Dear Grandmother, what has happened? What is it you have felt, to make you so sick?"

"You have found out my secret," Grandmother barely breathed, without opening her eyes. "Now that my secret is known, I must prepare to leave you soon."

"Dear Grandmother, don't die!" Older Brother begged. "Stay with us; don't leave us. How can we live without you?"

"I will always be with you," Grandmother assured him, and slowly her eyelids raised, and her eyes lay open in her gray face. "When I am gone, you must do exactly what I am going to tell you. Bury me in the field near the bayou; the field that never floods. Lay my body in the earth, and cover me with the rich soil. Then build a fence of sticks all around my grave, to keep out the wild hogs, and don't let anyone come near my burial place. Next spring, you will see something green come out of the earth where I am buried. The plant will grow tall, tall. Its top will blossom. There will be beautiful tassels along its sides. Leave my plant alone, and in the fall, harvest the heads that bear the tassels. Dry the grains, and store them in a clean dry place where the rats can not get them, until next spring."

"What shall we do then, Grandmother?"

"When the corn is dried and laid away, go out into the world, and find yourselves wives. Bring them home, and when spring comes let them plant the corn. Make little hills in rows in the fields, and plant four grains of corn and four beans in each hill. Then the corn and beans will grow together, and you may plant their little sister, the squash, between the rows. If your wives take good care of their gardens, then you will always live well, because you are both good hunters. As long as you have the corn, I will be with you."

Then Grandmother sighed, because she was old and tired and she had given up all her power. Before she died, she blessed her grandsons, and wished them well with their lives, their wives, and their gardens.

And the grandsons obeyed the old lady, and buried her as she had instructed them to do. Then, in the fall, when the corn was harvested and dried and stored, the two brothers went out and found wives for themselves.

So corn came to the Mikasukis, and so the Mikasukis learned to garden.

# Seneca Corn Rite

*Rituals performed by women in agricultural societies symbolized both their importance in providing for the community and their control over the food supply. Seneca Arthur C. Parker explains the corn ritual of the women of the Seneca, still performed in the early twentieth century. After this ceremony, the women distributed the corn pudding to the rest of the members of the tribe.*

The corn was carefully dropped in the hills so as not to break the germs which had nearly burst through. Among the Senecas, in planting corn the seeds of the squash and bean were sown in every seventh hill because it was thought that the spirits of these three plants were inseparable. They were called Diohe′ ko, these sustain us. In the Green Corn Thanksgiving the leader rises and says, "Diettino nio′ diohe′ ko, we give thanks to our sustainer."

Certain women banded themselves together in a society called the Toñwisas or Towísas Oä′no. They propitiated the spirits of the three sisters by certain ceremonies. At the closing of the ceremony the head-woman chants the Dio′hēko song as she leads her band about a kettle of corn pudding. She carries an armful of corn on the cob; in her right hand she holds some loose beans, and in her left some squash seeds, the emblems of fertility. The Towii′sas hold one ceremony each year, unless some calamity threatens the harvest.

# Pueblo Grinding Tools

*For over 10,000 years, grinding tools have been used in the Southwest to pulverize wild and domesticated seeds into meal. Anthropologist Katharine Bartlett recreates the way in which Pueblo women probably refined and improved the*

*process of grinding with the metate (from an old Aztec word
to describe the concave bottom stone) and the hand-held
mano (Spanish for hand).*

In the early times when hunting was the major occupation,
and wild nuts and seeds were gathered to augment the food
supply, each family probably had a crude metate, on which the
woman ground the seeds. Any flat rock served her purpose, yet
perhaps she might have found a particularly suitable one which
she cherished, and took with her as the family followed the
game. One metate was enough for her purpose. When she
prepared the seeds for the family to eat, she sat down on the
ground beside the flat stone, and with a few blows and a circular
motion of her mano, held in one hand, reduced the seeds to an
edible state.

At a later date, the people began to grow corn, which kept
them at home to tend to their crops. Corn became the staple food
and more and more was used. Then the woman instead of
casually sitting on the ground and grinding with one hand,
propped up her lower milling stone on several rocks, kneeled
behind it, took a long mano in both hands, set it flat on the
metate, and really got down to work. Her metate had a trough so
the meal did not spill off on the sides. In her pithouse home,
there was not much room and when she could, she worked
outside. Her metates had to be portable so that she could carry
them in and out, and so that they could easily be put out of the
way. She had several metates of varying grades of coarseness, for
now the family lived in one place and the heavy grinding stones
no longer had to be carried about as perhaps they formerly were.

By and by, the woman, who now had a masonry house with
several rooms, thought it would be nice to have one of her
metates that she used most often permanently set up. She had
plenty of room in her house, and she could easily spare enough
space, so she set one of her old troughed metates into the floor at
a steeper angle than she had been using it and surrounded it by a
slab box, neatly held in place with adobe. This was the first
mealing bin. By this time she had discovered that it was easier to
grind if she had something to brace her feet against, so the

mealing bin was backed up against a wall leaving just enough space for her to kneel in.

The next time she made a bin, she realized it was useless to spend time pecking out the trough in the metate as she had done, because now she had the bin to hold the meal. She used a flat slab of stone to grind on, and found it worked just as well. After this she began to use her mano in a new way so that it had two grinding surfaces. It did not become worn out so soon and the more triangular it became the easier it was to hold, and moreover it saved her the trouble of spreading the meal over the grinding stone as frequently as she had done. As houses increased in size, and rooms were built for storage and other special purposes, there was space enough in the living rooms for several metates to be set up permanently in bins, so that the meal could be lifted from one metate directly to the next as it became ground successively finer and finer. Also several women could grind at the same time and enjoy each other's company.

All this progress in milling stones took many hundreds of years to accomplish, yet each new step made the task easier or quicker or more sociable for the women who were condemned to spend most of their lives grinding corn.

## Zuni Grinding Song

*Bracing her feet against the wall, the woman grips the mano in her two hands, pushing and pulling it back and forth across the metate. As the women grind, they sing. Natalie Curtis, who collected Pueblo songs in the early twentieth century, describes the singing of the Zuni women at work and records one of their traditional grinding songs.*

The corn is placed on the stone and is ground by rubbing over it another cubelike stone. The woman kneels to the work and sways back and forth with rhythmic swing. As she grinds she sings. There are usually two or three metates in each house, and two or three women often grind and sing together. Sometimes a woman will invite many others to her house to grind, spreading for her guests a mid-day feast. The visitors grind the corn of their hostess, taking their places in turn at the metates. Those who are resting swell the chorus of the workers, and the flutelike voices rise high and clear over the rhythmic scraping of the stones.

| **Ockaya** | **Corn-Grinding Song** |
|---|---|
| Elu homa | O, my lovely mountain |
|    Yallanne! |    To'yallanne! |
| Elu homa | O, my lovely mountain, |
|    Yallanne! |    To'yallanne! |
|    Yallanne! |    To'yallanne! |
| Awehiwia' kwai-i, | High up in the sky, |
| Imuna Kwagia | Rain Makers |
| Lonan-eshto 'wiyane, | See Rain Makers seated, |
|    He-ya, ha-ya, he-ya! | Hither come the rain-clouds now. |
| Liwamani |    He-ya, ha-ya, he-ya! |
| Iyuteapa | Behold, yonder |
| Awiyane, | All will soon be abloom |
| Hawilana litla. | Where the flowers spring— |
| | Tall shall grow the |
| |    youthful corn-plants. |

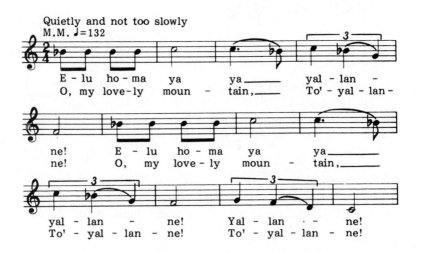

A - we-hiwi- a' kwai – i, Im - u - na kwa -
High up in the sky, see Rain - ma-kers seat -

gia, Lo - nan - esh - to 'wi - ya - ne,
ed, Hi - ther come the rain - clouds_ now,

He ya____ ha ya he ya!____

Li - wa - ma - ni i - yu -
Be - hold,____ yon - der all will soon

te-a -pa A - wi ya - ne Ha - wi -
be a-bloom Where the flow - ers__ spring, Tall shall

la - na li - i - tla.____
grow the youth - ful corn - plants.____

# Buffalo Bird Woman

*Hidatsa, Buffalo Bird Woman grew up along the banks of
the Missouri River, where she tended her plots of corn, bean,
and squash. It was about 1917 when she described to
anthropologist Gilbert L. Wilson how women of her family
once tilled in what is now North Dakota.*

liked to go with my mothers to the cornfields in planting
time, when the spring sun was shining and the brids singing

in the tree tops.* How good it seemed to be out under the open sky, after the long months in our winter camp! A cottonwood tree stood at a turn of the road to our field. Every season a pair of magpies built their nest in it. They were saucy birds and scolded us roundly when we passed. How I used to laugh at their wicked scoldings!

I am afraid I did not help my mothers much. Like any young girl, I liked better to watch the birds than to work. Sometimes I chased away the crows. Our corn indeed had many enemies, and we had to watch that they did not get our crop. Magpies and crows destroyed much of the young corn. Crows were fond of pulling up the plants when they were a half inch or an inch high. Spotted gophers dug up the roots of the young corn, to nibble the soft seed.

When our field was all planted, Red Blossom used to go back and replant any hills that the birds destroyed. Where she found a plant missing, she dug a little hole with her hand and dropped in a seed, or I dropped it in for her.

It was hard work, stooping to plant in the hot sun, and Red Blossom never liked having to go over the field a second time. "Those bad crows," she would groan, "they make us much trouble."

My grandmother Turtle made scarecrows to frighten away the birds. In the middle of the field she drove two sticks for legs, and bound two sticks to them for arms; on the top, she fastened a ball of castaway skins for a head. She belted an old robe about the figure to make it look like a man. Such a scarecrow looked wicked! Indeed I was almost afraid of it myself. But the bad crows, seeing the scarecrow never moved from its place, soon lost their fear, and came back.

In the months of midsummer, the crows did not give us much trouble; but, as the moon of Cherries drew near, they became worse than ever. The corn had now begun to ear, and crows and blackbirds came in flocks to peck open the green ears for the soft

*Buffalo Bird Woman was the offspring of a polygamous marriage; hence, her plural reference, mothers. Polygamy was apparently relatively uncommon among Native Americans, and usually indicated inequal wealth in these normally egalitarian societies.

kernels. Many families now built stages in their fields, where the girls and young women of the household came to sit and sing as they watched that crows and other thieves did not steal the ripening grain.

We cared for our corn in those days, as we would care for a child; for we Indian people loved our fields as mothers love their children. We thought that the corn plants had souls, as children have souls, and that the growing corn liked to hear us sing, as children like to hear their mothers sing to them. Nor did we want the birds to come and steal our corn, after the hard work of planting and hoeing. Horses, too, might break into the field, or boys might steal the green ears and go off and roast them.

A watchers' stage was not hard to build. Four posts, forked at the tops, upheld beams, on which was laid a floor of puncheons, or split small logs, at the height of the full grown corn. The floor was about four feet long by three wide, roomy enough for two girls to sit together comfortably. Often a soft robe was spread on the floor. A ladder made of the trunk of a tree rested against the stage. The ladder had three steps.

A tree was often left standing in the field, to shade the watchers' stage. If the tree was small and more shade was wanted, a robe was stretched over three poles leaned against the stage. These poles could be shifted with the sun.

Girls began to go on the watchers' stage when about ten or twelve years of age, and many kept up the custom after they were grown up and married. Older women, working in the field and stopping to rest, often went on the stage and sang.

There was a watchers' stage in my mothers' field, where my sister, Cold Medicine, and I sat and sang; and in the two weeks of the ripening season we were singing most of the time. We looked upon watching our field as a kind of lark. We liked to sing, and now and then between songs we stood up to see if horses had broken into the field or if any boys were about. Boys of nine or ten years of age were quite troublesome. They liked to steal the green ears to roast by a fire in the woods.

I think Cold Medicine and I were rather glad to catch a boy stealing our corn, especially if he was a clan cousin, for then we could call him all the bad names we wished. "You bad, bad boy," we would cry. "You thief—stealing from your own relatives! *Nah, nah*—go away." This was enough; no boy stayed after such a scolding.

Most of the songs we sang were love-boy songs, as we called them; but not all were. One that we younger girls were fond of singing—girls, that is, of about twelve years of age—was like this:

You bad boys, you are all alike!
Your bow is like a bent basket hoop;
Your arrows are fit only to shoot into the air;
You poor boys, you must run on the prairie barefoot, because you
have no moccasins!

This song we sang to tease the boys who came to hunt birds in the near-by woods. Small boys went bird hunting nearly every day. The birds that a boy snared or shot he gave to his grandparents to roast in the lodge fire; for, with their well-worn teeth, old people could no longer chew our hard, dried buffalo meat.

Here is another song; but, that you may understand it, I will explain to you what *eekupa* means. A girl loved by another girl as her own sister was called *eekupa*. I think your word "chum," as you explain it, has nearly the same meaning. This is the song:

"My *eekupa*, what do you wish to see?" you said to me.
What I wish to see is the corn silk peeping out of the growing ear;
But what *you* wish to see is that naughty young man coming!

Here is a song that older girls sang to tease young men of the Dog Society who happened to be going by:

You young man of the Dog Society, you said to me,
"When I go east with a war party, you will hear news of me
how brave I am!"
I have heard news of you;
When the fight was on, you ran and hid;
And you still think you are a brave young man!
Behold, you have joined the Dog Society;
But I call you just plain *dog!*

Songs that we sang on the watchers' stage we called *meeda-heeka*, or gardeners' songs. I have said that many of them were love-boy songs, and were intended to tease. We called a girl's sweetheart her love-boy. All girls, we know, like to tease their sweethearts.

At one side of our field Turtle had made a booth, diamond willows thrust in the ground in a circle, with leafy tops bent over and tied together. In this booth, my sister and I, with our mothers and old Turtle, cooked our meals. We started a fire in the booth as soon as we got to the field, and ate our breakfast often at sunrise. Our food we had brought with us, usually buffalo meat, fresh or dried. Fresh meat we laid on the coals to broil. Dried meat we thrust on a stick and held over the fire to toast.

Sometimes we brought a clay cooking pot, and broiled squashes. We were fond of squashes and ate many of them. We sometimes boiled green corn and beans. My sister and I shelled the corn from the cob. We shelled the beans or boiled them in the pod. My grandmother poured the mess in a wooden bowl, and we ate with spoons which she made from squash stems. She would split a stem with her knife and put in a little stick to hold the split open.

I do not think anything can taste sweeter than a mess of fresh corn and beans, in the cool morning air, when the birds are twittering and the sun is just peeping over the tree tops.

# Mary Jemison

*Mary Jemison (1743–1833) was born on the ship which brought her parents to America from Ireland. At thirteen, she was captured by the Seneca and spent the second half of the eighteenth century living with Native American women. In this account of her life, she explains why she preferred the life of the Seneca women to that of white women.*

I had been with Indians four summers and four winters, and had become so far accustomed to their mode of living, habits and dispositions, that my anxiety to get away, to be set at liberty, and leave them, had almost subsided. With them was my home; my family was there, and there I had many friends to whom I was warmly attached in consideration of the favors, affection and friendship with which they had uniformly treated me, from the time of my adoption.* Our labor was not severe; and that of one year was exactly similar, in almost every respect, to that of the others, without that endless variety that is to be observed in the common labor of the white people. Notwithstanding the Indian women have all the fuel and bread to procure, and the cooking to perform, their task is probably not harder than that of white women, who have those articles provided for them; and their cares certainly are not half as numerous, nor as great. In the summer season, we planted, tended and harvested our corn, and generally had all our children with us; but had no master to oversee or drive us, so that we could work as leisurely as we pleased. We had no ploughs on the Ohio; but performed the whole process of planting and hoeing with a small tool that resembled, in some respects, a hoe with a very short handle.

Our cooking consisted in pounding our corn into samp or hommany, boiling the hommany, making now and then a cake and baking it in the ashes, and in boiling or roasting our venison. As our cooking and eating utensils consisted of a hommany block and pestle, a small kettle, a knife or two, and a few vessels of bark or wood, it required but little time to keep them in order for use.

Spinning, weaving, sewing, stocking knitting, and the like, are arts which have never been practised in the Indian tribes generally. After the revolutionary war, I learned to sew, so that I could make my own clothing after a poor fashion; but the other domestic arts I have been wholly ignorant of the application of, since my captivity. In the season of hunting, it was our business, in addition to our cooking, to bring home the game that was taken by the Indians, dress it, and carefully preserve the eatable meat, and prepare or dress the skins. Our clothing was fastened together with strings of deer skin, and tied on with the same.

*My family: Jemison refers here to her adopted, Native American family.

In that manner we lived, without any of those jealousies, quarrels, and revengeful battles between families and individuals, which have been common in the Indian tribes since the introduction of ardent spirits amongst them.*

## Pima Past

*Anna Moore Shaw, Pima woman of Southern Arizona, learned from her mother the discipline of women's work in a tribe which, in the mid-nineteenth century, depended on both agriculture and food gathering for subsistence. In A Pima Past, Shaw described that work as her mother, Molly, had experienced it in her youth.*

Like the Nile, the Gila and Salt Rivers used to overflow their banks, depositing rich loam. Men and women cooperated and went to the farms to plant seeds. A wooden *gihk,* or shovel, with a sharp end, was used to dig holes. When the tiny seed was thrown in the hole, bare heels were ready to shove the dirt over the seed....

Even though she was only sixteen, Molly knew how to care for a household. As was expected of her, she took over the duties of foodgathering, cooking, and caring for Red Arrow and his family. She went about her work with industry, for she knew she must prove herself to her new family....

She knew how to roast beef, venison, antelope, horsemeat, fish, and locusts to perfection. She expertly jerked left-over meat in the sun for future meals.†

Molly's bean pot was always filled with good-smelling things, even in the summer when her days were often spent gathering wild foods in the desert. In late June and early July, she would

*Ardent spirits: rum.
†Jerked...meat: cut meat into long slices.

join the other women as they took their long *ku'ipad* [saguaro rib poles] out among the giant cacti to harvest the sweet red fruit.*
After boiling it into a syrup, she stored it away for the winter use in little ollas [jars] with round clay lids. The tiny black seeds were shaped into balls and stored; nothing was wasted. A portion of Molly's syrup always went into the large community ollas to ferment into wine for the rain making ceremonies. During this festival, Molly would join the other women on top of the olas kih, where they made fun of the men, who grew silly and clumsy from drinking the fermented fruit.†

After the saguaro gathering came foraging for the buds of the prickly pear and cholla cacti. After picking the fruit with two sticks used like scissors, she placed it in a rough willow basket made to fit her side. Then she roasted it all night on layers of sagebrush in a pit among the rocks. In the morning, she would carefully pull off the thorns, then dry and store the fruit for the winter months.

When caterpillars were plentiful, Molly would gather them in large quantities, cut off their heads, and squeeze out their insides. Then she boiled them in salted water, and when they were cooked, she salted them again before braiding them into long strands for storage.

Next her saguaro rib poles were brought out again—this time to harvest the bean pods of the mesquite tree. Off and on during the hot month of July, Molly would fill her *gioho* [burden basket] with *wihog* [mesquite pods]. She would smile as she watched the village youngsters climb the trees and stamp their feet to shake down the pods for their mothers. The mesquite bean pods were an important staple in the Pima diet. Molly would dry them in the sun, then pound them to a powder in a wooden mortar with a long stone pestle. The powder was made into cakes for nourishment during the winter famine....

In the late summer, when the Indian corn was ripe, she would gather a large pile of mesquite wood and place two or three dozen ears of green corn among the twigs. When a match struck the

---

*Saguaro:* cactus bearing edible fruit.
†*Olas kih:* round houses constructed of brush.

bottom of the wood pile, the corn was roasted. The process was repeated until the desired amount was prepared. When it was cool, Molly husked the corn and spread it in the sun on top of the brush ramada to dry.* The parched corn, called *ga'iwesa*, was ground on a metate with a mano, or rolling stone.

When the muskmelons and squash were ripe, Molly again went to the fields to help cut them into strips, then hang them to dry in the sun. She added the strips to her winter stores, to eat with or without lard when fresh vegetables were not available.

Because she was so industrious, Molly's huge storage baskets were filled by the time winter came. Besides wheat, saguaro syrup, cholla fruit, caterpillars, mesquite cakes, parched corn, melon strips, and squash, they contained dried salt bush leaves to flavor winter foods in the cooking pot. Next to the great storage baskets, animal skin bags held the jerky Molly had put up for the winter meals. There was honey for sweetening and salt for seasoning. From the ceiling hung bunches of willow twigs, cattails, and devil's claws for weaving baskets on winter days.

# Speech of the Cherokee Women

*The United States government promised the Cherokees that they could retain their ancestral lands in Georgia if they would adopt the ways of white men and women. For Cherokee women, this meant withdrawing from field work and confining themselves to traditional white farm women's work: caring for cows and chickens, spinning and weaving cloth, and tending small gardens. Despite the Cherokees' willingness to compromise, white settlers continued to demand their lands. In 1838, nearly 17,000 Cherokees were*

---

*Ramada:* a porch-like structure made of brush and elevated on poles, providing shade and drying space.

*forcibly removed from their homes by a combined force of*
*4,000 United States soldiers, state militia, and volunteers.*
*Families were taken by surprise, driven to stockades at*
*bayonet point, their homes looted and burned. A few*
*Cherokees fled to the mountains of North Carolina, where*
*their descendants still remain. The rest were forced to begin*
*what became known as the "Trail of Tears," an 800 mile*
*winter journey of over three months, in which at least 4000*
*Cherokees died.*

*Cherokee women had, from an early date, protested leaving*
*the ancestral lands. In 1818, after meeting in political council,*
*a delegation of the women urged the men of their nation to*
*resist removal to west of the Mississippi.*

**W**e have called a meeting among ourselves to consult on
the different points now before the council relating to
our national affairs. We have heard with painful feelings that the
bounds of the land we now possess are to be drawn into very
narrow limits. The land was given to us by the Great Spirit above
as our common right, to raise our children upon, and to make
support for our rising generations. We, therefore, humbly
petition our beloved children, the head men of warriors, to hold
out to the last in support of our common rights, as the Cherokee
nations have been the first settlers of this land; we, therefore,
claim the right of the soil.

We well remember that our country was formerly very
extensive, but by repeated sales it has become circumscribed to
the very narrow limits we have at present. Our Father the
President advised us to become farmers—to manufacture our
own clothes, and to have our children instructed. To this advice
we have attended in every thing as far as we were able. Now the
thought of being compelled to remove to the other side of the
Mississippi is dreadful to us, because it appears to us that we, by
this removal, shall be brought to a savage state again; for we have
by the endeavors of our Father the President, become too much
enlightened to throw aside, the privileges of a civilized life.

We therefore unanimously join in our meeting to hold our
country in common as hitherto.

Some of our children have become Christians; we have missionary schools among us; we have heard the gospel in our nation; we have become civilized and enlightened; and are in hopes that in a few years our nations will be prepared for instruction in other branches of sciences and arts, which are both useful and necessary in civilized society.

There are some white men among us, who have been raised in our country from their youth, are connected with us by marriage and have considerable families, who are very active in encouraging the emigration of our nation. These ought to be our truest friends, but prove our worst enemies. They seem to be only concerned how to increase their riches but do not care what becomes of our Nation, nor even of their own wives and children.

# TWO:
# Staying Put, Moving On
## Women East and West

IN THE EARLY DECADES of the nineteenth century, the American frontier advanced rapidly. The industrialization of the East which drove many farmers to seek western open spaces had a continuing and more direct effect upon Eastern farm families. In this section the focus is primarily upon Euro-American women—

those living on the settled Eastern farm lands, and those who joined the stream west.

As the examples in section 1 show, Native American women shared with men in supplying the food for their communities. While the women did much of the heavy labor, including careful hoeing and fertilizing, their field labor was not an excessive burden. They had ample time to process food, to create implements for food processing and containers for storage, to manufacture clothing, and to assist in the building of shelters. The variety of agricultural work done by the women, together with the hunting of the men, led to self-sufficient Native American communities.

Euro-American farm women had a different agricultural tradition. They concentrated their efforts on the processing of food and the manufacture of clothing. They also planted and cultivated gardens; but they did not work in the fields unless the men needed help. Although they could, and often did, plow and plant if men were not available, they did not consider this their primary work. This section shows the kind of work these women performed on self-sufficient farms and their attempts to adapt to the changing conditions brought about by industrialization, new methods of transportation, and the application of technology to agriculture.

The earliest European settlers, women and men of the Plymouth community, were not primarily farmers.[1] Coming in 1620 from urban areas, they were artisans and merchants who learned farming techniques from the Native Americans. Later, with the arrival of English migrants who were farmers rather than city people, the Native American techniques of hoe cultivation and fertilization were gradually abandoned. It was to acquire land that the farm families made the hazardous trip to the colonies. Availability of land and scarcity of labor in the colonies caused the new immigrants to adopt plow culture, which made possible the cultivation of grain on large areas of land.

Many women still worked in the fields, but as the hoe of the Native American woman was replaced by the heavy plow, men came to dominate agriculture. Women increasingly confined themselves to household tasks which included tending poultry, making butter and cheese, working in vegetable gardens, manu-facturing clothing, and caring for children. Except for the Hispanic farm family, in which three generations frequently lived together, the families were usually nuclear. That is, instead of an extended family, in which children remained in the household of their parents, and spouses joined the family, grown children were expected to move out of the household to form new households of their own. While this arrangement created discontinuity in families, it also allowed members and parts of families to move away in search of improved economic op-portunities.

Although the sexual division of labor and the household

arrangements of the Euro-American families differed from those of the Native Americans, in both cases men and women worked together to achieve self-sufficiency. Under the Euro-American system, however, men largely controlled the land, and women had no power to allocate it or to determine how it would be used. In areas influenced by the community property concepts of Roman law—areas eventually taken over by the United States from Mexico and France—women retained some rights in the land; but under the prevailing English common law, women had no right to own land unless they remained single, which few did until the late nineteenth century. Once a woman married, her husband held legal title to the land, and even at his death a widow had a right to only one-third of the land which had accumulated during their married life. Usually, the law did not permit a widow to sell any of her third; legally, it went to the male heirs at her death. During the course of the nineteenth century, women won the right to own land after marriage and to dispose of it freely after a husband's death.

Whether or not women directly controlled the land, their work was essential to the survival of the family farm. No farm could remain independent of the marketplace without the household production of women. The diversity of their production in food and clothing allowed the family to maintain itself with hard work and careful savings. Farm women sold surplus cloth woven in winter to country stores in exchange for most consumption items the family could not produce. Surplus income from the grain crop usually went to buy more land to insure that sons and daughters could set up their own self-sufficient farms.

The diary of Mary Poor describes the manifold kinds and great amount of work performed by women under this farm system. Everyone in the family worked hard, but there were compensations—villages close by for visiting and trading, kin settled on land close enough to visit, a wide range of skills and duties to prevent boredom, and an independence which farm women treasured. Even at eighty-four Mary Poor was paying her own way. She was not dependent upon her children, but upon her ability to work at tasks important for the farm economy.

By 1834, the year of Poor's last diary entries, the old self-

sufficient farm pattern was disintegrating rapidly in the Northeast, as industrialization went forward. Taxes, mortgages, scarcity of land, and the expenses of store-bought manufactured
items all made the family farm more dependent upon the larger
national economy. Agricultural productivity in some areas
decreased because men seldom devoted care to fertilizing or
developing crops which required much hand labor. Even without
a decline in productivity, competition from more productive
western land made the survival of the self-sufficient farm in the
Northeast difficult.[2]

Faced with these conditions, farm families had various choices,
such as learning to diversify their crops, sending daughters into
factories so that their wages might supplement the family
income, setting up communal farms, or migrating to the city.
They could also move west, in an attempt to reproduce the old
agricultural system on the frontier; and this was the favored
choice of agricultural families seeking self-sufficiency.

The diversity of women's work as they moved west is explored
in the pages that follow in writings by Abigail Scott Duniway,
about her life on the Oregon frontier, and by Guri Olsdatter,
about life on the frontier in Minnesota. Most of these frontier
farms had certain similarities: families were nuclear; men
normally plowed the fields; and women tended poultry, made
butter and cheese, worked in vegetable gardens, and cared for
small children. Few women any longer spun or wove. By 1840,
textiles manufactured by mother and daughter had disappeared
in New England, and soon after, women in all but the remotest
frontier areas had abandoned the production of linen and
woolens. Sales of butter and cheese, poultry and eggs, or income
from new "cottage industry" items like shoes and palm hats,
allowed women to buy the textiles they had once manufactured.[3]
By mid-nineteenth century, farm women were caught up in an
agricultural revolution, as farm families produced a cash crop
which would allow them to purchase necessities they could no
longer produce in competition with manufactured items. Manufactured farm implements allowed greater productivity. Purchase of farm implements, in turn, required increased capital.
The pattern was to repeat itself across the country as railroads
put more and more farm communities in touch with the market.

On the West Coast and in the Southwest, Hispanic women on the frontier lived on ranches and farms linked to the Mexican economy through long trails over which products from the frontier passed, and needed supplies for the northern frontier returned. Here a unique type of system, resembling in some respects the Southern plantation system, developed within the missions. An oral history by Eulalia Perez describes the major responsibilities in the day-to-day operation of these vast mission establishments, explaining what they produced for use as well as for export to Mexico.

Corn remained the subsistence crop of the western farms. It was used as a first crop on newly plowed lands and was good for family and livestock. Women cooked corn bread, corn pone, and hominy on the frontier. Under the impetus of the market economy, however, wheat soon became the main cash crop for most farm families in the North and West. Easy to transport, durable, and in demand in the urban areas of the East and in the South, wheat brought women onto the prairie and into isolated homesteads in an attempt to recreate with the men in their families the self-sufficiency and independence of the old farm system.

For those who remained behind, diversifying and increasing their agricultural production was one possible means of remaining on the land. Feminist Susan B. Anthony, herself from a farm family which had encountered economic pressures before moving to Rochester, New York, urged farmers that they not rely solely on grain crops, calling upon farm women to emulate their foremothers' spirit in transforming Eastern agriculture. Some farms in the Northeast did make this transition. Urban populations provided a market not only for wheat, but also for fruits and vegetables, pork, butter, and cheese. Cash from these—which the farm women had produced largely for family consumption in earlier days—allowed farmers to purchase an increasing number of commodities produced in the new industrial centers. Those farms which could not diversify dropped more deeply into debt. Farms not only had more mortgages, but mortgages which city financial institutions were unwilling to hold for long periods of time. Foreclosures and the fear of losing the family farm became more common in New England. When that loss threatened, daughters often climbed into wagons for the journey to mill towns like Lowell, where they worked amid the noise and lint of textile factories to help pay the mortgage with their wages.

Another alternative, that of farming communally, appealed to many farm people. Of the great variety of experiments, descriptions of two are included here. The first example, by Louisa May Alcott, describes a small communal venture of a nuclear family which failed after one year. Alcott, who later assumed the financial responsibility for providing for the family, never tried farming as a means of survival. Writing eventually became her means of bringing income into the family.[4]

The second example is an account of a far more successful venture, that of the Shakers. Founded by Mother Ann Lee in 1774, the Shaker communities abandoned the nuclear structure in favor of one which stressed celibacy and a new sexual division of labor. Men still performed most of the field work, and women did the work of food processing that they had done under the old farm system. But by organizing their work so that they also produced surplus items for the market, especially the herbs and medicines which the Shaker sisters manufactured, the Shaker communities were able to create self-sufficient communities which survived the industrialization of the nineteenth century. All members of these communities had to submit to the authority of elders, but women never had to submit to the authority of men in their work. Women's work groups were supervised by women, and there was strict equality of the sexes in the governing hierarchy. In the songs and dances inspired by the teachings of Mother Lee, women also had greater access to spiritual power than they had in most of the traditional religions and most of the religious communes of the time. Hundreds of women experimented with rural communal living during the early nineteenth century, but only those communes rooted in the new market economy in some manner survived more than a year or two. While they existed, the communes enabled women to experiment with forms of cooperative work similar to those of the Native American communities.[5]

Whether working on communes, on Eastern farms, or in isolated frontier log cabins, farm women labored long and hard. It was this tradition of hard work which the Black leader Sojourner

Truth recalled when she reminded the Akron women's rights convention in 1851 that being a woman had given her no privileges, and that women could not be denied political rights on the basis of physical weakness. The middle-class ideal of the fragile "lady" in need of male protection might have seemed to fit the white, urban feminists in Sojourner Truth's audience; but these women were not as far removed from the physical toil of their rural past as the male ideal would have it. Most leaders of the feminist movement and the women's labor movement of the early nineteenth century spoke to women who were still close to the farm tradition of self-sufficiency, independence, and hard work. When Susan B. Anthony later lectured in barns and from wagons on the need for women's rights, or when the strikers at Lowell warned farm daughters about the dangers of becoming "wage slaves," they could assume a common heritage in their rural past.

Ironically, these women were fighting for rights which Native American women already held in some Indian nations. In 1848, the Seneca nation established a written constitution providing for women's participation in electing officials and in ratifying all political decisions. It was in the same year, a hundred miles away at Seneca Falls, that white women assembled to demand the right to vote and be heard in the politics of their nation.

Meanwhile, on the frontier, the westward press for land was bringing Euro-American homesteaders and Native Americans into conflicts in which the women of each culture suffered great losses.[6] Neither Guri Olsdatter nor Iron Teeth, whose memories of life on the plains are reprinted here, could control the larger economic and political forces which brought their families into conflict in the Northwest.

## New England Farm Woman

*As a bride of twenty-three Mary Poor left Indian Hill Farm to move to the neighboring town of West Boxford, twenty-five miles from Boston. From 1770 to 1811 she farmed there with* *her husband; when he died she went to live with a daughter. Over the next three decades, the son-in-law sold off Mary Poor's land to pay for the costs of board, which included twenty-five cents for each pail of water brought to her room. In a diary, she left a record of the many tasks she performed during these years. The diary selections that follow were written between her eighty-third and eighty-seventh years, 1830–1834.\**

## 1830

*Jan. 5.* Cloudy, began to snow at ten o'clock.
*Jan. 6.* A snow storm, a great snow, folks breaking paths.
*Fri. Feb. 12.* Cold, a party here at night.
*Sat. Feb. 13.* Buried Mis Wood aged one hundred and one.
*Mon. Feb. 15.* Cloudy, the school done, all to school house.
*Thurs.* Cold, asewing, and a singing school at night.
*Mon.* Rain, Edward came home at six o'clock.
*Fri.* Moderate, aknitting, Edward sick.
*March 1.* Very warm, aweaving, Mary making candles.
*March 25.* Aknitting, all gone to the sing.
*April 7.* Cloudy, wind North-east, aknitting.
*Wed. 28.* Sister Pearl died yester morning.
*Thurs. 29.* Fair, at the funeral Sister Pearl.
*May 22.* Cool, Asa and Mary to the Cape.
*Aug. 30.* Eleanor, Edward, George to Plum Island.
*Sept. 4.* Eliza come [from Bradford Academy].
*Sept. 15.* Moses Spofford had a fall.
*Sept. 17.* Moses Spofford died at six o'clock this morning.
*Sun. 18.* All at home, rain and snow, rained all night.
*Nov. 1.* Pleasant, to see my sisters to Dan Adams.
*Nov. 2.* To Sam Kimball's and home, Hannah with me.
*Dec. 2.* Thanksgiving, all to meeting but Eliza and her mother.
*Dec. 5.* The schoolmaster came last night.

---

*The diary entries as published originally were not grouped chronologically. Order and dating of entries have been rearranged here for accuracy.

*Dec. 7.* A high wind, snow flies smartly.

*Dec. 8.* Cloudy, Jane Tyler married to our house yesterday.

## 1831

*Jan 13.* Awashing, Asa to Bradford. Two gentlemen to lodge.

*June 15.* Very warm, aknitting, and sewing, folks to work highway.

*June 22.* Pleasant, Eleanor and Eliza to Andover to meeting, four days meeting.

*Aug. 21.* Cool, ahurtleberrying, tired, Mr. Eaton here this morning [the pastor].

*Sun. Sept. 4.* To meeting all day. Three sermons preached.

*Oct. 17.* This day eighty-four years old, awashing, very warm.

*Dec. 20.* Pleasant, aspooling.

*Dec. 22.* Awarping my web, warm.

*Dec. 23.* Warm, atying in my web.

## 1832

*Wed. Feb. 8.* Cloudy, astarching caps, cold, Bets and Susan come.

*Thurs. Feb. 9.* Asnow, cold, amending my gown.

*Feb. 13.* Fair, windy, awashing, folks killed hogs, town meeting.

*Feb. 19.* Warm, amaking fish lines, knitting.

*Feb. 23.* Warm, began to spin Sam Spofford's flax.

*April 22.* Cool, amaking my apron.

*April 23.* Warm, aknitting, took up my roots.

*May 12.* Warm, ascouring my cupboard.

*Wed. May 18.* Abraiding rags, all unwell almost.

*Sat. May 21.* Cloudy, Mary sick, Dr. Mighill here.

*Aug. 6.* Wind North-east, amending.

*Sept. 20.* Awashing and clubbing yarn.

## 1833

*Tues. Feb. 6.* Warm, awashing, tired, areading and nothing else.

*Wed. 7.* Windy, apoking. Mary and Nathan to Rowley.

*Sat. 10.* Warm, asewing, Mary made a kittle of soap.
*Sun. 11.* Cold, at home all day, time mispent.
*Mon. April 23.* Asewing and scouring, Mary awashing.
*Tues. 24.* Rainy, acarding and sewing.
*Fri. June 1.* Cloudy, Edward and Asa to Andover. Mis Foster come.
*June 9.* Pleasant, up on the hill strawberrying in the morning.
*June 12.* Warm, up on the hill, aknitting, tired.
*June 21.* Warm, aknitting, George made my shoes.
*Tues. 10 July.* Cloudy, awashing, very tired, Mary weeding garding.
*Wed. 18.* Lame my side and arm, can't work.
*July 21.* Warm, aquilting and knotting.
*July 23.* Very warm, Mary papered my room.
*Thurs. 26 July.* Warm, acutting shoe linnings and poking about.
*Mon. Aug. 6.* Cloudy, awashing, very tired, areading and set still.
*Tues. Aug. 8.* Ahurtleberrying, got none.
*Wed. Aug. 22.* Warm, aknitting, folks to Haseltine meadow.
*Sat. 25.* Very warm, asewing, picked herbs for the sick.
*Sat. Sept. 1.* Aknitting, Eleanor to Joe Tyler's, quilting.
*Oct. 29.* Asa to Charlestown, awashing, got a new gown.
*Nov. 18.* Foggy, all day atwisting.

## 1834

*Thurs. Jan. 31.* Sick abed, cold, could not sit up.
*Feb. 2.* Sick, took a new cold, quite sick.
*Mon. Feb. 4.* Dr. Mighill came.
*Thurs. 7.* No better.
*Fri. 8.* J. F. for the doctor, he came.
*Sat. 9.* Dr. Mighill here, wrote for me.
*Sun. 10.* Sick, Doctor here at one o'clock.
*Mon. 11.* A little better.
*Tues. 12.* Better, cold, stormy.
*Wed. 13.* Storming, sick.
*Thurs. 14.* Sick abed.
*Fri. 15.* No better.
*Fri. 22.* Warm, no better.
*Sat. 23.* Warm, sick, I do nothing.

# Susan B. Anthony
# Talks to the Farmers

*In the flowing prose she soon sharpened to a weapon in
defense of women's suffrage, Susan B. Anthony counseled
farm men and women to diversify their crops. The occasion
was an 1856 agricultural fair in Yates County, New York.*

If the farmers of New York would save their children from the
sickly employments, and debasing vices of our cities, they
must conduct their pursuits on scientific principles, that shall
command the respect and attention of young men and women of
intelligence, taste, and refinement. If Central and Western New
York would regain its once famous standing as an agricultural
section of the United States, its farmers must not so exclusively
devote themselves to the raising of grains as they now do, and as
their fathers did before them, but they must turn their attention
to the cultivation of fruits. No part of this Union is better
adapted to the growth of all the varieties of the apple, pear, peach,
cherry, plum, and a few of the hardier kinds of the grape, than the
section of country stretching from Buffalo to Utica, and lying
between the highlands of the Southern tier of Counties, and
Lakes Ontario, Onondaga, and Oneida.

The increased value of its lands, the fabulous facilities of
transportation, its soil, the weevil, the midge and the rust, make
it vain for this region longer to attempt to compete successfully
with the great and teeming West, in the growing of wheat, corn
and similar grains. Necessity, therefore, as well as sound policy,
demands that we resort to the cultivation of fruits, and to elevate
this region to its once envied position, as the most productive
farming region of the state, and one of the best in the Union.

And by fruit, I mean, not only the larger kinds already
mentioned, but the smaller, as strawberries, raspberries, black-
berries, gooseberries, and currants. Men and women, and even
boys and girls, can prosecute all departments of fruit growing,
and in this way, farmers might make that division of labor in
their families, which is considered the perfection of industrial

pursuits. While the men are at work in the fields, ploughing, planting, and harvesting, the women, and girls and boys, may be employed in planting trees, bushes, and vines; in pruning, budding, and grafting; in gathering, barrelling, and canning the various fruits for the market. How much more delightful and profitable, and healthful too, would be such employments for the wives and daughters of our farmers, than spending three fourths of their time in the laborious work of making butter and cheese, and dividing the other fourth between the trivial employments of embroidering, knitting stockings, and piecing bed quilts.

And in this connection, allow me to administer a gentle rebuke to a portion of our farmers. It is always painful to pass the home of the owner of a valuable farm, and see that it is *not* adorned with a variety of shade trees, enriched by orchards of the most delicious fruits, rich gardens that yield, not only the earliest and choicest vegetables, but an abundance of the smaller fruits, and where no vines and flowers mingle their beauty and fragrance in the scene; reckless alike of the comfort and taste of wife and daughter. And yet, there are, doubtless, farmers in this county of Yates worth their ten thousand dollars, whose fruit trees, bushes, and vines would be extravagantly estimated at the sum of ten dollars. Their fields wave with golden grains, their hay is piled up like the pyramids of Egypt, their cattle graze on a thousand hills, their butter and cheese stand first in the market; and yet their whole stock in fruit consists of a half dozen deformed apple trees, whose product vies with pebbles in hardness, and with pickles in sourness, a scrubby pear tree or two, for whose gnarled crop the children and the pigs maintain a fierce contest, and three or four old cherry trees which have the good sense to hide their limbs in the nooks of the fences. Not a plum tree, a current or quince bush, or grape vine, not a strawberry, raspberry or blackberry can be seen around their premises. As to shade trees, the lady of the mansion may have a longing that way, but the lord of the manor thinks they would intercept his clear view of his barns and cattle stalls; and so his great uncouth dwelling braves the blazing heats of summer, and shivers in the bellowing blasts of winter, year after year, without a tree to protect it, or bear it company through the revolving seasons.

Now if the men will not reform this evil, but will persist in devoting their whole time and energy to the raising of grain and cattle, then should the women lay aside their patch work and take it in hand, and plant out fruit trees and bushes, shade trees, and ornamental shrubs.

Mrs. Worden, the sister of our greatest statesman—William H. Seward—has a beautiful home near Auburn. She planned and superintended, day by day, the building of her cottage, and planted with her own hands every tree and shrub, each vine and flower that adorns and beautifies her grounds.

And better still, your own illustrious pioneer Jemima Wilkinson. Within 20 miles of the spot where I now stand, she not only cleared up and managed an extensive farm but brought from Providence, Rhode Island, through the trackless wilds of the then great West, the necessary irons and stoves, and in 1790 built a saw mill, and in the year following erected the first grist mill west of Utica. And, for several years thereafter the settlers of your own, and the surrounding counties of Ontario, Seneca, Cayuga, and Tompkins, made their pilgrimages up to the New Jerusalem to pay tribute to the masterly enterprise and persevering industry of that wonderful woman. Surely, if Jemima might hew down the mighty forests, dam up the rivers, build the mills, saw the lumber, grind the corn, and most thoroughly contribute to the convenience, wealth and prosperity of those olden times, the *Jennies* and *Minnies* and *Lizzies* of these later days may cultivate vegetables and fruits for their own health and comfort and plant out shade trees and shrubs and flowers.

# Pioneering in the Northwest

*Abigail Scott left Ohio with her family in the early 1850s to cross the Great Plains over the Oregon Trail. Along the way her mother died of cholera, but Abigail Scott and her family pushed on to Oregon, where cousins were already settled.*

*After years as a women's suffrage activist in Oregon, she
recalled her hard life as a pioneer.*

T he following Spring found me installed as a district school
    teacher on the banks of the little river, Rickreall, near its
junction with the wider Willamette, in the village of Eola, then
known as Cincinnati, and looked upon for a time as a rival of the
City of Salem. It was here that I met my fate in the person of
Mr. Ben C. Duniway, a young rancher of Clackamas County, who
took me, a bride, to his bachelor ranch, where we lived for four
years. Two children Clara and Willis, were born to us here. It was
a hospitable neighborhood composed chiefly of bachelors, who
found comfort in mobilizing at meal times at the homes of the
few married men of the township, and seemed especially fond of
congregating at the hospitable cabin home of my good husband,
who was never quite so much in his glory as when entertaining
them at his fireside, while I, if not washing, scrubbing, churning,
or nursing the baby, was preparing their meals in our lean-to
kitchen. To bear two children in two and a half years from my
marriage day, to make thousands of pounds of butter every year
for market, not including what was used in our free hotel at
home; to sew and cook, and wash and iron; to bake and clean and
stew and fry; to be, in short, a general pioneer drudge, with never
a penny of my own, was not pleasant business for an erstwhile
school teacher, who had earned a salary that had not gone before
marriage, as did her butter and eggs and chickens afterwards, for
groceries, and to pay taxes or keep up the wear and tear of
horseshoeing, plow-sharpening and harness-mending. My recreation during those monotonous years was wearing out my
wedding clothes, or making over for my cherished babies the
bridal outfit I had earned as a school teacher.

My good husband was not idle; he was making a farm in the
timber and keeping a lot of hired men, for whom I cooked and
washed and mended, as part of the duties of a pioneer wife and
devoted mother.

As I look back over those weary years, the most lingering of my
many regrets in the fact that I was often compelled to neglect my
little children, while spending my time in the kitchen, or at the

churn or wash tub, doing heavy work for hale and hearty men—work for which I was poorly fitted, chiefly because my faithful mother had worn both me and herself to a frazzle with just such drudgery before I was born.

When our four years' probation on my husband's donation claim expired, he sold the place and bought the farm in Yamhill County, now known as the Millard Lownsdale Apple Ranch, where we lived for five years, until an unexpected incident occurred which changed the whole course of our future lives....

That Yamhill County farm was my good husband's pride. The location was beautiful, and with the large capital inherited by its subsequent purchaser, Mr. Millard Lownsdale, who was able to finance it for a long period of years before it brought financial returns, it became the pride of its owner, who developed its natural resources, as we could and would have done with equal, outside financial backing.

My labors on that farm became an added burden as our resources grew. I recall one day which, like hundreds of others, was occupied to the limit. After dishes were washed, beds made, rooms swept, and when dinner was over for the family and hired men; after the week's washing was finished and the churning done, and I was busy in an outside house picking ducks—for those were pioneer days, and even our pillows, like our stockings, were home-made—a man came up from the village to our woodpile, where my husband was at work, and asked him to become surety for a considerable sum, with interest at two percent per month, to be compounded semi-annually until paid. The two men parleyed awhile and then went into the house. It dawned upon me suddenly, as I was picking a duck, that it would ruin us financially if those notes were signed. I tried hard to be silent, being a nonentity in law, but my hands trembled, my heart beat hard, and I laid the pinioned duck on its back and repaired to the living room to investigate. My husband had already signed two notes, and was in the act of signing the third, when I leaned over his shoulder and said, tremulously: "My dear, are you quite certain about what you are doing?" The other fellow looked daggers at me, but said nothing, and my husband answered as he signed the last note: "Mama, you needn't worry: you'll always be protected and provided for!" I wanted to say: "I guess I'll always earn all the protection I get," but I remembered that I was nothing but a woman; so I bit my lips to keep silent and rushed back to my work, where for several minutes, I fear that duck flesh suffered, for I didn't pluck the feathers tenderly. But I cooled down after awhile, and to my credit be it said, I never alluded to the notes afterwards. But hard times came, crops failed, my butter and egg money all went to pay interest and taxes, and the months went on and on. A great flood swept away the warehouse on the bank of Yamhill River at holiday time, carrying off the year's harvest, and the unpaid notes, with accrued interest, compounded semi-annually at 2 percent per month, all fell due at once.

One busy day, when I had added to my other duties several rapid hurries down the hillside to scare the coyotes away from the sheep, and just as dusk was coming on—my husband having been away from home all day—the sheriff came to the house and served summons on me for those notes! Now, observe that, when that obligation was made, I was my husband's silent partner—a legal nonentity—with no voice or power for self-protection under the sun; but, when penalty accrued, I was his legal representative. I took the warrant smilingly from the sheriff's hand, and said, "It is all right. Won't you walk in?" He excused himself and went to a neighbor's house, nearly a mile distant, and served a wife with another paper. I afterwards learned that the good wife had, as the sheriff expressed it, "blowed him up," and he said to her, as he turned away: "You'd better go and see Mrs. Duniway and learn a lesson in politeness."

When the hired men came in to supper I was as entertaining as I knew how to be. I told them of some cute sayings of the children, and strove in many ways to conceal the fact that I had been used. I had yet to learn that the right to sue and be sued was the inalienable right of an American citizen.

As the night came down my husband came home, and, after he had eaten supper, and while he was playing with the children, the hired men having gone to their quarters, I confess I felt a little secret satisfaction when I served those papers on him. I had framed up a little "spiel," which I meant to practice on him when I should serve the papers, but he turned so pale and looked so care-worn, I couldn't even say, "I told you so!"

# Keeper of the Keys

*In the early nineteenth century Spanish missions of the
Southwest, Hispanic women managed large households
similar to those of the Southern plantation (see section 3)
and were called* llaveras, *keepers of the keys. Women like
Eulalia Perez supervised cooking, food processing,
manufacture of clothing, and the production of wine, olive
oil, and soap. An assistant was usually responsible for
running the mission hospital, serving as* partera *(midwife)
and* curandera *(healer). Young Native American women
learned to spin and weave, to sew, and also worked at
unloading supplies. Perez was born and raised in Loreta,
Mexico, moved to Alta California with her husband
sometime around 1810, and was* llavera *at the San Gabriel
Mission from 1821 to 1835. She continued to live near the
mission, dictating her recollections to Thomas Savage in 1877
at the age of ninety-seven.*

After consulting among themselves, the priests brought me
the mission keys. This was in 1821, if I remember
correctly. I do remember that my daughter Maria Rosario was
seven years old. She became very ill and was looked after by
Father José Sanchez, who gave her much skillful care; it was by
this good fortune that we did not lose her. I was at that time
the *llavera.*

The *llavera* had various duties. In the first place, she passed out
daily rations. To do this, she had to count nuns, the single men,
the day laborers, the saddle cowboys, the bareback cowboys, and
also the married couples. In short, she saw to the supplies for the
Indian people and for the priests' kitchen. She held the key to the
clothes storeroom which contained the cotton goods for clothing for single and married women and for children. She was also
charged with cutting clothes for the men.

It was my duty also to cut and sew clothing and other articles
to cover the cowboys from head to foot—that is, the saddle
cowboys. The bareback cowboys received no more than one
cotton blanket and a breechcloth. But the saddle cowboys

dressed like the Spanish-speaking inhabitants, the upper classes; they received a shirt, a vest, a jacket, trousers, a hat, boots, shoes, spurs. For their horse, a saddle, a bridle, and a lariat. Each cowboy also received a cumberbund of Chinese silk, a fine handkerchief, or whatever there might be in the storeroom.

Everything concerned with the making of clothes was done under my direction. I would cut and fit, while my five daughters sewed the pieces. When the work load was overwhelming, I would tell the priest, and he would then hire for pay some women from Los Angeles. In addition, I attended to the enormous laundry, the wine presses, and the crushing machines which rendered the oil from olives, which I worked myself. I handled the distribution of tanned hides, chamois, sheep skins, Moroccan leather, flax handkerchiefs, nails, thread, silk—all the items related to the making of saddles, as well as what was necessary in the belt and shoe-making shop.

Every eight days I delivered rations for the troops and the servants of the upper-classes—beans, maize, garbanzos, lentils, candles, soap. To help me, I had been given an Indian servant, Lucio. Whenever necessary, one of my daughters did the work I could not complete. Generally, the daughter who accompanied me everywhere was Maria del Rosario....

In the San Gabriel Mission there were many neophytes.* The married ones lived on their ranches while their children were young. There were two divisions for unmarried persons—one for the women, called the nunnery, and another for the men.

Little girls of seven, eight, and nine years were brought to the nunnery and reared there until they left to marry. They were cared for by an Indian nun, who was called "Mother Superior." The mayor† had charge of the division for the single young men. Every evening both divisions were locked up and I was given the keys, which I in turn gave to the Fathers.

A blind Indian named Andresillo stood at the convent door and called out the name of each girl to enter. If any girl was missing, a search was initiated the following day, and the girl

---

*Neophyte: a church convert, in this case Native American converts to the Catholic church.
†Mayor: a Catholic church elder.

would be brought to the convent. Her mother, if she had one, was also brought in and punished for having kept her daughter away, and the girl was locked up for having been careless about arriving punctually.

In the morning the girls were taken out; first they went to Mass with Father Zalvidea, for he spoke Indian; afterwards to the kitchen to have breakfast, which on feast days sometimes consisted of *champurrado* [a mixture of chocolate and maize *atole*, gruel] with sugar and bread. On ordinary days, they usually had *pozole* [hominy and meat]. After breaking fast, each girl went to a task which had been assigned beforehand. Her job might be at the loom, or in the sewing room, or unloading—whatever needed to be done.... All work ceased at eleven, and everyone came to the dining room to eat *pozole* and vegetables at twelve. At one they returned to their jobs. The work day ended at sundown when everyone returned to the dining area for a supper of *atole* and meat or plain *atole*....

It was I, with my daughters, who made the chocolate, the oil, the candy, the lemonade. I made so much lemonade that some of it was even bottled and sent to Spain.

# Transcendental Wild Oats

*When Louisa May Alcott was ten, her family moved to the country to set up a farm commune. Unlike the ventures of the more businesslike Shakers, who did well on their farm communes in the same region, the Alcott experiment at Fruitlands was not a success. Alcott enjoyed the time on the farm, as the following excerpt from her childhood diary of 1843 shows; but as an adult, realizing the huge burden her mother bore, she wrote in* Transcendental Wild Oats *a bittersweet account of the family's adventures. The character Sister Hope, in that account, is Alcott's mother; Abel Lamb is her father.*

**Louisa's Journal**

*September 1st* —I rose at five and had my bath. I love cold water! Then we had our singing-lesson with Mr. Lane. After breakfast I washed dishes, and ran on the hill till nine, and had some thoughts,—it was so beautiful up there. Did my lessons,—wrote and spelt and did sums; and Mr. Lane read a story, "The Judicious Father": How a rich girl told a poor girl not to look over the fence at the flowers, and was cross to her because she was unhappy. The father heard her do it, and made the girls change clothes. The poor one was glad to do it, and he told her to keep them, But the rich one was very sad; for she had to wear the old ones a week, and after that she was good to shabby girls. I liked it very much, and I shall be kind to poor people.

We had bread and fruit for dinner. I read and walked and played till supper-time. We sung in the evening. As I went to bed the moon came up very brightly and looked at me. I felt sad because I have been cross today and did not mind Mother. I cried, and then I felt better, and said that piece from Mrs. Sigourney, "I must not tease my mother." I get to sleep saying poetry, —I know a great deal.

*Thursday, 12th* —After lessons I ironed. We all went to the barn and husked corn. It was good fun. We worked till eight o'clock and had lamps.

**Transcendental Wild Oats:**
**A Chapter From An Unwritten Romance**

On the first day of June, 184–, a large wagon, drawn by a small horse and containing a motley load, went lumbering over certain New England hills, with the pleasing accompaniments of wind, rain, and hail. A serene man with a serene child upon his knee was driving, or rather being driven, for the small horse had it all his own way. A brown boy with a William Penn style of countenance sat beside him, firmly embracing a bust of Socrates. Behind them was an energetic-looking woman, with a benevolent brow, satirical mouth, and eyes brimful of hope and courage. A baby reposed upon her lap, a mirror leaned against her knee, and a basket of provisions danced about at her feet, as she struggled with a large, unruly umbrella. Two blue-eyed little girls, with hands full of childish treasures, sat under one old shawl, chatting happily together.

In front of this lively party stalked a tall, sharp-featured man, in a long blue cloak; and a fourth small girl trudged along beside him through the mud as if she rather enjoyed it.

The wind whistled over the bleak hills; the rain fell in a despondent drizzle, and twilight began to fall. But the calm man gazed as tranquilly into the fog as if he beheld a radiant bow of promise spanning the gray sky. The cheery woman tried to cover every one but herself with the big umbrella. The brown boy pillowed his head on the bald pate of Socrates and slumbered peacefully. The little girls sang lullabies to their dolls in soft maternal murmurs. The sharp-nosed pedestrian marched steadily on, with the blue cloak streaming out behind him like a banner; and the lively infant splashed through the puddles with a duck-like satisfaction pleasant to behold.

Thus these modern pilgrims journeyed hopefully out of the old world, to found a new one in the wilderness....

This prospective Eden at present consisted of an old red farmhouse, a dilapidated barn, many acres of meadow-land, and a grove. Ten ancient apple-trees were all the "chaste supply" which the place offered as yet; but, in the firm belief that plenteous orchards were soon to be evoked from their inner consciousness, these sanguine founders had christened their domain Fruitlands.

Here Timon Lion intended to found a colony of Latter Day Saints, who, under his patriarchal sway, should regenerate the world and glorify his name for ever. Here Abel Lamb, with the devoutest faith in the high ideal which was to him a living truth, desired to plant a Paradise, where Beauty, Virtue, Justice, and Love might live happily together, without the possibility of a serpent entering in. And here his wife, unconverted but faithful to the end, hoped, after many wanderings over the face of the earth, to find rest for herself and a home for her children....

The goods and chattels of the Society not having arrived, the weary family reposed before the fire on blocks of wood, while Brother Moses White regaled them with roasted potatoes, brown bread and water, in two plates, a tin pan, and one mug; his table service being limited. But, having cast the forms and vanities of a depraved world behind them, the elders welcomed hardship with the enthusiasm of new pioneers, and the children heartily enjoyed this foretaste of what they believed was to be a sort of perpetual picnic.

During the progress of this frugal meal, two more brothers appeared. One [was] a dark, melancholy man, clad in homespun, whose peculiar mission was to turn his name hind part before* and use as few words as possible. The other was a bland, bearded Englishman, who expected to be saved by eating uncooked food and going without clothes. He had not yet adopted the primitive costume, however; but contented himself with meditatively chewing dry beans out of a basket.

"Every meal should be a sacrament, and the vessels used should be beautiful and symbolical," observed Brother Lamb, mildly, righting the tin pan slipping about on his knees. "I priced a silver service when in town, but it was too costly; so I got some graceful cups and vases of Britannia ware."

"Hardest things in the world to keep bright. Will whiting be allowed in the community?" inquired Sister Hope, with a housewife's interest in labor-saving institutions.

"Such trivial questions will be discussed at a more fitting time," answered Brother Timon, sharply, as he burnt his fingers with a very hot potato. "Neither sugar, molasses, milk, butter, cheese, nor flesh are to be used among us, for nothing is to be admitted which has caused wrong or death to man or beast."

"Our garments are to be linen till we learn to raise our own cotton or some substitute for woollen fabrics," added brother Abel, blissfully basking in an imaginary future as warm and brilliant as the generous fire before him.

"Haou abaout shoes?" asked Brother Moses, surveying his own with interest.

"We must yield that point till we can manufacture an innocent substitute for leather. Bark, wood, or some durable fabric will be invented in time. Meanwhile, those who desire to carry out our idea to the fullest extent can go barefooted," said Lion, who liked extreme measures.

"I never will, nor let my girls," murmured rebellious Sister

*That is, last name first, as is customary among Hungarians.

Hope, under her breath.

"Haou do you cattle'ate to treat the ten-acre lot? Ef things ain't 'tended to right smart, we shan't hev no crops," observed the practical patriarch in cotton.

"We shall spade it," replied Abel, in such perfect good faith that Moses said no more, though he indulged in a shake of the head as he glanced at hands that had held nothing heavier than a pen for years. He was a paternal old soul and regarded the younger men as promising boys on a new sort of lark.

"What shall we do for lamps, if we cannot use any animal substance? I do hope light of some sort is to be thrown upon the enterprise," said Mrs. Lamb, with anxiety, for in those days kerosene and camphene were not, and gas unknown in the wilderness....

Any housewife can imagine the emotions of Sister Hope, when she took possession of a large, dilapidated kitchen, containing an old stove and the peculiar stores out of which food was to be evolved for her little family of eleven. Cakes of maple sugar, dried peas and beans, barley and hominy, meal of all sorts, potatoes, and dried fruit. No milk, butter, cheese, tea, or meat appeared. Even salt was considered a useless luxury and spice entirely forbidden by these lovers of Spartan simplicity. A ten years' experience of vegetarian vagaries had been good training for this new freak, and her sense of the ludicrous supported her through many trying scenes.

Unleavened bread, porridge, and water for breakfast; bread, vegetables, and water for dinner; bread, fruit, and water for supper was the bill of fare ordained by the elders. No teapot profaned that sacred stove, no gory steak cried aloud for vengeance from her chaste gridiron; and only a brave woman's taste, time, and temper were sacrificed on that domestic altar.

The vexed question of light was settled by buying a quantity of bayberry wax for candles; and, on discovering that no one knew how to make them, pine knots were introduced, to be used when absolutely necessary. Being summer, the evenings were not long, and the weary fraternity found it no great hardship to retire with the birds. The inner light was sufficient for most of them. But Mrs. Lamb rebelled. Evening was the only time she had to herself, and while the tired feet rested the skilful hands mended torn frocks and little stockings, or anxious heart forgot its burden in a book.

So "mother's lamp" burned steadily, while the philosophers built a new heaven and earth by moonlight; and through all the metaphysical mists and philanthropic pyrotechnics of that period Sister Hope played her own little game of "throwing light," and none but the moths were the worse for it....

About the time the grain was ready to house, some call of the Oversoul* wafted all the men away. An easterly storm was coming up and the yellow stacks were sure to be ruined. Then Sister Hope gathered her forces. Three little girls, one boy (Timon's son), and herself, harnessed to clothes-baskets and Russia-linen sheets, were the only teams she could command; but with these poor appliances the indomitable woman got in the grain and saved food for her young, with the instinct and energy of a mother-bird with a brood of hungry nestlings to feed.

This attempt at regeneration had its tragic as well as comic side, though the world only saw the former.

With the first frosts, the butterflies, who had sunned themselves in the new light through the summer, took flight, leaving the few bees to see what honey they had stored for winter use. Precious little appeared beyond the satisfaction of a few months of holy living.

At first it seemed as if a chance to try holy dying also was to be offered them. Timon, much disgusted with the failure of the scheme, decided to retire to the Shakers, who seemed to be the only successful community going.

"What is to become of us?" asked Mrs. Hope, for Abel was heart-broken at the bursting of his lovely bubble.

"You can stay here, if you like, till a tenant is found. No more wood must be cut, however, and no more corn ground. All I have must be sold to pay the debts of the concern, as the responsibility rests with me," was the cheering reply.

"Who is to pay us for what we have lost? I gave all I had, —furniture, time, strength, six months of my children's lives, —and all are wasted. Abel gave himself body and soul, and is

---

*The Oversoul, a term coined by Ralph Waldo Emerson, is a key concept in transcendental philosophy.

almost wrecked by hard work and disappointment. Are we to have no return for this, but leave to starve and freeze in an old house, with winter at hand, no money, and hardly a friend left; for this wild scheme has alienated nearly all we had. You talk much about justice. Let us have a little since there is nothing else left."

But the woman's appeal met with no reply but the old one: "It was an experiment. We all risked something, and must bear our losses as we can."...

So one bleak December day, with their few possessions piled on an ox-sled, the rosy children perched atop, and the parents trudging arm in arm behind, the exiles left their Eden and faced the world again.

# Shaker Sisters

*Shaker communities were among the most successful religious communities of the nineteenth century. Farming supplied their own needs, while the sale of seeds, medicines, and processed foods provided a cash income. Highly structured, but including women at all levels of decision making, the Shaker life was attractive to hundreds of women who found it secure and productive. The following account by Marcia Bullard, written in 1906, describes the Shaker women's work of herb-gathering and processing as it had been done forty years earlier. The last living sisters closed the community in the early 1970s.*

Forty years ago it was contrary to the "orders" which governed our lives to cultivate useless flowers, but, fortunately for those of us who loved them there are many plants which are beautiful as well as useful. We always had extensive poppy beds and early in the morning, before the sun had risen, the white-capped sisters could be seen stooping among the scarlet blossoms to slit those pods from which the petals had just fallen. Again after sundown they came out with little knives to scrape off the dried juice. This crude opium was sold at a large price and its production was one of the most lucrative as well as the most picturesque of our industries.

The rose bushes were planted along the sides of the road which ran through our village and were greatly admired by the passersby, but it was strongly impressed upon us that a rose was useful, not ornamental. It was not intended to please us by its color or its odor, its mission was to be made into rosewater, and if we thought of it in any other way we were making an idol of it and thereby imperiling our souls. In order that we might not be tempted to fasten a rose upon our dress or to put it into water to keep, the rule was that the flower should be plucked with no stem at all. We had only crimson roses, as they were supposed to make stronger rosewater than the paler varieties. This rosewater was sold, of course, and was used in the community to flavor apple pies. It was also kept in store at the infirmary, and although in those days no sick person was allowed to have a fresh flower to cheer him, he was welcome to a liberal supply of rosewater with which to bathe his aching head.

Then there were the herbs of many kinds. Lobelia, pennyroyal, spearmint, peppermint, catnip, wintergreen, thoroughwort, sarsaparilla and dandelion grew wild in the surrounding fields. When it was time to gather them an elderly brother would take a great wagonload of children, armed with two sheets, to the pastures. Here they would pick the appointed herb—each one had its own day, that there might be no danger of mixing—and, when their sheets were full, drive solemnly home again. In addition to that which grew wild we cultivated an immense amount of dandelion, dried the root and sold it as "chicory." The witch hazel branches were too tough for women and children to handle, so the brethren cut them and brought them into the herb shop where the sisters made them into hamamelis.* We had big beds of sage, thorn apple, belladonna, marigolds and camomile, as well as of yellow dock, of which we raised great quantities to sell to the manufacturers of a well-known "sarsaparilla." We also made a sarsaparilla of our own and various ointments. In the herb shop the herbs were dried and then pressed into packages by

---

*Hamamelis refers to a medicine prepared from the bark of the witch hazel tree.

machinery, labeled and sold outside. Lovage root we exported both plain and sugared and the wild flagroot we gathered and sugared too. On the whole there was no pleasanter work than that in the "medical garden" and "herb shop."

# I Have Plowed
# and Planted and Gathered

*Despite the hard work of rural women, the myth of women's frailty flourished in the ideology of middle-class, men who used the argument of women's inability to care for themselves to counter demands by middle-class women for a variety of human rights. At an early women's rights convention in Akron, Ohio, in 1851, the Black leader Sojourner Truth listened to such an argument made by one of the men at the meeting. Then, in the dialect that was her inheritance from Africa and slavery, and with the wit and passion that commanded rapt attention whenever she spoke, she made this reply.*

Dat man ober dar say dat women needs to be helped into carriages, and lifted ober ditches, and to have de best place every whar. Nobody eber help me into carriages, or ober mud puddles, or gives me any best place, and ar'n't I a woman? Look at me! Look at my arm! I have plowed, and planted, and gathered into barns, and no man could head me—and ar'n't I a woman? I could work as much and eat as much as a man (when I could get it), and bear de lash as well—and ar'n't I a woman? I have borne thirteen children and seen 'em mos' all sold off into slavery, and when I cried out with a mother's grief, none but Jesus heard—and ar'n't I a woman?...

If the first woman God ever made was strong enough to turn the world upside down all alone, these women together ought to be able to turn it back, and get it right side up again! And now they is asking to do it, the men better let them.

# A Norwegian Farm Woman

*Although the life of Scandinavian women on the northern
Plains is often depicted by novelists as one of tragedy and
defeat, in reality the women proved themselves hardy
survivors, as Guri Olsdatter reveals in this letter written from
Minnesota to her family·in Norway. The attack described by
Olsdatter was an attempt by the Sioux warriors to push back
the settlers, when the government violated its agreement to
allow Native Americans to maintain their nations west of the
Mississippi.Like most of the settlers, Olsdatter believed that
the Sioux were "savages" wantonly murdering peaceful
whites. She had no recognition that Native Americans
considered the land theirs and that, to them, the whites were
marauding invaders.*

*Harrison P. O., Monongalia Co., Minnesota
December 2, 1866*

**D**ear Daughter and Your Husband and Children, and My
Beloved Mother: I have received your letter of April
fourteenth, this year, and I send you herewith my heartiest
thanks for it, for it gives me great happiness to hear from you and
to know that you are alive, well, and in general thriving. I must
also·report briefly to you how things have been going with me
recently, though I must ask you to forgive me for not having told
you earlier about my fate. I do not seem to have been able to do so
much as to write to you, because during the time when the
savages raged so fearfully here I was not able to think about
anything except being murdered, with my whole family, by these
terrible heathen. But God be praised, I escaped with my life,
unharmed by them, and my four daughters also came through
the danger unscathed. Guri and Britha were carried off by the
wild Indians, but they got a chance the next day to make their
escape; when the savages gave them permission to go home to
get some food, these young girls made use of the opportunity to
flee and thus they got away alive, and on the third day after they

had been taken, some Americans came along who found them on a large plain or prairie and brought them to people. I myself wandered aimlessly around on my land with my youngest daughter and I had to look on while they shot my precious husband dead, and in my sight my dear son Ole was shot through the shoulder. But he got well again from this wound and lived a little more than a year and then was taken sick and died. We also found my oldest son Endre shot dead, but I did not see the firing of this death shot. For two days and nights I hovered about here with my little daughter, between fear and hope and almost crazy, before I found my wounded son and a couple of other persons, unhurt, who helped us to get away to a place of greater security. To be an eyewitness to these things and to see many others wounded and killed was almost too much for a poor woman; but, God be thanked, I kept my life and my sanity, though all my movable property was torn away and stolen. But this would have been nothing if only I could have had my loved husband and children—but what shall I say? God permitted it to happen thus, and I had to accept my heavy fate and thank Him for having spared my life and those of some of my dear children.

I must also let you know that my daughter Gjaertru has land, which they received from the government under a law that has been passed, called in our language "the Homestead Law," and for a quarter section of land they have to pay sixteen dollars, and after they have lived there five years they receive a deed and complete possession of the property and can sell it if they want to or keep it if they want to. She lives about twenty-four American miles from here and is doing well. My daughter Guri is away in house service for an American about a hundred miles from here; she has been there working for the same man for four years; she is in good health and is doing well; I visited her recently, but for a long time I knew nothing about her, whether she was alive or not.

My other two daughters, Britha and Anna, are at home with me, are in health, and are thriving here. I must also remark that it was four years on the twenty-first of last August since I had to flee from my dear home, and since that time I have not been on my land, as it is only a sad sight because at the spot where I had a happy home, there are now only ruins and remains left as reminders of the terrible Indians. Still I moved up here to the neighborhood again this summer. A number of families have moved back here again so that we hope after a while to make conditions pleasant once more. Yet the atrocities of the Indians are and will be fresh in memory; they have now been driven beyond the boundaries of the state and we hope that they never will be allowed to come here again. I am now staying at the home of Sjur Anderson, two and a half miles from my home. I must also tell you how much I had before I was ruined in this way. I had seventeen head of cattle, eight sheep, eight pigs, and a number of chickens; now I have six head of cattle, four sheep, one pig; five of my cattle stayed on my land until February, 1863, and lived on some hay and stacks of wheat on the land; and I received compensation from the government for my cattle and other movable property that I lost. Of the six cattle that I now have three are milk cows and of these I have sold butter, the summer's product, a little over two hundred and thirty pounds; I sold this last month and got sixty-six dollars for it. In general I may say that one or another has advised me to sell my land, but I would rather keep it for a time yet, in the hope that some of my people might come and use it; it is difficult to get such good land again, and if you, my dear daughter, would come here, you could buy it and use it and then it would not be necessary to let it fall into the hands of strangers. And now in closing I must send my very warm greetings to my unforgetable dear mother, my dearest daughter and her husband and children, and in general to all my relatives, acquaintances, and friends. And may the Lord by his grace bend, direct, and govern our hearts so that we sometime with gladness may assemble with God in the eternal mansions where there will be no more partings, no sorrows, no more trials, but everlasting joy and gladness, and contentment in beholding God's face. If this be the goal for all our endeavors through the sorrows and cares of this life, then through his grace we may hope for a blessed life hereafter, for Jesus sake.

Always your devoted
Guri Olsdatter

# Iron Teeth

*To Sioux and Cheyenne women, the invasion of their homelands meant both the death of loved ones and also the end of their self-sufficient, independent way of life. In the selection that follows, Iron Teeth, a Cheyenne woman, describes the growing struggle of her people for food and land, their resistance to the government's effort to bring them into the reservation system, their doomed last attempt to re-establish themselves in Montana. Pioneer Guri Olsdatter could look forward to a comfortable life behind the frontier, and land for her daughters. For Iron Teeth, the future held no promises.*

We used to plant corn, when I was a little girl. With sharpened sticks we punched holes in the ground, dropped in the grains of corn, went hunting all summer, then returned to gather our crops. But the Pawnees and the Arikaras got to stealing or destroying our plantings, so we quit it and followed all the time after the buffalo. We gathered wild turnips, wild sweet potatoes and different kinds of wild berries. One time, as we were passing near some white settlements, our women got a few watermelons. They cut them up and put them into pots for boiling. After a while, when they looked into the pots they found the food all changed into water. . . .

The first issue of government presents to the Cheyennes was when I was fifteen years old. The place was near the fork of what we called Horse River and Geese River. Soldier houses had just been built there [Fort Laramie, 1849]. We were given beef, but we did not eat any of it. Great piles of bacon were stacked on the prairie and distributed to us, but we used it only to make fires or to grease robes for tanning. We got soda, but we did not know what to do with it. The green coffee looked to us like some new kind of berries. We boiled these berries just as they were, green, but they did not taste good. We liked the sugar presented to us. They gave us plenty of it, some of it light brown and some of it dark brown.

We got copper kettles, coffee-pots, butcher knives, sewing-awls, colored calicoes, bedticking cloth and boxfuls of thread for sewing. The thread was in skeins, not on spools. We were given plenty of brass buttons, colored beads, brass finger-rings, and red and blue face-paints. Blankets, of pretty colors, were issued to all of us. Our chiefs told us, "These presents are given to us so that we may become civilized, like the white people."...

My father gave me a tamed yearling colt when I was about ten years old. When we were traveling, my mother would put packs upon the colt with me. Usually I had behind me and dangling down the colt's sides two badger skins filled with dried choke-cherries. When I grew older I liked to break wild horses. My sister and I used to take them to some sandy spot beside a river. Sometimes, before mounting one we would lead it out into the water. A horse cannot buck hard in deep water.

I was married to Red Ripe when I was twenty-one years old. But the Indian women of the old times did not change their names on account of marriage; so all throughout my lifetime I have kept the same name, Iron Teeth. My husband was a good hunter and did not need my help for gathering meat for his family, but I often went hunting with him. One time, when we were after a small band of buffalo, I rode around to turn them toward the hilltop, because a buffalo cannot run fast uphill. I struck a bull with my hatchet. The bull whirled and knocked down my pony. I fell sprawling, but my husband drove away the angered animal and saved me....

Soldiers built forts in our Powder River country when I was about thirty-two years old [Fort Phil Kearny, Fort C. F. Smith, and others, in 1866]. The Sioux and the Cheyennes fought against them. After a few years peace was made. The Cheyennes settled at the White River agency, in our favorite Black Hills country. This was to be our land forever, so we were pleased. But white people found gold on our lands. They crowded in, so we had to move out. My husband was angry about it, but he said the only thing we could do was go to other lands offered to us. We did this.

Many Cheyennes and Sioux would not stay on the new reservations, but went back to the old hunting grounds in Montana. Soldiers went there to fight them. In the middle of the summer we heard that all of the soldiers had been killed at the

Little Bighorn River [Custer battle]. My husband said we should go and join our people there. We went, and all of our people spent the remainder of the summer there, hunting, not bothering any white people nor wanting to see any of them. When the leaves fell, the Cheyenne camp was located on a small creek far up the Powder River.

Soldiers came [November 29, 1876] and fought us there. Crows, Pawnees, Shoshones, some Arapahoes and other Indians were with them. They killed our men, women and children, whichever ones might be hit by their bullets. We who could do so ran away. My husband and my two sons helped in fighting off the soldiers and enemy Indians. My husband was walking, leading his horse, and stopping at times to shoot. Suddenly, I saw him fall. I started to go back to him, but my sons made me go on, with my three daughters. The last time I ever saw Red Ripe, he was lying there dead in the snow. From the hilltops we Cheyennes saw our lodges and everything in them burning.

We wallowed through the mountain snows for several days. Most of us were afoot. We had no lodges, only a few blankets, and there was only a little dry meat food among us. Men died of wounds, women and children froze to death. After eleven days of this kind of traveling we found a camp of Oglala Sioux. They fed us, but the rest of that winter was a hard one for all of us. When the spring came, I went with the band of Cheyennes who surrendered to Bear Shirt [General Miles] at Fort Keogh.

I was afraid of his soldiers, at first. These were the same kind of men who in past times had killed our people and burned our villages. I had in mind particularly a time, twelve years before this, when they had killed and scalped many of our women and children, in a peaceable camp near Mexico [Sand Creek, in southeastern Colorado]. At that time I had seen one of our women crawling along on the ground, shot, scalped, crazy, but not yet dead. After that, every time I saw white soldiers I thought of her.

# THREE:
# In Bondage to Cotton
## Women of the South

THIS SECTION FOCUSES ON WOMEN who lived and worked on the land in the South, from the years before the Civil War to the years of its aftermath. The rise and decline of a distinctive type of large Southern farm known as the cotton plantation dominated the fate of most rural women during this period.

64

Between 1815–1860, the cotton plantation spread until it covered a wide crescent from the Carolinas to the prairies of Eastern Texas. Cotton plantations gave the South its regional unity, and bound Black and white together in a unique set of social relationships. As cotton became the major export crop of the South and its most profitable investment, the expansion of slavery into the western territories became an issue between North and South. In 1861–1865, the issue was resolved by civil war—a war which ended slavery and the plantation system based upon it. The voices of Black and white plantation women alternate in the selections that follow, contrasting the life patterns that developed on the plantation. Within this system

which neither group of women had created, Black and white women exhibited impressive power. The pride in management of the white woman, and the struggle of the Black woman to reinforce her family and strengthen community ties in the face of the abusive power of white plantation owners, are the major themes.

The selections in this section show the work Black and white women performed on the cotton plantation, as well as the changes caused by the Civil War and the emancipation of Black plantation workers. Plantation owners emerged from the war with their property in land virtually intact. When post-war cotton prices soared to new highs on the international market— from a pre-war average of eleven cents a pound to forty-three cents a pound in 1866—owners hired Black wage labor to replace Black slave labor. Eventually, owners began to parcel out land in thirty- to fifty-acre tracts to freed Black families, who worked the land and paid rent with a share of the crop. By 1880, most Black women had moved into this new sharecropping system. White plantation women, on the other hand, moved from their impor-tant role in plantation management into a much more restricted role as managers of their nuclear family households. This pattern held until the migration of Black agricultural workers out of the South and the mechanization of cotton production in the 1930s and 1940s.

It should be remembered that a majority of Southern white women and men before the Civil War lived not on plantations, but on self-sufficient farms similar to those described in section 2. Most of the nearly 200,000 farms of the cotton South had few slaves and produced little cotton. Hundreds of thousands of young white males left these farms to fight and die in the Civil War; but women, older men, and children continued to farm successfully throughout the war, with little change in agricul-tural methods.[1] Both before and after the war, these small farms were located on marginal lands or scattered between the large cotton plantations which dominated the economic and social life of the South. While life on the cotton plantations is well documented, few records describing life on these small farms remain. The account by Tilatha Wilson English gives us an example of the work performed by young women on one such farm in Texas.

About a million Black women became freedwomen in 1865, two-thirds of whom lived in the rural cotton South, mainly on plantations. The few thousand free Black women in the pre-war South worked in urban areas as servants. Of the majority who were rural and enslaved, almost ninety percent worked in the fields.[2] Before 1830, Southern Black women worked as spinners and weavers, but Northern textile production gradually eliminated this occupation for most Black women. Historians in the past have sometimes given the impression that Black women typically worked in the "Big House," as the home of the plantation owner was usually called. In fact, by 1860 the typical Black Southern woman worked in the fields, where her intensive labor was crucial. Without the field work of Black women and their reproduction of the Black labor force, cotton cultivation would not have been profitable to Southern plantation owners.[3]

By 1860, Black women and men had lived in the South for over two hundred years, and Black communities had already evolved distinctive Afro-American cultures. Several identifiable aspects of western African culture were important ingredients in the evolution of Afro-American plantation life. Women of West Africa had a long tradition of sharing field work with the men, one which has continued into the twentieth century. This tradition resembled that of Native American women, but differed from that of Euro-American women, who typically did not work regularly in the fields. In West Africa, women had organized their work in the fields and had marketed surplus farm products locally. They had also contributed to the development of strong kinship ties within the African household, which was in some cases, like Native American clans, matrilineal.[4] Blacks adapted their African traditions to the conditions of forced labor imposed upon them under slavery, working out strategies by which they could place certain limits upon white control over their culture and work, and, as selections in this section show, did manage to minimize arbitrary discipline by the white planter. The planter, nevertheless, was legally protected in the use of force to regulate Black slave labor and also to sell it, thereby separating families. This power supplied the major weapon in securing acquiescence of Black workers to the plantation regime.[5]

Although the accounts of Linda Brent and Mrs. John Little were published for a nineteenth century abolitionist audience, they do not exaggerate the concerns of Black women about the disruptions of families caused by the selling of wives, husbands, children, parents, brothers, and sisters. Each separation warned Black people of the planter's ability to destroy family relations. As the cotton plantation economy spread south and west, slave owners in the upper South sold slaves to the deep South. Hundreds of miles might thus lie between family members. But family ties were difficult to maintain at shorter distances, too. A separation of even thirty miles might be a severe obstacle to keeping in contact with family members. Black workers had little free time, and their travel was restricted. They could seldom be off the premises for a period longer than from Saturday sundown to Monday sunup. They required the planter's permission to visit; and they traveled on foot. Written communication was denied them, as they were denied literacy. Wives and husbands separated by relatively short distances might have no choice but remarriage. Despite these factors, many slaves formed nuclear families and maintained stability in their marriages.

Because of the threat of separation through sale, Black parents taught their children survival skills beginning at an early age. Strong family ties were an important ingredient in this teaching. Daughters and sons early learned about family traditions and about relatives, however distant, upon whom they could depend; they learned that loyalty to the family was expressed through caring for its members. Through such means, Black people developed kinship networks which could provide support for families broken by slavery. The result was a spiritual and physical strength which enabled Afro-Americans to survive the burdens of slavery and to create and hand on a unique Black culture.[6]

Black daughters, who usually went into the fields to work with their parents between the ages of six and twelve, had already been taught to fend for themselves and also to cooperate with other Black workers. Cooperation, self-reliance, and the ability to earn or negotiate respect were important elements of a young girl's training. Black females learned that assertive speech— sometimes referred to as "sassiness"—was one technique through which they might negotiate respect, not only from members of the Black community, but from owners and overseers as well. Role-playing—particularly the role of "good slave"—was another technique for acquiring some control over social relations. Still another was the according of special respect only to those who had earned it—whether they be white or Black. The title of "Aunt" for old Black women signified the respect due from younger people to their elders.[7]

A Black daughter who was in the fields at twelve beside her parents would within a few years be working a fourteen-hour day. As a woman, she plowed, planted, hoed, and harvested six days a week. On some plantations, she might have half a Saturday free to work in her own garden plot at raising vegetables; or she might work to obtain credit for extra food or clothing for her family. Like many European peasant and some American farm communities, the Southern rural Black community of the period sanctioned premarital sexual relations; but most young people were expected to, and did, settle into monogamy and marriage.[8] Black women knew, however, that the Black community would respect a decision not to marry, and would accept them as part of the community regardless of that decision. Most Black field hands bore many children, receiving four to six weeks off, following a birth, before returning to work.[9] On the larger plantations, the older Black women normally provided child care, health care, and food preparation within the slave community as well as for the white plantation family.

For the Black women, the possibility of physical abuse, ranging from rape to beatings, was an ever present threat. As ex-slave Anne Coley later explained in an interview, Black women developed group techniques to protect themselves from abuse. Black women might attack an overseer who mistreated one of them, and even institute work stoppage by disappearing into the brush until the offending overseer had been discharged or properly disciplined by the owner. The Black woman thus was able to rely upon support from her own kin, the Black community, and her Black sisters in her daily life within the plantation structure.

Black women also looked to the white plantation women for cooperation and even for certain kinds of services, as Sara Hicks, a Northern woman who went South to marry the son of a plantation widow, soon discovered. Isolated within a nuclear family, tied to a small planter class, yet surrounded by a large Black community, the white plantation woman had a difficult role to fill. While the daughter of a wealthy plantation family might spend her youth in relative idleness—reading, visiting, and perhaps writing in her journal—upon marriage she was expected to learn quickly the duties of a plantation mistress. The marriage choices of most young women were controlled by means of their families' admitting to the inner circle of close family friends only selected people. Marriage within the family consolidated property in land and slaves. The pervasiveness of marriages of first cousins among white plantation families signified limited marriage choices.[10] A dowery in slaves was expected of the planter-class Southern woman, as Hicks also learned upon her arrival in the South. Divorce was not a socially accepted means of resolving marital conflict, nor was separation.

The plantation mistress was invaluable in the cotton economy. On a large plantation, she managed the extended household of family and slaves; and when her husband was absent through business, politics, or death, she might manage the entire plantation. She often had to organize the labor of Black workers, both in the field and in the house. A white male overseer usually carried out her instructions in the field; but in the house, she instructed Black artisans and servants herself. She superintended the gardens, poultry, and dairy animals. The letters of Rachel O'Connor, a widow, and Hicks, a wife, show the involvement of women in the details of plantation management, regardless of their marital status. A plantation mistress also developed nursing skills; worked at cutting and sewing clothing for all members of the plantation household; and assisted with cleaning and processing of food. Although she worked hard and had many responsibilities, she had the freedom to arrange her own time, and she could assign Black women to carry out the hardest labor. If she arose early and worked in the garden or sewed in the morning, she might take a nap in the afternoon, or visit friends before supper. She did not have the burdens of preparing food for each meal, of regular housework, or of child care. Black women usually performed these chores for her.[11]

White women had great power within the plantation structure, but almost no public power. As married women, they had no legal right to hold property in most states of the South. While property holdings of Southern women did increase during the early nineteenth century, Southern plantations were dominated by patriarchal relations, a situation in which the oldest white male determined most of the legal and social relationships. Thus, although white women were often treated with respect and accorded great social status, their legal rights were few, and their political rights were fewer. Angelina Grimké, opposed to slavery from youth, found no effective public means of voicing her concern until she left her South Carolina plantation home. After she and her sister Sarah had moved North, they both became well-known abolitionists and eloquent defenders of women's rights. Other Southern white women remained silent. Even women like Hicks, who came from the North, seemed soon to adjust to the pattern of white control of Black lives on the cotton plantation, and to their own place in the system. Women in the South did not exercise the right to speak publicly, to assemble in public to discuss political issues, or to petition. Nor did they demand suffrage. White women most often saw their role as a missionary one—care of their Black charges. As a consequence, a number of white women did extend personal help to Black women in securing physical comfort, sometimes even physical freedom from slavery. Occasionally, white women taught Black girls and boys to read and write, even though it was prohibited by law. Yet white women publicly upheld the labor system upon which their society rested, and did little to change it. Thus the personal and managerial power they exercised within the plantation structure did not extend into the public realm. Like the Black woman, the white woman exercised control over her

work and her life only through such private means as her status
in the family and the community allowed her.

The Civil War brought down the plantation system as it had
existed. The advance of the Northern troops into the South
signaled the movement of much of the Black population away
from the plantation. An account by the Black leader Harriet
Tubman gives a vivid picture of the Black plantation women as
they left the farms. Many believed that the United States
government would help them to establish their own independent,
self-sufficient farms, but plantation owners retained legal title to
the land, and had no intention of allowing the Black majority to
move into land ownership. The plantation owners attempted to
continue their crop production and at the same time maintain
control over the land in a number of ways. One was by allowing
Black people to farm some land at a cash rental or for a share of
the crops raised on these plots. Another was through hiring the
freed Blacks as wage laborers; but in the swift change out of the
old system, they lacked the cash to pay well or to pay regularly,
or, often, to pay at all. Black people, particularly Black women,
refused to work the plantations under these conditions. Plantation owners tried other means of obtaining labor, among them an
apprenticeship system for Black children.[12] In a selection below,
Aunt Nellie tells of being bound out under apprenticeship laws.
The institution of harsh vagrancy laws—the Black Codes of
1865–1866—made it virtually impossible for apprentices and
Black workers generally to travel, thus supplying convict labor.
Even so, plantation owners were forced to sell some of their land;
but the number of freedmen and freedwomen who were able to
buy was not great.

During this period of reconstruction, the Freedman's Bureau
helped some families, with distribution of rations, medical
attention, and other forms of assistance; but the resources of the
shortlived Bureau (1865–1872) were not equal to the needs; and
of the four million Black Southerners freed after the war, one-
half of them children, only about one half of one percent
received aid.[13] Black families took in orphans and cared for
themselves during this period of transition. Eventually, many
freed Blacks moved onto family-sized farms of thirty to fifty

acres each, which they rented or sharecropped, in a newly emerging system that barely yielded them subsistence. On these farms, Black women continued to work in the fields; but now, in addition, they spent more time occupied in duties similar to those of Euro-American farm women. Instead of sharing child care and cooking, which had once been performed by the older Black women for all, each Black woman had to care for her own houshold. In spite of these doubled burdens, most Black women continued to marry. Aunt Nellie was in the minority when she rejected marriage.

For Black women, sharecropping seemed the best alternative available in a region still dominated by the political might of white men. Sharecropping and such land ownership as could be obtained were ways of life that helped to preserve strong family structures in the years after the war. Inheriting from her father part of a small family farm, Aunt Nellie continued to work it with her children. Aunt Kee, whose husband preferred to work for wages, sharecropped with a son. Both Aunt Nellie and Aunt Kee clearly preferred hard subsistence farming to either laboring for wages in the fields or leaving the land for the city. As Aunt Kee said in explaining her decision to remain working on the Southern land: "I'd rather belong somewhur."

## Overthrow the System

*Angelina Grimké grew up·on a South Carolina plantation where Black women labored in field and house while Angelina led a privileged, sheltered life. Angelina began to question her family, friends, and Presbyterian church members about the slave labor system while still in her teens. Like her older sister Sarah, she became a member of the Society of Friends (Quakers), and in 1829, at the age of twenty-four, she followed Sarah Grimké North. In 1836, Angelina Grimké addressed this appeal to the white women of the South, describing how, through their own efforts, they might overthrow the system that enslaved Black people.*

I t is through the tongue, the pen, and the press, that truth is principally propagated. Speak then to your relatives, your friends, your acquaintances on the subject of slavery; be not afraid if you are conscientiously convinced it is *sinful*, to say so openly, but calmly, and to let your sentiments be known. If you are served by the slaves of others, try to ameliorate their condition as much as possible; never aggravate their faults, and thus add fuel to the fire of anger already kindled, in a master and mistress's bosom; remember their extreme ignorance, and consider them as your Heavenly Father does the *less* culpable on this account, even when they do wrong things. Discountenance *all* cruelty to them, all starvation, all corporal chastisement; these may brutalize and *break* their spirits, but will never bend them to willing, cheerful obedience. If possible, see that they are comfortably and *seasonably* fed, whether in the house or the field; it is unreasonable and cruel to expect slaves to wait for their breakfast until eleven o'clock, when they rise at five or six. Do all you can, to induce their owners to clothe them well, and to allow them many little indulgences which would contribute to their comfort. Above all, try to persuade your husband, father, brothers and sons, that *slavery is a crime* against God and man, and that it is a great sin to keep *human beings* in such abject ignorance; to deny them the privilege of learning to read and write. The Catholics are universally condemned, for denying the Bible to the common people, but, *slaveholders must not* blame them, for *they* are doing the *very same thing*, and for the very same reason, neither of these systems can bear the light which bursts from the pages of that Holy Book. And lastly, endeavour to inculcate submission on the part of the slaves, but whilst doing this be faithful in pleading the cause of the oppressed.

"Will *you* behold unheeding,
Life's holiest feelings crushed,
Where *woman's* heart is bleeding,
Shall *woman's* voice be hushed?"

...Some of you *own* slaves yourselves. If you believe slavery is sinful, set them at liberty, "undo the heavy burdens and let the oppressed go free." If they wish to remain with you, pay them wages, if not let them leave you. Should they remain, teach them, and have them taught the common branches of an English education; they have minds and those minds, *ought to be improved.* So precious a talent as intellect, never was given to be wrapt in a napkin and buried in the earth. It is the *duty* of all, as far as they can, to improve their own mental faculties, because we are commanded to love God with *all our minds,* as well as with all our hearts, and we commit a great sin, if we *forbid or prevent* that cultivation of the mind in others, which would enable them to perform this duty. Teach your servants then to read &c, and encourage them to believe it is their *duty* to learn, if it were only that they might read the Bible.

But some of you will say, we can neither free our slaves nor teach them to read, for the laws of our state forbid it. Be not surprised when I say such wicked laws *ought to be no barrier* in the way of your duty....

But some of you may say, if we do free our slaves, they will be taken up and sold, therefore there will be no use in doing it. Peter and John might just as well have said, we will not preach the gospel, for if we do, we shall be taken up and put in prison, therefore there will be no use in our preaching. *Consequences,* my friends, belong no more to *you,* than they did to these apostles. Duty is ours and events are God's. If you think slavery is sinful, all *you* have to do is to set your slaves at liberty, do all you can to protect them, and in humble faith and fervent prayer, commend them to your common Father. He can take care of them; but if for wise purposes he sees fit to allow them to be sold, this will afford you an opportunity of testifying openly, wherever you go, against the crime of *manstealing.* Such an act will be *clear robbery,* and if exposed, might, under the Divine direction, do the cause of Emancipation more good, than any thing that could happen....

And what, I would ask in conclusion, have *women* done for the great and glorious cause of Emancipation? Who wrote that pamphlet which moved the heart of Wilberforce to pray over the

wrongs, and his tongue to please the cause of the oppressed
African? It was a *woman*, Elizabeth Heyrick. Who labored
assiduously to keep the sufferings of the slave continually
before the British public? They were *women*. And how did they
do it? By their needles, paint brushes and pens, by speaking the
truth, and petitioning Parliament for the abolition of slavery.
And what was the effect of their labors? Read it in the
Emancipation bill of Great Britain. Read it, in the present state of
her West India Colonies. Read it, in the impulse which has been
given to the cause of freedom, in the United States of America.
Have English women then done so much for the negro, and shall
American women do nothing? Oh no! Already there are sixty
female Anti-Slavery Societies in operation. These are doing just
what the English women did, telling the story of the colored
man's wrongs, praying for his deliverance, and presenting his
kneeling image constantly before the public eye on bags and
needle-books, card-racks, pen-wipers, pin-cushions, &c. Even the
children of the north are inscribing on their handy work, "May
the points of our needles prick the slaveholder's conscience.". . .

The *women of the South can overthrow* this horrible system
of oppression and cruelty, licentiousness and wrong. Such
appeals to your legislatures would be irresistible, for there is
something in the heart of man which *will bend under moral
suasion.* There is a swift witness for truth in his bosom, which
*will respond to truth* when it is uttered with calmness and
dignity. If you could obtain but six signatures to such a petition
in only one state, I would say, send up that petition, and be not in
the least discouraged by the scoffs and jeers of the heartless, or
the resolution of the house to lay it on the table. It will be a great
thing if the subject can be introduced into your legislatures in
any way, even by *women*, and *they* will be the most likely to
introduce it there in the best possible manner, as a matter of
*morals* and *religion*, not of expediency or politics. You may
petition, too, the different ecclesiastical bodies of the slave
states. Slavery must be attacked with the whole power of truth
and the sword of the spirit. You must take it up on *Christian*
ground, and fight against it with Christian weapons, whilst your
feet are shod with the preparation of the gospel of peace. And *you*

*are now* loudly called upon by the cries of the widow and the orphan, to arise and gird yourselves for this great moral conflict, with the whole armour of righteousness upon the right hand and on the left.

## The Slaves' New Year's Day

*According to ex-slave Linda Brent, she was able to write this account because she was owned by a kind woman for twelve years who taught her to read and spell. She wrote the account to arouse the women of the North to a realization of the conditions of the two million women in the South still in bondage. In order to escape sexual exploitation by her master, Brent had run away and hid in an attic crawl space in her grandmother's house.\* Unable to escape, she spent seven years in this confined area before leaving for the North. She describes here the practice of hiring out slaves in the 1830s.*

**H**iring day at the south takes place on the 1st of January. On the 2nd, the slaves are expected to go to their new masters. On a farm, they work until the corn and cotton are laid. They then have two holidays. Some masters give them a good dinner under the trees. This over, they work until Christmas eve. If no heavy charges are meantime brought against them, they are given four or five holidays, whichever the master or overseer may think proper. Then comes New Year's eve; and they gather together their little alls, or more properly speaking, their little nothings, and wait anxiously for the dawning of day. At the appointed hour the grounds are thronged with men, women, and children, waiting, like criminals, to hear their doom pronounced. The slave is sure to know who is the most humane, or cruel master, within forty miles of him.

---

\*A crawl space is a small storage area in which there is often not room for an adult to stand erect.

It is easy to find out, on that day, who clothes and feeds his slaves well; for he is surrounded by a crowd begging, "Please, massa, hire me this year. I will work *very* hard, massa."

If a slave is unwilling to go with his new master, he is whipped, or locked up in jail, until he consents to go, and promises not to run away during the year. Should he chance to change his mind, thinking it justifiable to violate an extorted promise, woe unto him if he is caught! The whip is used till the blood flows at his feet; and his stiffened limbs are put in chains, to be dragged in the field for days and days!

If he lives until the next year, perhaps the same man will hire him again, without even giving him an opportunity of going to the hiring-ground. After those for hire are disposed of, those for sale are called up.

O, you happy free women, contrast your New Year's day with that of the poor bond-woman! With you it is a pleasant season, and the light of the day is blessed. Friendly wishes meet you every where, and gifts are showered upon you. Even hearts that have been estranged from you soften at this season, and lips that have been silent echo back, "I wish you a happy New Year." Children bring their little offerings, and raise their rosy lips for a caress. They are your own, and no hand but that of death can take them from you.

# A Louisiana Plantation

*The cotton South flourished in the rich soil of Louisiana. There the wealth that could buy both land and the labor of Black slave workers was controlled by a small upper class. Rachel Swayze O'Connor belonged to this class by birth and marriage. Married first at fifteen, widowed at eighteen and married again, she accompanied her second husband to the raw frontier north of New Orleans to make a new start.*

*Twenty-five years later, at forty-eight, her husband and two*
*sons dead, Swayze O'Connor decided to put her plantation in*
*her brother's name, but manage it herself. By her death in*
*1846, she had expanded the plantation to over 1,000 acres*
*and eighty-one slaves. In this letter of 1833, she reveals the*
*combination of agricultural knowledge and business*
*shrewdness which led to her prosperity. That Swayze*
*O'Connor saw Black slaves as property—describing their*
*conditions much as she does the conditions of livestock and*
*crops—is also evident in the letter.*

*January 19, 1833*

**M**y Dear Brother,
I received yours of the 8th instant this evening. I will start
Arthur on Monday morning with your mares to Mrs. Dunken's
plantation below Baton Rouge if the weather continues fair so
that he can travel. I hope you may get them home safe. They are
beautiful and in fine order. I really like to look at them and see
the young mare play. You will have to keep them separate owing
to the oldest being so cross to the other, and may perhaps cripple
her by either being in a stable or pasture together. I wish the old
mare's colt may do well. Young Douglas said she would have it in
April. Lewis Davis left here this morning. He requested of me to
ask you the first time I wrote to bring one hogshead of your best
sugar over for himself and Mr. A. Doherty. Charlotte and
Clarissa will not agree to let them buy any other. They are great
hands for preserves which require good sugar to make them nice
and they have set their hearts on getting some of yours. The girls
have often threw hints to me since you sent this last sugar to me
but I let them hint away and took care of my sugar in the
meantime.

Old Mr. Chaney's property was sold yesterday and I got Mr.
Davis to come down to buy the corn for you if it sold reasonable.
He bought eighty barrels at one dollar per barrel and got afraid to
bid for any more. They say it is good corn. We shall commence
hauling it on Monday, and soon finish as the distance is so short.
They finished rolling logs last evening. Mr. Mulky is wishing for

you to come. I believe he wants to get some new fashion ploughs and I do not know what else but he knows it to be useless to apply to me unless you direct me to get them for him. I have no cause to complain of him now. He is very industrious and behaves well and appears to confine himself more to the truth than usual. I have great hopes of his making you a good crop. The news of the cholera has died away again which makes me anxious to see you come. I am really glad your sugar crop proves to be so good. You will get a high price for it this year. I have understood that the most of the sugar planters have done badly. You had another young negro born this morning. Charity has a fine daughter. . . .

I have, of late, discovered that cotton seed will make cows give much more milk when boiled. I have tried it for some time past and are better for my guinea hogs also. I wish you could buy one of them large kettles at Plackque mine for me to cook seed in. I can soon make butter to pay for it.

My guinea sows will soon have pigs and I must feed them with something. I have eighteen pretty lambs and nine young calves not more than a month old. So you see all is doing wonderful well and I am really thankful for it. I have been very fortunate in saving the meat that we killed. So far all is safe and sound and you would be surprised to see so much raised here.

Clarissa is getting quite healthy. She says you must go to see them when you come and then she will come and stay with you until you start home. They are doing very well and I expect she wants to show you how smart they are. Mr. Howell has bought the middle place that formerly belonged to Brother Caleb and 24 negroes from Mr. Barron and is to pay twenty-five thousand and five hundred dollars four years for it. He sold his plantation to old Mr. Robert for [11,000?] dollars. I have heard that Mr. Courtney often inquires for you and appears anxious to see you and that Wm. F. has written to Harold's son to try to have the cotton sold. I hope they are paying up in mind a little for the trouble they caused me last fall. I am sorry my sister has a sore finger but I hope it may not keep sore long. I shall be glad to receive another letter when she is able to write, but do not complain. She has been very good to write. The last came quite unexpected. Her family is large and keeps her busy, of course, and I take it truly kind in her to write occasionally. That is, whenever she can spare the time, I shall be thankful.

George has been very low this winter. I nearly lost hopes for a while. At length I concluded to send to Dr. Bell for some of Dr. Chapman's cough drops which relieved him very soon and he enjoys better health at present than he has for some time. My love to my dear and good sister and [unclear]. It is now midnight and midlen cold and my fire getting low. I will conclude and wish my beloved and best of brothers a good night. I remain

Your affectionate sister,
R. O'Connor

# A Texas Farm Woman

*Most white women in the South lived on family farms that did not grow cotton. Many of these women were part of the westward movement taking place on the Southern frontier. Tilatha Wilson English left Kentucky with her family when she was two. After several years in Illinois and Arkansas, the family moved west again, eventually settling on 640 acres near Grayson, Texas in 1845. When her mother died, English and a younger sister—both in grade school—took over the household chores here described.*

The first year we came to Grayson, my father bought a prairie team, which was six yoke of oxen and a big prairie plow, all on time and my two oldest brothers began breaking prairie; they broke a small field then began to break land for the man to pay for the team.... There was no mill nearer than Bonham, so most everbody got a little steel mill and ground their corn at home, sifted out the fine and used it for bread and cooked the rest for hominy. They did not raise any wheat for a few years, but when people got their land in cultivation they raised lots of wheat but hardly knew what money was. Everybody was poor who came to get homes....

...When we would hear of preaching any where near, we would go. I have walked five miles to church and back the same day, and wore homemade dresses, bonnets and shoes. My father sometimes made buckskin and sometimes cloth, and sometimes leather shoes—just anything he could get to make them out of, and we would be mighty proud of them, and most everybody dressed alike. People loved each other then; it was not as it is now. Pride and style have taken the place of religion. I am an old spinner and weaver. I have had to quilt, card, spin and weave ever since I was large enough. We had to pick out all the seed from our cotton with our fingers for several years after we came to Texas, make up our own clothing, and raise our own indigo to color the cloth. I never saw a sewing machine or cook stove until after the war. I was married, and had three children before I saw a cook stove and in making up our cloth after we got it we would sew it all with our fingers and make the buttons out of thread. I have made many a button out of thread. You think, no doubt, that we had a hard time, and so I reckon we did, but we enjoyed it, and it was happiness to us all, for we loved each other, and were always glad to see and help each other and when one got sick we would go eight or ten miles to see them or sit up with them, if it was needed...

We raised gourds to use for almost everything; big gourds (we called them fat gourds). Lots of them could hold a half bushel. We put lard in them or anything we wished. Spanish gourds were large at both ends and small in the middle. We would saw off both ends about half way, clean them out good, tie a cloth over one end, and it made a good strainer. We had gourds to milk in, drink water out of, and other things too numerous to mention.

When our fire would go out we had to go to a neighbor and get fire or catch it some way. I have many times taken a skillet lid and an old case knife, and knocked fire out of it. I have spun fire many a time, and I will tell you how I did it. I took deep copper thread and doubled it several times, and twisted it a little, then held it in the whirl of the wheel and turned the wheel right fast, and it would mighty quick set it on fire. I would have some cotton ready and stick in it. I would soon have plenty of fire....

...I used to knit my folks gallouses* and knit the button holes in them. I used to plait wheat straw and make my men folks summer hats, and take home-made jeans and make them caps for winter...

I know some that say they would not like such times as we old timers had, but if I was young again I would love to be in such a place and would go to it, if there was such a place.

## Hoeing Cotton

*A fugitive slave in Canada, whose name was given only as Mrs. John Little by the compiler of this 1856 oral history, describes learning to hoe cotton for the first time. Born in Virginia, Little was taken while young to Alabama, where, after her owner died, her parents were sold. Little said, "My mistress beat me like sixty." Later, she too was sold, but persuaded her new owner to purchase her husband as well.*

I was employed in hoeing cotton, a new employment: my hands were badly blistered. "Oh, you must be a great lady," said the overseer, "Can't handle the hoe without blistering your hands!" I told him I could not help it. My hands got hard, but I could not stand the sun. The hot sun made me so sick I could not work, and, John says if I had not come away, they would surely have sold me again. There was one weakly woman named Susan, who could not stand the work, and she was sold to Mississippi, away from her husband and son. That's one way of taking care of the sick and weak. That's the way the planters do with a weakly, sickly "nigger,"—they say "he's a dead expense to 'em," and put him off as soon as they can. After Susan was carried off, her

*Suspenders for trousers.

husband went to see her: when he came back he received two
hundred blows with the paddle.

## A North Carolina Plantation

*Sarah Francis Hicks waited eight years before marrying
Dr. Benjamin Wilson because he was a slave holder and not a
professing Christian. In 1853 they married in her hometown
of New Hartford, New York, and moved to the North
Carolina plantation which his mother owned. These letters to
Sarah Hicks Wilson's parents document a Southern woman's
farm responsibilities and the emphasis placed upon Black
slaves as her dowry. Although Hicks Wilson believed that
eventually emancipation should occur, she shared the
common prejudices about Black slaves, and was in no sense
an egalitarian, either on questions of race or class. She
considered mistaken those Northerners who were making
demands for the immediate abolition of slavery.*

*Clifton Grove, Oct. 22, 1853.*
*Saturday Morning*

**M**y dear Parents:
Your letter enclosing others has been received and ere this
you have received one from me informing you of our safe arrival
here. It would be wrong, perhaps, for me to form or express an
opinion in regard to the manners and customs of the people, after
only two weeks tarry among them. I shall not speak for or against,
but will state things as I have seen them and you may form your
own opinions. The woods present a beautiful appearance now, the
rainbow hues of autumn contrasting beautifully with the deep
dark green of the pines. Many of the trees are hung with vines of
the honeysuckle, woodbine and others. Now to mingle the bitter
with the sweet, in those woods are snakes of various sizes, both

harmless and poisonous, among the latter are large adders and occasionally a rattlesnake. Scorpions, too, they tell me, are plentiful. There is one thing I miss sadly, and that is our beautiful grass. The soil is sandy and the grass is of a different character entirely, being coarse and full of weeds. But when the ground is planted and cultivated with the different products of the country, it presents a fine appearance. The cotton fields are beautiful, the corn will range from ten to twelve feet in height, and the sweet potatoes and yams look fine. Ambition is satisfied here by numbering its thousands of dollars, acres of land and hundreds of negroes. Houses, furniture, dress are nothing. For instance, the Dr.'s brother, a very wealthy man, lives in a brown wood house without lathing or plastering. To be sure, he has a handsome sofa, sideboard and chairs in his parlor, which contrast strangely with the unfinished state of the house. However, he purposes building soon. This, I might say, is the common style of house, and ours, which is finished, the exception. As to household arrangements, I have discovered no system. Wash, bake or iron, just as the fit takes.... Baking is all done in bake kettles and cooking at a fire place. Chimneys are all built on the outside of the houses. The Negroes are certainly not overtasked on this plantation. One house girl at the North will accomplish more than two here. But I think the great fault lies in the want of system. Mother Williams works harder than any Northern farmer's wife, I know. She sees to everything. The Dr. has another place, seven miles from here, mostly pine land. That with his other business demands a good share of his time. He has gone with his brother to Greenville to engage his turpentine, which is selling for $4.00 per barrel. I don't expect him back until Monday. As to the treatment of servants, the overseer that Ben employed while he was away, struck one of the Negroes, and his mother would not speak to him afterwards, and had him discharged. They are not diffident, either. One of the field hands asked me to fix a dress for her the other day. Another servant wanted to know if Massa Ben and I couldn't ride over to Snow Hill and get her a new dress. They have plots of ground they cultivate and have what they make from them. They can go to Church (Preaching, as they say) on the Sabbath. Indeed, a majority of the congregation is colored. On Sundays they dress up and many of them look very nice. They leave off work at sundown during the week. You will not wonder, finding everything here so entirely different, if I should feel like a stranger in a strange land. It must take time for me to become accustomed to such an utter change, but with a husband who has proved so devoted, I could not be unhappy anywhere. I think I can appreciate Miss Ophelia's feelings for I have not approached any of the little negroes very closely yet, like her I should wish a good application of soap and water, comb & clean clothes. I have just received a letter from Malvina full of good kindly feelings. In it she said "I meant to write to your mother ere this." Will you tell her that a rush of engagements has prevented me. Give her my very best love and tell her that I very often think of the family alone in the dear pleasant homestead. "Mother sends her regards with many thanks for the liberal supply of wedding cake she received." By the way, the cake that John brought, came safely and we have had it on the table twice. The house was full for a week after we came with relatives. We had a very pleasant time & we felt rather lonely after they all left. I expect my furniture is in New Bern, but we cannot get it until the river rises. Ben, I expect, will go away next week to Beaufort, where he is talking of purchasing a lot and perhaps of building a residence at some future time. My paper is full and I have just room to say to both Write often to your

Sara


*Clifton Grove, March 17, 1854*
*Friday*

**M**y dear Parents:
    Yours was received on Wednesday & I hasten to reply. You may imagine that the very thought of seeing you filled me with joy, but there are circumstances which surround us, & which, I feel due to you as well as to us to explain, some things that we feel must be changed before you come in order to make a visit pleasant. We ordered a stove some time since from New York, hoping to receive it & be installed at our own house keeping (a

proposition of Mother Williams) by this time, but we hear nothing from Luther or the stove. I do feel that I want to see you very much. I want your council particularly, but under the circumstances, I do not feel at liberty to make friends of mine guests at Mother's. I feel quite sensitive enough at being here myself.... There is one thing that to me throws light on the whole matter, although Ben is hardly willing to allow it. A Southern lady generally receives a number of servants as her marriage dower. I have no doubt that Mother had looked forward to her son marrying such an one & thus adding to the rather small number of hands (Sister Mary having removed about twenty last spring, they being her portion) & leaving about the same number here, which are not sufficient to work so large a farm. Then, too, I can look back and see wherein I have erred. Had my wardrobe been plainer I would have pleased her better. But I do not imagine that she is wholly destitute of kindness to me. I have received favors from her, but Ben's marrying seems to have turned her against him. She proposes for him to attend the business this year, divide profits next fall, and then each attend to their own. 250 acres are his now, the rest not until she is through with it.... Ben talks some of moving to Snow Hill in the fall to a house in which he owns an interest and renting his land here. He does not like to remove any of his hands from his turpentine land, the income from that being much larger than from the plantation & he would have to in order to farm to any advantage. His most valuable farm hand is now sick with dropsy & will probably never be any better. In attending to her I find that I can be useful, also in sewing.

...The Dr. says we must have some cool weather yet and he thinks you may come with safety in the middle of May. But you must use your own judgment. The Dr. hated to have me write this letter, but I told him I had always told you everything and I knew you would not love us less for dealing frankly now. I know none of us would enjoy the visit as well as if you wait. Company disturbs Mother Williams and her ways are so entirely different from what I have been used to that it seems quite impossible for me to help her. We are hoping to hear from Lucinda and Luther daily. Unless the stove and box that we have sent for come within a few days, we may not get them until the fall, as the creek is fast falling and will soon be too low for flats to come up from New Bern. Love to all and much, very much from your daughter, Sara and her husband.

*Clifton Grove, Monday, Oct. 2nd, 1854*

**M**y dear Parents:
　　Yours was received on Saturday & I hasten to reply today, that we may enjoy a chance of enjoying some of your good apples before going to Raleigh, or at least before Ben does. They will be very acceptable, I assure you. Please direct them to the Dr. care of B. F. Havens, Washington, N. C. Ben is sending (or going to) turpentine to Greenville and can get it more easily than from New Bern. I wish as sincerely as you possibly can that we lived nearer you. What changes the next few years may make in our arrangements, it is impossible to divine. I could wish they might find us in a pleasant home in the North. And, yet, to gain that end I should be very unwilling to sell our servants. I know that they are kindly cared for now, and they might easily fall into worse hands. The recent discussions upon the slavery question have kindled the smouldering fires of animosity both in the North and the South. How I wish the Abolitionists of the North could see these things as I see them. If they knew what they were about they would act differently. As they are doing, they are tightening the bonds of the slave and putting farther off his emancipation.... Brother James has a son very sick which will detain him from visiting the North at present. Baby is crying and I must close. With love, in which the Dr. joins me, I am your affectionate daughter,

Sara

*May 22nd, 1855*
*Evening*

**M**y dear Parents:
　　I am still alone. Ben has not returned from the South yet, unless he has passed & gone on North, which is not unlikely, as

Mr. Hannum had large interests in New York, and they intended to get security if it is to be had. However, don't worry about us, for with proper economy, and even though we lose this, we can still be independent. You inquire in regard to the kitchen, etc. It is a rough affair for temporary use, but much better than none. The cooking is all done in the new stove now. It would be better if it were a wood stove, but it is a coal stove. However, I suppose Luther hadn't time to be particular & it answers our purposes much better than none. The kitchen is over by Old Lucy's house & connected with it to Lizzie's house. Lettuce and Charity stay with Lizzie & Ann stays in the house. Mother Williams is not very well, but still will not call herself sick. She scolds about as much as ever. But I don't care as much for it, for I know I have tried to do right.... She will never forgive Ben for not marrying "Niggers," never, never, never.* He tends his own land, and since he has been away, I see to his business. I am up before sunrise to give out the keys. He told me how to order & sometimes I steal Mother's thunder. I watch and see what her hands are doing & then I order ours as if I knew it all. For instance, I set them to setting out sweet potatoe sprouts the other day. I did not know anything about it, but I watched, and then I told them I wanted to "throw three furrows together and set the sprouts in the middle furrow," and our patch looks as good as Mother's. Now they are plowing and hoeing the corn. If Ben doesn't come this week, I shall make them thin it out and leave only one stalk in a hill except in the richest places. Don't you think I'll make a farmer. Then I have a vegetable garden, which I superintend. I have collards (most like cabbage) almost a foot high and leaves as big as the palm of your hand, peas that are running, Irish potatoes that are in blossom, cucumber with leaves half as large as my hand and mustard going to seed. We have had radishes a month or more. Another year, I'm going to see what I can do. If I live and am well, I am going to have the best garden in the County. I want some Shanghai chickens, and am going to try for a pair if I go home this summer. I don't think you need look for me before

*Hicks is referring again, as on page 87, to her mother-in-law's disappointment that Hicks did not bring a dowery of slaves to the marriage.

August. Lilly stands alone and says "mama" and has four teeth. I received a letter from Luther last night in the same mail with yours. The fruit trees are loaded with fruit; we shall have bushels and bushels of peaches, plums and apples a plenty. We had red cherries last week. They are all gone now. Love to all from your daughter

Sara


# Never Did Hev
# No More Overseers

*The view from the "Big House," as the owner's home was called by slaves, reflected the privileged and protected lives of the white women who managed the plantations. From the "Street," as Blacks called the area in which they lived, plantation life had a different aspect. Few Black women worked in the "Big House," and the lives of those who did were not typical. Most Black women worked all day in the cotton fields, usually under the authority of white overseers. Ultimately, Black women had to depend upon themselves for protection. They resisted and sometimes ended the mistreatment of overseers through collective action.*

*Annie Coley was born twenty miles north of Camden, South Carolina (the location of the Chestnut plantation referred to in the selection, "Diary from Dixie"). During the 1930s, when the Federal Writers Project collected the narratives of ex-slaves, Coley recounted the incident she describes here, of group action taken by Black women against an abusive overseer.*

*The Black dialect spoken by Coley, like that of several speakers in this collection, is an Africanized form of English adopted under slavery. Blacks who received schooling, like Linda Brent, wrote standard English; but oral histories such as*

*the following usually retain the richness and variety of the
spoken word.*

We worked in de fiels, in de cotton en de corn, from early
mawnin' twel sundown. Sat' days, all day, jes' de same.
Sundays we could rest. Big Boss giv each cullud man a piece of
groun' to mek a crap of cawn en cotton for hisself. Sundays each
niggah worked out his own crap....

We bought Sunday clo'se with our cotton money. Boss giv us
plenty good work clo'se. We got to rest three days at Christmas.
We had a big dinner, but Boss giv us thet out'n his smokehouse.

When the War came, ole Boss was dead. Little Boss, who was
Jesse Truesler, went to de Army, and was wounded. He was de
onliest chile, so ole Miss went to live with her sister at Camden.
Then my pappy moved to Camden too, but we chilluns cried to
go back home; we didn' get no more milk en butter now. But
pappy wouldn' go back though little Boss had come home...

My Boss' overseer was a po' white man, but he was good to us
cullud folks....

But ole Boss Jones had a mean overseer who tuk 'vantage of the
womens in the fiel's. One time he slammed a niggah woman
down that was heavy, an cause her to hev her baby—dead. The
niggah womens in the Quarters jumped on 'im and say they
gwine take him to a brushpile and burn him up. But their mens
hollered for 'em to turn him loose. Then big Boss Jones came en
made the womens go back to the Quarters. He said, "I ain'
whipped these wretches for a long time, en I low to whip 'em dis
evenin'." But all de womens hid in the woods dat evenin', en Boss
never say no more about it. He sent the overseer away en never
did hev no more overseers.

## Diary from Dixie

*White women on plantations experienced privation during
the Civil War, sometimes facing starvation as refugees, but*

*affected mainly by the disruption of their settled and secure lives. Mary Boykin Chestnut, who was brought up to be a Southern lady, describes in the first diary entry below the comfortable life of her mother-in-law on an antebellum cotton plantation in Camden, South Carolina, during 1861. The second entry, from 1865, comments on the destruction brought about by the war. Throughout these drastic changes, Chestnut could not detect, or chose not to report, any changes in the Black population. To her, apparently, they had always been and would always remain happy to serve within the paternalistic structure of slavery. "William the faithful" is her ideal Black servant, concerned only that he had failed to protect the possessions of his white master. William Walker was probably playing a role, to stabilize his relationship with the white plantation owners.*

*September 24, 1861*

**M**rs. Chestnut has a greediness of books such as I never saw in anyone else. Reading is the real occupation and solace of her life. In the soft luxurious life she leads, she denies herself nothing that she wants. In her well-regulated character she could not want anything that she ought not to have. Economy is one of her cherished virtues, and strange to say she never buys a book, or has been known to take a magazine or periodical; she has them all. They gravitate toward her, they flow into her room. Everybody is proud to send, or lend, any book they have compassed by any means, fair or foul. Other members of the family who care nothing whatever for them buy the books and she reads them.

She spends hours every day cutting out baby clothes for the Negro babies. This department is under her supervision. She puts little bundles of things to be made in everybody's work basket and calls it her sewing society. She is always ready with an ample wardrobe for every newcomer. Then the mothers bring their children for her to prescribe and look after whenever they are ailing. She is not at all nervous. She takes a baby and lances its gums quite coolly and scientifically. She dresses all hurts, bandages all wounds. These people are simply devoted to her, proving they can be grateful enough when you give them anything to be grateful for. Two women always sleep in her room in case she should be ill, or need any attention during the night; and two others sleep in the next room—to relieve guard, so to speak. When it is cold, she changes her night clothes. Before these women give her the second dress, they iron every garment to make sure that it is warm and dry enough. For this purpose, smoothing irons are always before the fire, and the fire is never allowed to go down while it is cool enough for the family to remain at Mulberry. During the summer at Sand Hill it is exactly the same, except that then she gets up and changes everything because it is so warm! It amounts to this, these old people find it hard to invent ways of passing the time, and they have such a quantity of idle Negroes about them that some occupation for them must be found. In the meantime, her standing employment is reading, and her husband is driving out with a pair of spanking thoroughbred bays, which have been trained to trot as slowly as a trot can be managed.

*March 15, 1865*

L awrence says Miss Chesnut is very proud of her presence of mind and her cool self-possession in the presence of the enemy. She lost, after all, only two bottles of champagne, two of her brother's gold-headed canes, and her brother's horses— including Claudia, the brood mare that he valued beyond price— and her own carriage. A fly-brush boy called Battis, whose occupation in life was to stand behind the table and with his peacock feathers brush the flies, was the sole member of his dusky race at Mulberry who deserted "old Marster" to follow the Yankees.

*May 2nd, 1865*

I I am writing from the roadside below Blackstock's, *en route* to Camden. Since we left Chester, solitude; nothing but tall, blackened chimneys to show that any man has ever trod this road before us. This is Sherman's track! It is hard not to curse him.

I wept incessantly at first. "The roses of the gardens are already hiding the ruins," said Mr. Chesnut, trying to say something. Then I made a vow. If we are a crushed people, I will never be a whimpering, pining slave.

We heard loud explosions of gunpowder in the direction of Chester. I suppose the destroyers are at it there. We met William Walker. Mr. Preston left him in charge of a carload of his valuables. Mr. Preston was hardly out of sight before poor helpless William had to stand by and see the car plundered. "My dear Missis, they have cleaned me out, nothing left," moaned William the faithful.

May 4th—From Chester to Winnsboro, we did not see one living thing, man, woman or animal, except poor William trudging home after his sad disaster. The blooming of the gardens had a funereal effect. Nature is so luxuriant here; she soon covers the ravages of savages. The last frost occurred the seventh of March, so that accounts for the wonderful advance of vegetation. It seems providential to these starving people; so much that is edible has grown in two months.

## Farm Women Refugees

*Slave women had evolved a way of life on most plantations in which close family ties, kinship networks, and group action provided some security against the arbitrary divisions of families by slave owners, the rapes, the crippling beatings which occurred. The Civil War brought freedom from enslavement, but also a new type of insecurity, as thousands of Black women left plantations, many believing that the government would provide them with farms of their own.*

*When Union gunboats appeared on the Mississippi, the word quickly spread, and women left their quarters. Harriet*

*Tubman, who accompanied expeditions up the river as guide
and intelligence gatherer, later described the scene to a
chronicler, who wrote it down this way.*

They came down every road, across every field, just as they had
left their work and their cabins; women with children
clinging around their necks, hanging to their dresses, running
behind, all making at full speed for "Lincoln's gunboats." Eight
hundred poor wretches at one time crowded the banks, with
their hands extended towards their deliverers, and they were all
taken off upon the gun-boats, and carried down to Beaufort.

"I nebber see such a sight," said Harriet; "we laughed, an'
laughed, an' laughed. Here you'd see a woman wid a pail on her
head, rice a smokin' in it just as she'd taken it from de fire, young
one hangin' on behind, one han' roun' her forehead to hold on,
'tother han' diggin' into de rice-pot, eatin' wid all its might; hold of
her dress two or three more; down her back a bag wid a pig in it.
One woman brought two pigs, a white one, an' a black one; we
took 'em all on board; named de white pig Beauregard, an' de
black pig Jeff Davis. Sometimes de women would come wid twins
hangin' roun' der necks; 'pears like I nebber see so many twins in
my life; bags on der shoulders, baskets on der heads, and young
ones taggin' behin', all loaded; pigs squealin', chickens screamin',
young ones squallin'." And so they came pouring down to the
gun-boats. When they stood on the shore, and the small boats
put out to take them off, they all wanted to get in at once. After
the boats were crowded, they would hold on to them so that they
could not leave the shore. The oarsmen would beat them on their
hands, but they would not let go; they were afraid the gun-boats
would go off and leave them, and all wanted to make sure of one
of these arks of refuge. At length Col. Montgomery shouted from
the upper deck, above the clamor of appealing tones, "Moses,
you'll have to give 'em a song."* Then Harriet lifted up her voice
and sang:

---

*Tubman was often called "Moses" because of her success in helping hundreds of
slaves to escape to the "Promised Land" in the North and Canada. She was also
famed for her melodious and powerful singing voice.

Of all the whole creation in the east or in the west,
The glorious Yankee nation is the greatest and the best.
Come along! Come along! don't be alarmed,
Uncle Sam is rich enough to give you all a farm.


# Freedom's Here
# and Slavery's Past

*Not all Black women fled the plantations as refugees or*
*to find families broken up under slavery. Aunt Nellie, who*
*had been raised by a grandmother, was about ninety when*
*she told Bernice Kelly Harris her life story, in which she*
*explained what had happened to the nine children in her*
*family, told about another freedwoman who used song to*
*remind a former owner of her new status, described her own*
*love of working the land and the reasons she never married.*

**A**fter freedom, Old Marster bound we chil'en out,* and we
worked fust one place and 'nother. He tuk us to Jackson
where de man asked us: "Do you alls wants to be bound to Mr.
Ellis?" We said we did; so we was scattered round from one to de
other den, workin' at anything come to hand.

Old Mr. John Long had a 'oman at his place named Tildy dat
used to sass him after freedom. When he'd come ridin' long in his
rockaway [a kind of carriage], Tildy'd git close to de road and sing:

"Thank God A'mighty dat freedom's here and slavery's past,
Thank God A'mighty de slavery chain is broke at last."

Den as de rockaway got 'gainst de house, she'd break out:

"Sweet Jesus, swing yo' chariot down,
Now we's free, halleluiah, swing yo' chariot down.
For I don't want to stay here no longer."

---

*Bound out: system in which children were apprenticed to a family where they
worked, usually for room and board. The practice had died out in the North.

Mr. Lon'd cuss and holler at her: "By God, dat ain't my song. I *do* want to stay here." Look like it made him mad to be 'minded 'bout gwine away from here. He stayed drunk half de time; his house was full o' shot holes, for he kep' one o' his men side o' him to load de gun while he shot. He hated to see Tildy out in de yard, 'cause he knowed she was gwine sass him 'bout leavin' here, but he'd always holler back from de rockaway, "I *do* want to stay here."

De fust work I ever 'member doin' was breshin' yards, doin'· round in de house, takin' my little basket to de field and pickin' cotton. Since den I's done a mess o'work—cleanin' house; plowing, honey, jes like a man; choppin', pullin fodder,* pickin' cotton.... Tain't much I ain't done, honey.... When my daddy died, he left a little farm yonder on de road to be divided in three shares 'tween we three dat was livin'. I got twenty acres, some of it open land, bought me a steer, and started farmin' for myself. My five chil'en was big enough to insist me den; so we made out to make a livin', wid what I brought in from workin' round by de day. I cooked or washed or ironed one at every house in Gumberry. Long den I walked de two miles to Seabord to wash and iron for Miss Annie, den come back home and went right to work till dark. Anytime I picked 250 pounds o' cotton a day.... Mo'nin's I got up 'fore day, cooked de somethin' t'eat, put a little cold rations in a tin bucket to take wid me to de field, and picked or pulled fodder or chopped till night, anything dere was to do. It's been hard work for me all my days; I didn't mind it neither, for I loves to work. When I was growin' up, I never had a day's sickness in my life, and work was as good a time as I wanted. We had plenty good times long wid de work. It was balls and dances when I was young; den it was one think and t'other as I growed older. Sweethearts? Whu-wh- whu! I had some, but I ain't never loved none of 'em. I mought, but dey'd say somethin' to make me mad, and love'd take out and run like a wild rabbit. I wa'n't studyin' 'em. Whu-wh- whu! I did study some about gettin'

---

*Pulling fodder, practiced in the cotton South during August, consisted of stripping green leaf blades from growing cornstalks to be used as fodder. The practice developed as a way to utilize Black labor not needed in the cotton fields during this season.

married, but after de chil'en was done on hand I didn't want 'em 'bused by no strange man.

## I'd Rather Belong Somewhur

*Long after emancipation, daughters and sons separated from their parents under slavery sought to reunite families. In 1939, Aunt Alice Kee still vividly remembered her own mother's 1888 search for lost parents. Recounting her life story to interviewer Bernice Harris, Kee also explained why she preferred to remain in the South working on the land rather than move to New York. Saving money from "maulin [splitting] wood, ditchin', plowin' and hoe work," Kee wanted to buy a farm, but her husband spent the money. Although she tried to convince him to sharecrop, her husband's choice was migratory work for day wages. Later, she sharecropped with a son.*

In 1888 my mother and Pa left Cedar Rock and started to Suffolk to find my mother's folks. Deir money give out at Seaboa'd; so dat's whur we had to stop and go to work. When my mother finally did git to Suffolk, she found out her mammy had been dead two years....

De fust place we landed at in Seaboa'd was Mr. Jim Crocker's. We worked for him by de day, makin' two and three dollars a week. My mother died whilst we was here, leavin' a baby jus' six months old. I didn't know she was dyin'; I'd never seen death befo'. So when time come for de baby to nu's, I carried it to de bed. Dat's de way my mammy died—a-nu'sin' de baby....

I raised de baby best I could and done fer de other chil'en near like a mother as I knowed how. Pa married again, and Miss Jennie was mean to us. I worked in de field every mornin', put de clothes in soak at twelve o'clock whilst I was restin', went back to de field till night, den washed and ironed our clothes and Miss

Jennie's too. Miss Jennie wouldn't let me have no soap for our clothes; de neighbors give me little scraps o' lye soap to make out wid. Some womens told me to leave home and work for myself. My sister did git a job wid a lady dat tuk her to New York wid her. De neighbors said I better do dat too. I studied 'bout it. One day I leaned on my plow handles and looked at it good. It come to me it wa'n't de thing to do. I didn't want to git on de scrap pile. De Prodigal Son done dat and had to come back home wid rags and a empty stomack. I'd rather belong somewhur; a piece o' home was better'n no home. So I stuck to it.

# FOUR:
# On the Last Frontier
## Women Together, Women Divided

IN THE PERIOD from 1865 to 1910 a flood of farm people advanced across the western half of the United States to the Plains, the Rockies, and the Pacific. That advance signalled for Native Americans the final chapter in the loss of control over

their lands and their way of life. In this sense, those years marked a last frontier: the invasion and taking of Native American territory begun three centuries earlier was completed.

On the last frontier, a struggle to control and work on the land was waged by Euro-Americans, including the two distinctive Hispanic and Mormon cultures; by Blacks; and by Native Americans. The selections in this section document the lives of the women of these five cultures as they participated in the struggle to remain on the land.

Native Americans lost control of the land in several uneven stages during the years of westward movement. In the seven-

teenth century, English colonial charters had given colonists in North American a free hand to take land from non-Christians, but because Native Americans remained relatively powerful, Europeans and Native Americans usually sealed land transfers with formal treaties, as did all sovereign nations. After the establishment of the United States in 1789, the new Congress announced that it had sole power to ratify these treaties. As the tribes east of the Mississippi gradually lost the power to maintain their independence, the federal government forcibly relocated most of them in the West on lands obtained by treaty with the tribes farther west. Treaties made by the United States with European nations and with Mexico extinguished the claims of those countries to portions of the West, but did not establish uncontested control over the land occupied by Native Americans. Then in 1871, Congress abolished the treaty system, replacing it with a reservation plan that imposed control on the Native American nations.[1]

The lands once occupied by Native Americans in the West then provided the land known as the "public domain," controlled by the government of the United States and made available for individual family farms. Homesteading laws varied over the years, but generally allowed the head of a family to file a claim on a plot of land, usually 160 acres, to pay a small sum per acre, and to gain ownership after clearing a portion of the land, building a home, and living on the land for a certain number of years. The new Homestead Act of 1862 explicitly provided that women as well as men could file for a homestead, provided "she" was a single citizen over twenty-one years of age, an immigrant who had filed papers to become a citizen, or the head of a household. Earlier homestead acts had carried no such explicit provision for women to become land owners. In the next half century, Euro-American women moved onto the land in unprecedented numbers, filing their own claims and "proving up" (staying the necessary length of time to gain clear title to homesteaded land). The Homestead Act gave Euro-American women an important stake in the land for the first time in history.

Over this same period, in the eastern part of the United States, farm families became increasingly tied to commercial farms that produced cash crops to feed the growing urban masses. Younger sons and daughters continued to homestead east of the Mississippi until 1885, after which, most of the public lands were gone; the peak of homesteading in the West came between 1900 and 1915. Between 1868 and 1917 over 170 million acres of public land were transferred to private ownership under the homestead acts. During the years to 1910, the farm population continued to grow numerically: the majority of Americans still lived on farms. By 1910, however, most of the new lands open to homesteading had been broken by the plow. Centuries of westward farm movement came to an end.[2]

The United States government expected northeastern industrial expansion to be based upon the expansion of the family farm in the West. In its *Annual Report* of 1862, the Department of Agriculture had even formulated an ideal of a husband-wife partnership in the family farm, a partnership to be cemented by romantic love. Deviations, whether in the form of slavery, Mormon polygamy, or communal farming by Native Americans, were not to be tolerated. The Republican party had received widespread support for opposing expansion of slavery in the West because Northerners feared that free family farms could not compete with Black slave plantation labor. To stop the westward expansion of slavery, the North fought the Civil War and accepted the liberation of Black Americans, who were even, for a few years, encouraged by government action to homestead in family units. It was through federal intervention, also, that the practice of polygamy was outlawed among Mormons in the West. On reservations, Native Americans often evolved successful ways to farm collectively, but the federal government always favored individual family farms, and after 1887 encouraged Native Americans to take up family plots and sell the rest of their reservation lands to Euro-American farmers and ranchers. By 1910, Native American tribes had also lost much of their remaining reservation land under this policy.[3]

Throughout the period from 1865 to 1910, the family farm remained the national ideal, a uniform agrarian base that could underpin a growing urban-industrial power. Individuals presumably would gain these family farms through rising on the "agricultural ladder." The theory of the agrarian ladder was that farm sons and daughters would begin as wage laborers on neighboring farms, save their earnings to become farm tenants or renters, and then eventually become owners of a farm themselves. Most of them would marry, beginning a new cycle of farm families. According to this theory, Americans of all ethnic groups would end up on family farms.[4]

The ideal, however, fell short of realization, especially for nonwhite Americans. Black families seeking to establish themselves on land of their own encountered many obstacles. A path had seemed to be opening for them when, in 1866, Republicans passed a special Southern Homestead Act to make remaining public domain in the states of Alabama, Arkansas, Florida, Louisiana, and Mississippi available to Blacks and to white Southern loyalists. These homesteads were to provide "cities of refuge," for freed families. Although the soil was poor and the land timbered, this law might have given thousands of Black families their own farms. But the Bureau of Freedmen, which was to help transport and settle the families, was able to give aid only in Florida, where three-fourths of the 4,000 Black homesteading families finally settled.

A few hundred Black families succeeded in obtaining land in Alabama. Among them was the Brown family, whose story, excerpted in the following pages, was later recreated by descendant Margaret Walker, poet and novelist. Still other Black people headed for Texas, but made it only as far as Louisiana, where several thousand families settled on open land without filing claim on it. After the Southern Homestead Act was repealed in 1876, most of the remaining land went to timber syndicates. So Black families went farther west, to Oklahoma, Texas, Kansas, and Colorado, where they set up hundreds of small independent farming communities.[5]

Once settled in the West, the work of Black farm women became crucial for the physical and psychological survival of family and community. Farm women were active in recreating the main Black rural social institutions—the churches. They planned church socials and community holidays. Women often farmed while men migrated to nearby towns in search of wage labor, or worked on the railroad. As Dearfield settler Irma Ingram recalls, in the interview passages reproduced here, women "worked everywhere": in the home, in the fields, and tending the dairy. For these few, the vision of an independent Black community became a reality.

For most Black families, however, the vision was impossible to realize. Land farther west required more money to reach and to farm. The Brown family and the Dearfield pioneers had enough farm equipment for field and house, and the skills to be self-sufficient. Most families did not. Black families had difficulty raising the money to go west individually. Euro-American opposition to Black settlers stalked even well-planned group enterprises, making the trek westward difficult, and survival precarious. And not all Blacks who went west shared the dreams of Vyry and Innis Brown or the Dearfield inhabitants; on the contrary, they saw farm labor as a continuing identification with the detested badge of slavery. Increasingly, then, Blacks in the West looked for opportunities in its urban areas.

If Black families found it difficult to settle on the land, Hispanic families already settled in the West found it increasingly difficult to remain on the land by the late nineteenth century. In 1846, when the United States army invaded and occupied the areas of northern Mexico now known as the Southwest, perhaps 100,000 members of Hispanic ranch and farm families already lived there. Most of the Hispanic population lived in villages, sharing communal pastures and farming individual plots of land located around the edges of the villages. Even in the larger communities, like Los Angeles and Santa Fe, many of the residents owned farms or worked as farm laborers. Artisans provided a variety of local products like cloth and shoes, and villages usually supported musicians and teachers. But the establishment of territorial governments and new land policies by the United States gradually deprived the Hispanic people of most of their land.

Through fraud, manipulation of laws, and newly imposed land taxes, non-Hispanic Americans obtained large grants of land formerly owned by Hispanics, both in California and in New Mexico. Land taxes made it difficult for Hispanic villages and families to hold onto the old land grants, while rising land prices stood in the way of the purchase of land for sons and daughters. To retain smaller farms, Hispanic men sought work in mines outside their communities, while women assumed more responsibility for running family farms. It was still possible for some families moving north from Mexico to find land, as the account in this section by Maria Duran Apodaca shows. But as the Southwest was increasingly dominated by non-Hispanic Americans—or, as they came to be called, *Anglos*—fewer and fewer Hispanic people could compete successfully with them for land.

Anglo domination was not invariable in the Southwest, however. New Mexico attracted fewer immigrants than California; and in those areas of New Mexico where the Hispanic population formed a majority, and where there was little competition from Anglos for natural resources, wealthy Hispanic families (the *ricas*) managed to retain both their influence and their property. Families such as the Bacas, for example, retained large estates, known as *haciendas*. Women of these families, described in this section by Fabiola Cabeza de Baca, enjoyed a security and stability unavailable to many poor Hispanic women. They had the advantages of education; and in the absence of established social institutions, they functioned as teachers and *médicas*, becoming responsible for most rural health care in the Southwest. Their high status in the society, then, meant hard daily work, rather than a release from it.

Many of the Hispanic villages of New Mexico also remained intact through the nineteenth century. The women of these villages left few records of their own, but other historical documents show that they inherited a tradition of hard farm work. While the poor woman might, like the *rica*, achieve high status as a *curandera* (healer) or a *partera* (midwife), it was more likely that she would spend her days working in the fields, irrigating, tending and butchering animals, and also processing food and preparing clothing. Women picked and dried chiles and made *carne secca* (jerkey); poorer women might even grind flour and produce their own simple pottery. Women also usually hauled the wood and water they needed for their work. Much of this labor was performed in extended family households, giving the women companionship and kin networks which isolated farm women did not have. Many times property was divided equally among daughters and sons; and widows retained half of the property owned with their husbands. Assigned work gave men and women their places in these villages.[6]

Under the impact of Anglo immigration, however, these cultural traditions began to break down. The nuclear family began to replace the extended family among Hispanics. As American economic and social institutions became more dominant, Hispanic women were caught between the new economic constraints and older community traditions. Daughters had worked within the family, where brothers and fathers assumed responsibility for their welfare. When young women worked outside the family, that responsibility decreased in reality, even though it might remain a masculine ideal. Hispanic women who began to work outside the family gradually assumed responsibility not only for their own welfare but also the additional task of helping their families retain control over dwindling land holdings.[7]

While most Black and Hispanic families were to find insurmountable barriers to settling and remaining on the land, the pull of the west continued to draw large numbers of Euro-American families from Prairie states like Illinois. Their resettlement on the Plains brought its own kind of hardship, beginning with leaving kin behind. But the vision of getting a home of their own persuaded women like Eva Hendrickson, whose recollections appear in the following pages, to undertake the arduous trail westward. Among arriving Euro-American families, too, it was often necessary for men to do day labor for neighbors, or in town, and to leave women to manage the new farms. Women ran the farms, made clothing, processed food, and provided health care and midwifery skills; because schools were often not established nearby, they also educated children.

On many western farms, women duplicated the practice of their eastern sisters in producing butter for urban markets. By 1860, eastern farm families had already come to depend on butter for a cash income to supplement income from grain surplus. As spinning and weaving had earlier been their prime household industry, making butter now became the chief occupation of farm women and girls. With the increasing urban consumer demand in the nineteenth century, women on small farms developed a decentralized butter industry, in which they carried surplus butter to country stores to exchange for necessities—just as, in an earlier era, they had carried yards of homespun cloth, until it was replaced by industrial textiles. As each frontier became settled in the West, more women turned to buttermaking as a way of supplementing the farm income. By 1910, women on the plains of Montana were using butter money to buy windmills necessary for survival of farms in the waterless land. As Elinore Stewart's account shows, she was enthusiastic about her homesteading because she grew most of her own food, and because her ten cows could provide enough butter to pay for flour and gasoline—two items she could not produce on her ranch in Wyoming.[8]

Farm daughters, whether immigrant or American-born, were likely to be deprived of any but the most rudimentary education. Better education was available in the urban centers on the frontier; and young farm women often felt inferior to town girls, who, unlike farm daughters, could go to school, working neither in the fields, nor laboring in the towns to pay off farm mortgages. The Nebraska frontier, which novelist Willa Cather knew so well, was harsh. Although her fictional Bohemian farm woman in *My Ántonia* survived, and helped to establish a prosperous farm of her own, forty-three percent of the homesteaders in Nebraska failed. Sickness, poverty, and natural disasters accounted for half of these failures. Failure in Nebraska might bring a move north to the Dakotas or to Alberta, Canada, or south to Colorado. In some areas of Colorado, women homesteaders had higher success rates than men at proving up their claims. But everywhere, failure, more often than success, encouraged the process of moving west.[9]

For those women who stayed on the land, either with kin or alone, the bitterest problem was the isolation which accompanied settlement on the arid farm and ranch lands of the West. But if the fictional Ántonia survived and flourished, so, too, did real women like the hardy Emma Marble, a New Mexico homesteader. Her reminiscences tell us of the loneliness which drove many women to leave their claims for extended visits with one another, while their husbands were cattle-herding or working the mines. Some women found the lack of village life an insurmountable disadvantage. They left for town—sometimes with their husbands and sometimes alone. The telephone finally linked women together, enabling later women homesteaders to ease their loneliness.[10]

Half-a-century before the telephone reached the farm, over 10,000 people, most of them in family units, participated in what Mormons call the "Great Migration of 1849." Crossing the plains into the Great Basin of Utah, they established Salt Lake City. Among these migrants were many single women converts for whom the church had promised to provide, in return for hard work and faith.

Mormon doctrine had always emphasized the importance of work for women in the community. As was the case in Judaism, Mormonism viewed the hard secular work of women as a way of liberating the men to pursue religious work. Women had to be prepared to survive on the the frontier, for the men went on missions for a period of at least one year. Lucy Hannah White Flake's account of homesteading, excerpted here, conveys the feeling of the immense responsibilities of Mormon farm women. In return for their work, the Mormon women gained a community support structure which was unique to western women. Groups of families moved to a new area together, setting up villages with houses clustered together, and fields outside the village. Villages then organized into districts, to meet farming needs, and into wards, to meet spiritual needs. Community and church reinforced each other in providing for the needs of families. Mormon women, for example, had perhaps the best obstetrics care of any frontier rural women of the late nineteenth century: each ward selected three women to train as midwives for six months in Salt Lake City, who then returned to serve their communities. As with Hispanic women, these skills brought status to individual women, as well as excellent female medical care to all. Mormon granaries could provide surplus food needed for new villages; and during the early settlement years, the practice of polygamy gave single women homes they might not otherwise have had.[11]

Polygamy was the most controversial of Mormon religious practices in the nineteenth century, one which attracted outside criticism, and was finally suppressed by the federal government. Practiced officially for fifty years, from 1840 to 1890, this "patriarchal order of marriage" never involved more than ten percent of Mormon men, but affected all Mormon women. An early revelation of Mormon founder Joseph Smith, polygamy became more firmly rooted as the church struggled to care for, and retain, young unmarried women between the ages of twenty-five and thirty-five years of age who came west to the Mormon Zion. By the late 1850s, polygamy had become a prerequisite for any man who wished to advance in the church; but bishops approved taking of more than one wife only by men who could afford to care for more than one household. Most plural wives shared their husbands with one other woman, and often the first wife chose the second wife. The marriage ceremony customarily involved the wife giving the bride to her husband.

In this "patriarchal order," husbands could be arbitrary in the distribution of material goods—including food—as well as their time and affection. However, accounts by Mormon daughters also record the advantages of polygamous households, such as learning a wide range of skills from several mothers and receiving good care even when one mother might be ill.[12] The benefits to adult women of sharing work and responsiblity were similar to those offered by communal Native American households.

Anti-polygamy acts passed by Congress caused much suffering among Mormon women. Some women lived with their children in hiding from the law for a decade. At the same time, persecution of the church for polygamy and the need for women to support each other in difficult times led to strong women's groups. Persecution may also have influenced the decision of the Mormon church to support women's suffrage. Support of suffrage was a way to retain a faction of the church which favored suffrage, as well as to refute outside critics who charged that Mormon women were enslaved by a polygamous family system.

Wyoming Territory had enfranchised 1000 women in December 1869—but two months later Utah Territory enfranchised 43,000 women, most of whom were Mormons. During the next forty years, many of these Mormon women became ardent suffragists. They published women's newspapers, organized suffrage groups, and campaigned to extend suffrage to other western states where Mormon women lived. Lucy Hannah White Flake's account reflects some of this ferment. However, once the Mormon church abandoned the doctrine of polygamy, it ceased to support further expansion of women's political rights, and began to oppose the women's movement which had developed within the church.[13]

Mormons had less conflict with Native Americans than did most Euro-Americans. Mormon women acted as doctors and midwives to Native American women in the West. They took in Native American orphans, raising them with their own children, learned Native American languages, fed Native American delegations, and developed programs to help Native American women in their regions. But if the Mormons caused less violence than did other Euro-Americans, their presence nevertheless led to the same pattern of competition for use of the land.[14]

On the Plains, in the Rockies, and on the Pacific Coast, the invasion of the Euro-Americans produced a bloody conflict over control of land and resources. Open war between the United States army and Native American tribes continued until the 1890s. Vigilantes and border ruffians engaged in vicious guerilla warfare. Euro-Americans decimated California's native population—in the case of the Yahi, systematically searching out and destroying the whole tribe. Epidemics had already seriously reduced the Native American population before soldiers and renegades eliminated their armed resistance. Then settlers moved in, disrupting or destroying the natural resources from which Native Americans had derived their food supply. In the West, where water was scarce, control of water was essential for the women's corn fields. When settlers plowed lands, they also disrupted the supply of wild food gathered by Native American women to supplement their cultivated gardens. Livestock ate the grasses upon which smaller game had subsisted, and both professional hunters and settlers participated in the slaughter of buffalo that Native American men had hunted. The sheer numbers of Euro-Americans, in combination with their settled, year-round family farm system of diversified crops and irrigated or dry land farming techniques, and their access to government protection, insured that their land system would prevail.[15]

Southwestern tribes struggled against extinction on the last frontier by combining subsistence farming with a market product. Pueblo women turned to pottery, and Navajo women to weaving, to bring in the extra cash needed to buy items they could no longer produce. The Osages in Oklahoma produced thousands of pounds of butter for the market each year. Elsewhere, the government demanded a continuation of the old policy established in the early nineteenth century, that Native American men engage in agriculture and Native American women withdraw from agriculture, even though this did not accord with their cultural practices. During these hard times in the West, Native American women often led their people in attempts to develop new ways to survive on the land. Chiparopai, leader of the Mohave, most eloquently summed up the fears of Native American women on the last frontier as the Euro-Americans gradually encircled their people: "When you come, we die."

# Jubilee

*Margaret Walker based the novel* Jubilee *(1966) on the life of her great-grandmother who left a Georgia plantation shortly after the Civil War and settled on a small farm in Alabama. The story of the family's migration west and first summer is retold here.*

**N**ine months after Lee's surrender the South was still trying to extricate itself from the wreckage of war. The roads and railroads were in many cases in a poor state of repair, and in some places were utterly beyond use. People were moving from place to place, nevertheless, at great inconvenience. The fact that Vyry and Innis Brown with two small children, Minna and Jim, were on the road in January of 1866 looking for a place to settle where they could begin a new life was typical of hundreds of thousands of emancipated Negroes.

It was bitterly cold. Vyry heated smoothing irons and wrapped them in rags to keep the children's feet warm while they sat in the wagon. Jim and Minna peeped out of the rear over the tail board while Vyry and Innis rode up front with more hot bricks and irons to keep them warm.

There was plenty of food for them, and provisions for the mule. Vyry had an abundance of other things she considered necessary to give them a comfortable start in life. She had iron pots and kettles, a wash pot, skillets, smoothing irons, candle molds and tallow candles, tin plates and cups and dippers of gourd and tin, a china wash bowl and pitcher and a slop jar. She had quilts and croker sacks* of cotton and feathers for beds and pillows, a precious spinning wheel, lots of potash soap, and most important of all she had sacks of seed. She filled the chest with her most valuable keepsakes from the plantation and Big House and tied it on the wagon. She baked sugar cakes for the children and roasted peanuts and she filled sacks with hickory nuts, pecans, and black walnuts....

At night they stopped to make a camp fire and cook supper, then they went to bed in the wagon with the mule tied to a tree. Early in the morning Vyry would make a hot mush gruel for breakfast and fill their stomachs with hot food and hot sweetened water before they began another day. She kept cold pones of corn bread and cold roasted sweet potatoes with hog meat for their middle of the day meal. But sometimes they did not stop along the way to eat this, hoping to move a few miles farther during the daylight hours....

Once they had completed the log cabin for shelter, Innis Brown and Vyry made long rows for a field which they planted

*Croker sacks: coarse sacking, as gunny or burlap.

with cotton seed and corn, sugar cane, rice, and potatoes. They exulted in the rich bottom land, although it was largely sandy loam, and they carried buckets of water up from the river to water the rows, for the spring and summer were very dry that year. Vyry detected a spring in the woods with clear fresh water to drink, and for this they were most grateful. In the spring they explored the woods. There would be wild fruits and berries and wild greens to add to their diet of corn meal and hog meat. As they walked through the forest where they lived, the children picked flowers and Vyry found her precious herbs and roots for teas and medicine, such as mullein, pinetop, penny royal, and sheep sorrel in profusion. . . .

At the end of the summer Vyry looked at her rows of canned vegetables, preserves, jam, and jelly and her provisions for the winter with great satisfaction. They dug potatoes and stored them in hills. She dried onions, and chopped cabbage and hot peppers for sauerkraut. She gathered okra and tomatoes and string beans and peas and corn and canned them. She dried meat and even dried some fish. She knew the value of rock salt and how to stretch her brown sugar and sugar cane syrup. Innis Brown laughed at her gathering her usual supply of nuts from the forest, measuring the peanuts she had grown, and saving sugar cane for the children to chew. "Ain't nobody gwine starve with you around!"

## A Woman Works Everywhere

*Dearfield, thirty miles east of Greeley, Colorado, was an all-Black farming community founded in 1910. Like many twentieth-century homestead and subsistence farms, the Dearfield farms could not survive without a cash income. The men therefore usually took wage-jobs, and the women farmed.*

*By the 1950s, Dearfield had dwindled to one inhabitant, a woman who remained in the settlement hoping that others would return, and again "share with each other." When she died, Dearfield vanished—except in the memories of the former inhabitants. In the excerpts that follow, from an interview conducted in 1976 by the Dearfield Oral History Project, three Black women who grew up in Dearfield explain the work of women in this farming community.*

**Irma Ingram:** My father was a foreman on the railroad, and he farmed too. My older brother and mother did a lot of the farming because that was the only way we could make it.... I don't remember any of the women ever working out, only at potato harvest time....

There was too much for women to do in their homes and fields to hire out—those dry fields—took all their effort. Money came from crops and men working outside. You know, Negroes were always at the "poverty level" but they did not consider themselves poor, they always had food, and necessities....

Every household expected the woman in the home to do the work. A woman works everywhere, she worked in the home, would put her cooking on before she went to the field, and then come back and tend to it, serve it, and if necessary go back out to the fields, or milk the cows, she would do that. A woman can adapt herself to every place and they were that kind of women. To make a life you endure most anything, women do.... That was a hardship area, you had to irrigate from windmills, with all that blowing sand. They'd come from fertile lands, better farms, but they went there to stick it out.

**Olietta Moore:** Mother was widowed and went to work in Denver to support her family. She homesteaded 160 acres in Dearfield so that Grandpa would have a place to garden and putter around on. They worked in the fields, raised corn, they would bring it to Denver and give it away to friends.

My aunt owned property there too.... My aunt was highly educated, many black people were, but they weren't hiring Negro teachers, mostly they worked as domestics, because it was better in Colorado than in the south.

People got along well. It was a peaceful sort of situation: struggling people working hard, they didn't have time for trouble. There was a spirit of helpfulness....

I remember places in Dearfield where they had dances, a dancehall. There were moonlight picnics, with lanterns, and big chicken fries. The people were friendly, neighborly.

**Irma Ingram:** For recreation was dancing, and church socials, and the women would get these together, there were picnics, and the younger folks had card parties. Denver was just about seventy miles away and the people of Denver liked to come up for social weekends. People didn't mix racially, but white folks would come up to hunt and fish.

Parents went to the school, to hear the children's recitations, and the picnics, the families all got together and worked at that, the ladies did the cooking and things.

All holidays were celebrated by the whole community. On Labor Day there was a white family, the McPhersons, they always gave a barbeque for the whole community, before school started. That's one time black and white and all got together and had a real good time....

Everyone had large families and they took care of each other. And I remember we always left a light on at night so if someone was lost they could find their way.

**Sarah Fountain** (a teacher): I was staying with the Clarks, friends of my family, and they accepted me as family. I'd wash and dry after dinner, wash my clothes in a tub and washboard. I made my own clothes and cooked.... You just assume certain duties if you're a girl.... Mother Clark protected me. She'd say to these young fellows who'd take me off on the ponies, "You be back home before dark," just like my mother would say, and I always was.

People were friendly, you know there's a deep respect for teachers. They liked me and I liked them and they accepted me as their teacher. I had to use a little whip once in a while—for discipline—the younger ones. It was all right with the parents that I did, make 'em mind. They were plain folks, they wanted their children educated, some of them were educated themselves.

The church was just up the hill from the school and we practiced singing there. I organized the students into a church choir. They permitted us to do that, practice, because it was the community church, everything belonged to everybody. I do believe women are more responsible for getting the church going, they're behind it. I knew some women in Denver who could get money from the wealthy people they worked for—they went all out to get money for their churches. They are the backbone of the church. It was women who kept that [Dearfield] church clean, went out and kept it in order. There were the women's church organizations, you know, the sewing and missionary group, it was well-organized. The children worked into the church programs, they would sing and I played piano. At school we played games, I was a YWCA person, had conducted a Y camp in the mountains, all kinds of games, volleyball and football. I taught them everything in the books and everything I knew. The girls taught me to knit and embroider. I had membership in the YWCA Girl Reserves since its inception in Denver—it emphasized community activities—helped me to help these children.

Most people went out there with high hopes and left with bitter disappointment. It all dried up and blew away.

## Women of the Llano

*Fabiola Cabeza de Baca grew up on the Llano, a plateau area in northwestern New Mexico. The selection that follows is from* We Fed Them Cactus, *an account both autobiographical and based on oral tradition, in which Baca described the lives*

*of late nineteenth-century Hispanic* ricas *(well-to-do-women)*
*of the Llano. In terms reminiscent of a Southern plantation*
*mistress, she tells here of the* rica's *work among* hacienda
empleados *(employees). The shared culture of Southwest*
*Hispanics allowed much closer relations among people of*
*different classes than were known between whites and*
*Blacks in the South; however, Baca probably over-emphasized*
*the democracy of the hacienda.*

T he women on the Llano and Ceja\* played a great part in the
history of the land. It was a difficult life for a woman, but
she had made her choice when in the marriage ceremony she had
promised to obey and to follow her husband. It may not have
been her choice, since parents may have decided for her. It was
the Spanish custom to make matches for the children. Whether
through choice or tradition, the women had to be a hardy lot in
order to survive the long trips by wagon or carriage and the
separation from their families, if their families were not among
those who were settling on the Llano.

The women had to be versed in the curative powers of plants
and in midwifery, for there were no doctors within a radius of
two hundred miles or more.

The knowledge of plant medicine is an inheritance from the
Moors and brought to New Mexico by the first Spanish colo-
nizers. From childhood, we are taught the names of herbs, weeds
and plants that have curative potency; even today when we have
doctors at our immediate call, we still have great faith in plant
medicine. Certainly this knowledge of home remedies was a
source of comfort to the women who went out to the Llano, yet
their faith in God helped more than anything in the survival.

Every village had its *curandera* or *médica* and the ranchers
rode many miles to bring the medicine woman or the midwife
from a distant village or neighboring ranch.

Quite often, the wife of the *patrón†* was well versed in plant

---

\**Ceja:* the edge or lip of the plateau.
†*Patrón:* master, boss, or landlord.

medicine. I know that my grandmother, Doña Estéfana Delgado de Baca, although not given the name of *médica*, because it was not considered proper in her social class, was called every day by some family in the village, or by their *empleados*, to treat a child or some other person in the family. In the fall of the year, she went out to the hills and valleys to gather her supply of healing herbs. When she went to live in La Liendre, there were terrible outbreaks of smallpox and she had difficulty convincing the villagers that vaccination was a solution. Not until she had a godchild in every family was she able to control the dreaded disease. In Spanish tradition, a godmother takes the responsibility of a real mother, and in that way grandmother conquered many superstitions which the people had. At least she had the power to decide what should be done for her godchildren.

From El Paso, Texas, she secured vaccines from her cousin, Doctor Samaniego. She vaccinated her children, grandchildren and godchildren against the disease. She vaccinated me when I was three years old and the vaccination has passed many doctors' inspections.

As did my grandmother, so all the wives of the *patrones* held a very important place in the villages and ranches on the Llano. The *patrón* ruled the *rancho*, but his wife looked after the spiritual and physical welfare of the *empleados* and their families. She was the first one called when there was death, illness, misfortune or good tidings in a family. She was a great social force in the community—more so than her husband. She held the purse strings, and thus she was able to do as she pleased in her charitable enterprises and to help those who might seek her assistance.

There may have been class distinction in the larger towns, but the families on the Llano had none; the *empleados* and their families were as much a part of the family of the *patrón* as his own children. It was a very democratic way of life.

The women in these isolated areas had to be resourceful in every way. They were their own doctors, dressmakers, tailors and advisers.

The settlements were far apart and New Mexico was a poor territory trying to adapt itself to a new rule. The Llano people had no opportunity for public schools, before statehood, but there were men and women who held classes for the children of the *patrones* in private homes. They taught reading in Spanish and sometimes in English. Those who had means sent their children to school in Las Vegas, Santa Fe, or Eastern states. If no teachers were available, the mothers taught their own children to read and many of the wealthy ranchers had private teachers for their children until they were old enough to go away to boarding schools.

## North from Mexico

*The Durans moved north from the state of Chihuahua in Mexico to the Territory of New Mexico in the 1880s where they farmed a small plot of land. In 1978, when Maria Duran Apodaca was 90, she explained to interviewer Aracelli Pando how her family obtained their land and what it was like growing up in the 1890s.*

**M**y parents were from Juarez but after New Mexico became a territory they came over here. Things were so different then. They had no rules about crossing. You would cross over from Juarez and then if you wanted to live here they would tell you, "OK, from here to there is yours." And they would stake it out. The properties were chosen by sight. A relative of my father was already here and he had a lot of land near the mountains. He told my father, "From there to there is yours. Put in the stakes." It didn't cost my father anything.

That's where we planted. It was a good *sembrado* [plot of land]. My father worked it with only a *cavador* [hoe] and *ancha* [ax]. We did not have a horse. We had nothing. Everything was done *a mano* [by hand]. We planted *maize* [corn], *traigo* [wheat], *chile, frijoles* [beans]. We would *cosecha* [harvest] it to eat during the winter. Now that's not the way. People have to live with everything in cans.

We were very poor. We had a house of only two rooms. It was not adobe; it was made out of sticks. We called them *jacals*. I can remember when I was eight years old, I had measles in that *jacalito*. I barely remember it as if in a dream, that skin, that is where they would lay me. There was only one bed and skins for all of us. Skins of goat or cow.

I never stepped inside a school. I learned how to read because my mother taught me. She knew how to read but she didn't know how to write. One of my half brothers taught me how to write. When the school opened I was already too big to go. I was eleven.

When I was young, I helped make food and washed clothes but I also worked in the orchard and hoed weeds. My father got sick and I would lead him around with his hand on my shoulder. Before this a man used to bring coffee beans around to sell. They had to be roasted. Then a man named José Rodriguez built the first grocery store here in San Miguel. My father and I would go to the store and buy lard. I was about ten when the store opened.

After my father died, the three of us women stayed with my mother. My youngest sister helped with the housework but myself and Josefa worked outside. We worked on *el sembrado* [the cultivated land]. We worked very hard. We planted and did everything like my father had. We would grind dried chile in the *metate*. We would roast green chile outside, peel it, and put it out to dry on the bark of the tree. We would clean the bark real good and put it there to dry. We called it *chile pasado*.

We grew lima beans. Sometimes my mother would pick them and cook them in water for dinner. And to drink we had *atole* [toasted corn and water]. Sometimes, we'd have *frijoles* or cooked corn. Now the weather is not as cold and the winter months go by fast. But then! The craziness of December and January. How we would pray that those months would end. It was so cold. And then we had to go out and cut wood. We had *fagones* [indoor ovens].

I was real young when I got married. I think I was nineteen years old. After I married I didn't work in *el sembrado*. My father had divided the land into four parts for the girls and my mother. And on my share my husband planted corn and wheat. The land was mine but my husband planted on it. We would take the flour to *el molino* [the mill] in Las Cruces to have it ground. We got the best two thirds and paid with the other third. We wouldn't get it in bags.

Now, God know where they get the flour. They don't mill it around here any more.

## Memories of the Plains

*When Eva Hendrickson was five, her father was killed in a railroad accident. Unable to support four children, her mother split up the family. Later, her mother reestablished a home for the children, but at twelve Eva Hendrickson began to support herself by doing domestic work for board and clothing. At sixteen, she married, and the following year, in 1880, left Illinois with her husband for Nebraska. Later in her life, she dictated her recollections. In the excerpts here, she recalls her life in a "soddie," the prairie houses built out of sod by the early Nebraska pioneers.*

**T**he next Summer was such a busy one. As soon as the fruit got ripe Mother Klepper and I began canning and drying. Currants and gooseberries were canned. Then cherries, we had 2 trees on the place we lived on. After we canned those I picked some on shares at one of the neighbors and canned them. As soon as the apples were ripe enough we commenced drying them. The peaches were next. We canned some and dried some. We had no nice glass jars. Used tin cans and sealed the lids down with sealing wax. But we must put up all the fruit we could as there were no fruit trees in Furnas County. Well, September came and it was time to make preparations to start west. On

September 19th we had our sale. Sold all the furniture. Packed all the bedding we didn't need to bring with us in a big goods box, packing pictures dishes and glassware among the bedding to keep it from breaking. This box we shipped to Orleans, Nebraska.... We loaded our wagons. We put in trunks, boxes of fruit, a chest with some clothing, bedding and pillows that we would need to sleep on and sacks of grain for the horses. In the front of our wagon we had a grub box, a big one, and some cooking utensils, where they would be handy to get. On September 22 the wagons were all loaded and nice new covers on. And about 2 p.m. we were ready to start. Some friends were there to see off, and say good bye, telling us, "you will be back next fall." But we know we are going to stay. Some would say, "Eva how can you leave all your people and go away out to Nebraska. It's so far away." I told them "I do hate to leave my dear mother, sister and brother; but I am going with my husband. And we are going to get us a home of our own where we can be to ourselves." That meant so much to us. So saying good bye to our loved ones we started. And were on our way out west....

There was no place for me to make a garden only what would grow in the sod. One day Jim says to me: "Eva on that North fire guard in the draw is a good place to plant some pumpkin seed." So I took the spade and some seeds and went up there. I would stick the spade down thru the sod, put in a few seeds, and mash the sod down on them with my foot. I had planted several hills when all at once I heard a queer buzzing noise so close to me. I looked and right in front of me, all coiled up was a big rattle snake ready to strike. Oh, I was so scared I never tried to kill it, just went hustling back to the house as fast as I could go. And never went back there until the pumpkins were ripe. It was the first rattler I ever heard. But I never forgot that sound. Jim broke out five acres of sod that spring and we planted that in corn, chopping it in. I took the ax and Jim the spade. That first summer was a long one for me. Jim got a job of breaking sod for a Mr. Watts that lived near Deviges, Kansas, about three and one-half miles from home. He would go early in the morning and not get home till dark. I did all the chores....

We were very poor. And our food was of the plainest. But we never went hungry. We would have biscuits made out of wheat flour for breakfast, and corn bread for dinner and supper. We had butter and molasses. Once they got some rye and took it to the mill and I tried to make biscuits out of that. We managed to eat them while hot, but, oh dear, when they got cold the dog couldn't hardly chew them. I can see the old black things yet.

We had some hard rains that summer. And once or twice it rained so hard the ditch above the dugout wasn't deep enough to carry all the water off. It run in at the window, and out at the door. Made our dirt floor rather soft. And the roof leaked something awful....

December 15th 1881, our baby girl was born. No good Dr. and nurse then, when a young mother needed them so bad. Just an old lady that was in the neighborhood that took the place of midwife. A good neighbor lady came and stayed with us a few days. Then Jim's sister stayed a day or two until I was able to sit up. We were so proud of our little black-eyed baby girl. We named her Mary Belle. Jim and I both had a sister Mary, and Belle was the lady's name that was so good to stay with us. Our hardest summer was past. We raised some seed corn that year and there was wheat too where the ground had been cultivated but wheat wouldn't grow on sod like corn would.

That year Jim broke more sod, and in the fall he plowed the 5 acres he had broke in the spring, and sowed it to wheat. The next year when harvest time came, he couldn't get a Reaper to cut the wheat so he got a man to cut it with an old fashioned cradle and Jim bound it. Then we had wheat enough for our bread. No more rye biscuits....

In 1882 and 1883 crops were some better. Jim worked for anyone who would give him a days work and that helped so much. I did what I could to help, such as washing for single men who were living on their claims, and did sewing. I did some sewing for one of the Jones girls and bought the first real bedstead we ever had....

In 1890 we had another crop failure. No rain to speak of. How the hot winds did blow and there was nothing raised but a little dried up fodder. Then we wondered again, how we would get thru the winter. But there was always some way provided. In 91 and 92 we had good crops, lots of good corn, but no market for it; 10-12-15 cents a bushel. As fuel was scarce, a good many burned corn that year. But it was very little corn we ever burnt. It seemed wicked to burn something that was needed for food.

# My Ántonia

*Novelist Willa Cather based* My Ántonia *on the life of a young Bohemian immigrant girl she had watched grow to womanhood near Red Cloud, Nebraska, the town to which Cather moved with her parents at age ten, in 1883. Here she describes Ántonia as a farmer and as a country girl at work in the small town, through the eyes of Jim, a young neighbor boy. Ambrosch was Ántonia's brother; Jake was the hired hand on the farm owned by Jim's family.*

When the sun was dropping low, Ántonia came up the big south draw with her team. How much older she had grown in eight months! She had come to us a child, and now she was a tall, strong young girl, although her fifteenth birthday had just slipped by. I ran out and met her as she brought her horses up to the windmill to water them. She wore the boots her father had so thoughtfully taken off before he shot himself, and his old fur cap. Her outgrown cotton dress switched about her calves, over the boot-tops. She kept her sleeves rolled up all day, and her arms and throat were burned as brown as a sailor's. Her neck came up strongly out of her shoulders, like the bole of a tree out of the turf. One sees that draught-horse neck among the peasant women in all old countries.

She greeted me gaily, and began at once to tell me how much ploughing she had done that day. Ambrosch, she said, was on the north quarter, breaking sod with the oxen.

'Jim, you ask Jake how much he ploughed to-day. I don't want that Jake get more done in one day than me. I want we have very much corn this fall.'

While the horses drew in the water, and nosed each other, and then drank again, Ántonia sat down on the windmill step and rested her head on her hand.

'You see the big prairie fire from your place last night? I hope your grandpa ain't lose no stacks?'

'No, we didn't. I came to ask you something, Tony. Grandmother wants to know if you can't go to the term of school that begins next week over at the sod school-house. She says there's a good teacher, and you'd learn a lot.'

Ántonia stood up, lifting and dropping her shoulders as if they were stiff. 'I ain't got time to learn. I can work like mans now. My mother can't say no more how Ambrosch do all and nobody to help him. I can work as much as him. School is all right for little boys. I help make this land one good farm.'

She clucked to her team and started for the barn. I walked beside her, feeling vexed. Was she going to grow up boastful like her mother, I wondered? Before we reached the stable, I felt something tense in her silence, and glancing up I saw that she was crying. She turned her face from me and looked off at the red streak of dying light, over the dark prairie.

I climbed up into the loft and threw down the hay for her, while she unharnessed her team. We walked slowly back toward the house. Ambrosch had come in from the north quarter, and was watering his oxen at the tank.

Ántonia took my hand. 'Sometime you will tell me all those nice things you learn at the school, won't you, Jimmy?' she asked with a sudden rush of feeling in her voice. 'My father, he went much to school. He know a great deal; how to make the fine cloth like what you not got here. He play horn and violin, and he read so many books that the priests in Bohemie come to talk to him. You won't forget my father, Jim?'

'No,' I said, 'I will never forget him....'

Since winter I had seen very little of Ántonia. She was out in the fields from sunup until sundown. If I rode over to see her where she was ploughing, she stopped at the end of a row to chat for a moment, then gripped her plough-handles, clucked to her team, and waded on down the furrow, making me feel that she was now grown up and had no time for me. On Sundays she helped her mother make garden or sewed all day. Grandfather was pleased with Ántonia. When we complained of her, he only smiled and said, 'She will help some fellow get ahead in the world.'

Nowadays Tony could talk of nothing but the prices of things, or how much she could lift and endure. She was too proud of her strength. I knew, too, that Ambrosch put upon her some chores a girl ought not to do, and that the farm-hands around the country joked in a nasty way about it. Whenever I saw her come up the furrow, shouting to her beasts, sunburned, sweaty, her dress open at the neck, and her throat and chest dustplastered, I used to think of the tone in which poor Mr. Shimerda, who could say so little, yet managed to say so much when he exclaimed, 'My Ántonia!'....

There was a curious social situation in Black Hawk. All the young men felt the attraction of the fine, well-set-up country girls who had come to town to earn a living, and, in nearly every case, to help the father struggle out of debt, or to make it possible for the younger children of the family to go to school.

Those girls had grown up in the first bitter-hard times, and had got little schooling themselves. But the younger brothers and sisters, for whom they made such sacrifices and who have had 'advantages,' never seem to me, when I meet them now, half as interesting or as well educated. The older girls, who helped to break up the wild sod, learned so much from life, from poverty, from their mothers and grandmothers; they had all, like Ántonia, been early awakened and made observant by coming at a tender age from an old country to a new.

I can remember a score of these country girls who were in service in Black Hawk during the few years I lived there, and I can remember something unusual and engaging about each of them. Physically they were almost a race apart, and out-of-door work had given them a vigour which, when they got over their first shyness on coming to town, developed into a positive carriage and freedom of movement, and made them conspicuous among Black Hawk women. . . .

The daughters of Black Hawk merchants had a confident, unenquiring belief that they were 'refined,' and that the country girls, who 'worked out,' were not. The American farmers in our county were quite as hard-pressed as their neighbours from other countries. All alike had come to Nebraska with little capital and no knowledge of the soil they must subdue. All had borrowed money on their land. But no matter in what straits the Pennsylvanian or Virginian found himself, he would not let his daughters go out into service. Unless his girls could teach a country school, they sat at home in poverty.

The Bohemian and Scandinavian girls could not get positions as teachers, because they had had no opportunity to learn the language. Determined to help in the struggle to clear the homestead from debt, they had no alternative but to go into service. Some of them, after they came to town, remained as serious and as discreet in behaviour as they had been when they ploughed and herded on their father's farm. Others, like the three Bohemian Marys, tried to make up for the years of youth they had lost. But every one of them did what she had set out to do, and sent home those hard-earned dollars. The girls I knew were always helping to pay for ploughs and reapers, brood-sows, or steers to fatten.

One result of this family solidarity was that the foreign farmers in our country were the first to become prosperous. After the fathers were out of debt, the daughters married the sons of neighbors—usually of like nationality—and the girls who once worked in Black Hawk kitchens are today managing big farms and fine families of their own; their children are better off than the children of the town women they used to serve. . .

The country girls were considered a menace to the social order. Their beauty shone out too boldly against a conventional background. But anxious mothers need have felt no alarm. They mistook the mettle of their sons. The respect for respectability was stronger than any desire in Black Hawk youth.

# Homesteading in Wyoming

*Elinore Rupert was a widowed washwoman with a young daughter when she decided in 1909 to leave Denver for Wyoming to homestead. Accepting a position as housekeeper with a Scottish cattleman, she carried out her plan to homestead, meanwhile continuing over the summer to manage the cattleman's household. She ran the mower (something she had learned as a young orphan girl on her grandmother's farm); milked cows; did the cooking at night; put up jelly and jam; and, after the harvest was finished, went off camping with her daughter. Four years later, after marrying the rancher, she wrote to her former employer advising homesteading as an alternative to going out to wash.*

*January 23, 1913.*

Dear Mrs. Coney, —
I am afraid all my friends think I am very forgetful and that you think I am ungrateful as well, but I am going to plead not guilty. Right after Christmas Mr. Stewart came down with *la grippe* and was so miserable that it kept me busy trying to relieve him. Out here where we can get no physician we have to dope ourselves, so that I had to be housekeeper, nurse, doctor, and general overseer. That explains my long silence.

And now I want to thank you for your kind thought in prolonging our Christmas. The magazines were much appreciated. They relieved some weary night-watches, and the box did Jerrine more good than the medicine I was having to give her for *la grippe*. She was content to stay in bed and enjoy the contents of her box.

When I read of the hard times among the Denver poor, I feel like urging them every one to get out and file on land. I am very enthusiastic about women homesteading. It really requires less strength and labor to raise plenty to satisfy a large family than it does to go out to wash, with the added satisfaction of knowing that their job will not be lost to them if they care to keep it. Even if improving the place does go slowly, it is that much done to stay done. Whatever is raised is the homesteader's own, and there is no house-rent to pay. This year Jerrine cut and dropped enough potatoes to raise a ton of fine potatoes. She wanted to try, so we let her, and you will remember that she is but six years old. We had a man to break the ground and cover the potatoes for her and the man irrigated them once. That was all that was done until digging time, when they were ploughed out and Jerrine picked them up. Any woman strong enough to go out by the day could have done every bit of the work and put in two or three times that much, and it would have been so much more pleasant than to work so hard in the city and then be on starvation rations in the winter.

To me, homesteading is the solution of all poverty's problems, but I realize that temperament has much to do with success in any undertaking, and persons afraid of coyotes and work and loneliness had better let ranching alone. At the same time, any woman who can stand her own company, can see the beauty of the sunset, loves growing things, and is willing to put in as much time at careful labor as she does over the washtub, will certainly succeed; will have independence, plenty to eat all the time, and a home of her own in the end.

Experimenting need cost the homesteader no more than the work, because by applying to the Department of Agriculture at Washington [she or] he can get enough of any seed and as many kinds as he wants to make a thorough trial, and it doesn't even cost postage. Also one can always get bulletins from there and from the Experiment Station of one's own State concerning any problem or as many problems as may come up. I would not, for anything, allow Mr. Stewart to do anything toward improving my place, for I want the fun and the experience myself. And I want to be able to speak from experience when I tell others what they can do. Theories are very beautiful, but facts are what must be had, and what I intend to give some time.

Here I am boring you to death with things that cannot interest you! You'd think I wanted you to homestead, wouldn't you? But I am only thinking of the troops of tired, worried women, sometimes even cold and hungry, scared to death of losing their places to work, who could have plenty to eat, who could have good fires by gathering the wood, and comfortable homes of their own, if they but had the courage and determination to get them.

I must stop right now before you get so tired you will not answer. With much love to you from Jerrine and myself, I am

Yours affectionately,
Elinore Rupert Stewart

*November, 1913.*

**D**ear Mrs. Coney, —
This is Sunday and I suppose I ought not to be writing, but I must write to you and I may not have another chance soon. Both your letters have reached me, and now that our questions are settled we can proceed to proceed.

Now, this is the letter I have been wanting to write you for a long time, but could not because until now I had not actually proven all I wanted to prove. Perhaps it will not interest you, but if you see a woman who wants to homestead and is a little afraid she will starve, you can tell her what I am telling you.

I never did like to theorize, and so this year I set out to prove that a woman could ranch if she wanted to. We like to grow potatoes on new ground, that is, newly cleared land on which no crop has been grown. Few weeds grow on new land, so it makes less work. So I selected my potato-patch, and the man ploughed it, although I could have done that if Clyde would have let me. I cut the potatoes, Jerrine helped, and we dropped them in the rows. The man covered them, and that ends the man's part. By that time the garden ground was ready, so I planted the garden. I had almost an acre in vegetables. I irrigated and I cultivated it myself.

We had all the vegetables we could possibly use, and now Jerrine and I have put in our cellar full, and this is what we have: one large bin of potatoes (more than two tons), half a ton of carrots, a large bin of beets, one of turnips, one of onions, one of parsnips, and on the other side of the cellar we have more than one hundred heads of cabbage. I have experimented and found a kind of squash that can be raised here, and that the ripe ones keep well and make good pies; also that the young tender ones make splendid pickles, quite equal to cucumbers. I was glad to stumble on to that, because pickles are hard to manufacture when you have nothing to work with. Now I have plenty. They told me when I came that I could not even raise common beans, but I tried and succeeded. And also I raised lots of green tomatoes, and, as we like them preserved, I made them all up that way. Experimenting along another line, I found that I could make catchup, as delicious as that of tomatoes, of gooseberries. I made it exactly the same as I do the tomatoes and I am delighted. Gooseberries were very fine and very plentiful this year, so I put up a great many. I milked ten cows twice a day all summer; have sold enough butter to pay for a year's supply of flour and gasoline. We use a gasoline lamp. I have raised enough chickens to completely renew my flock, and all we wanted to eat, and have some fryers to go into the winter with. I have enough turkeys for all of our birthdays and holidays.

I raised a great many flowers and I worked several days in the field. In all I have told about I have had no help but Jerrine. Clyde's mother spends each summer with us, and she helped me with the cooking and the babies. Many of my neighbors did better than I did, although I know many town people would doubt my doing so much, but I did it. I have tried every kind of work this ranch affords, and I can do any of it. Of course I *am* extra strong, but those who try know that strength and knowledge come with doing. I just love to experiment, to work, and to prove out things, so that ranch life and "roughing it" just suit me.

# Homesteading in New Mexico

*During the first decades of the twentieth century, New Mexico opened thousands of acres for homesteading. Most of the families who attempted dry farming failed, depending on natural rainfall rather than irrigation of the arid land.*

*Ranchers, who found their 160 homesteaded acres of land insufficient to feed cattle, then purchased land from the failed farmers at bargain prices. The ranchers usually survived and flourished. By the 1950s, the Bar T Ranch, homesteaded by Emma Marble, covered 164 sections of southwestern New Mexico.*

*Early ranchers often improved land and ran their cattle on it without having clear title. Writing half-a-century later, Emma Marble described how, as a young bride-to-be, she homesteaded the Bar T Ranch in 1899, and how, later, the women of the surrounding ranches collaborated to outwit the government land inspector.*

Under the law a person could only make one homestead filing. An unmarried woman had the right, but a married woman did not. John and I were not yet married, so I filed a claim, and in the center of the hundred and sixty acres that I chose were the shanty, corral, the cottonwood tree and the well of the Bar T Ranch....

To prove title to a homestead claim, the law required a residence thereon seven months a year for five years. John had enlarged the shanty to two rooms, and had run a water pipe from the well to the kitchen door. But how I did miss the comforts of my old Lordsburg home! Especially the refinement of the Estey organ which my mother had bought for $250 in Virginia City in 1876, and had brought to Shakespeare and then to Lordsburg, and the many little elegancies which the diligent saving of Arbuckle coffee coupons had brought us!

The loneliness—it was terrible! My nearest neighbor was nine miles away. Because of a terrifying childhood experience, I was afraid to ride horseback, so I could not saddle up and go visiting. As John and his cowhands had to be on the range all day long, I was alone most of the time. I looked forward to round-up times, twice a year, because John took me along in the wagon. I looked forward to the occasional visit to Lordsburg for the few supplies we bought. I longed for the windmill to have a breakdown so John would have to take the part—and me—to the village....

Like other homesteaders, we had a garden. Anything to save

money. The soil produced bountifully under irrigation from the earth tank into which the windmill pumped the water. Snakes are still plentiful in that part of New Mexico, but were much more numerous then.... But it was either shoo the snakes [from the garden] or go hungry, for canned goods cost so much we could have them only as an occasional luxury.

I baked twice a day.... Sourdough biscuits, cooked in a Dutch oven—oh, delicious! So few people know the sourdough as today, or the confection of that other specialty of the round-up, son-of-a-gun—to give its milder name. Pies too, whenever we had fresh fruit—deep and fragrant and juicy pies.

For tea, a wild growth of the range made a brew which tasted like the Lipton product—squaw tea, or Mormon tea, it is called. Another weed flavored our candy when we could expend sugar in that direction—hoarhound. We butchered our own beef, of course, and I kept hens for eggs. Coffee, sugar, salt soda and a few other items were the only foodstuffs we bought, but we fared like kings on the bounty of our land and labor.

In time, I received title to my homestead claim. This was the first patented land of the Bar T. Ranch.

In 1908, came the first great blow to loneliness—also, a new protection for us homesteaders against being caught off our claims when unfriendly visitors came—the telephone. Not such a telephone as you use today; not as convenient, not as certain, but clear in its transmission. We loved it, for us it was a miracle come into our little world.

The Arizona and New Mexico Railroad Company had, by that year, built a line from Lordsburg to Hachita. The rails passed close to our home ranch, and close to about a dozen other homesteaders. The right-of-way was enclosed by a strong barbed wire fence.

After the fence was completed, two of our few purebred bulls were killed by the train. Cattle were cheap and money was a scarce item in those days. Most people turned out their own bull calves.* It had been a great sacrifice to save the money to buy this new blood for our herd. The railroad did not want to pay our price

---

*Turned out their own bull calves: used bulls from their own herd, instead of buying a bull of an improved breed to upgrade the stock.

for the bulls, so their agent, E. C. Clapp, suggested that we settle for the privilege of using the top barbed wire of their right-of-way fence as a telephone wire.

John Muir connected our neighbors with the barbed wire trunk line, and they bought the instruments and necessary batteries.

That telephone worked! —in dry weather. It hummed a great deal when the green mesquite would grow and touch the wire, and there was considerable interference at times.

We had our own call rings, and the theory was that we would answer only when our own ring sounded, but whenever the bell rang every woman on the line rushed to a receiver. Every now and then someone would cut into a conversation. News and gossip were common property, like the sunlight, and we never had any privacies when we went to the telephone.

That telephone probably saved the claims for many homesteaders.

When the new families moved in, they soon saw the impossibility of making a living on their land. The men, after building shacks and digging wells, went to work for the mines at Pyramid, leaving the women and children on the land. Sometimes the men would be gone for weeks and months. The women, of course, were mighty lonely, and visiting back and forth to relieve the monotony or to help someone in a jackpot,* they often would leave their claims unoccupied for periods of time.

The government land inspector made trips over the Territory at frequent and unexpected intervals to see if the homesteaders were living up to the law. There was only one road to travel. As soon as he reached Lordsburg, our friends there would flash the news over the barbed wire telephone. Then there was a scurrying of homesteaders back to their shanties, a gathering of fresh ashes and tin cans, from neighbors, to spread around unoccupied premises to give them the appearance of being lived in. The progress of the Government man as he covered his beat in a rented buckboard was noted all along the line, and duly flashed over the telephone. He always found the women working at some household task and as surprised as all get-out to see him!

*In a jackpot: slang for being in a situation in which help from others is needed.

# I Will Just Write
# My Morning Chores

*Mormon women settled in the arid states of Utah, Idaho, and
Arizona. Like Lucy Hannah White Flake, whose thoughts
about life on the windswept land of Arizona follow here,
many kept diaries of their early experiences. Flake was born
in Illinois in 1842, walked from the Missouri River to Salt
Lake with her family as a child of eight, and married at
sixteen. She bore ten children before moving to Arizona in
1877; three more while there. Five of these children had died
by the time of these entries, written when she was in her fifties.
She records an immense quantity of work on the farm, but also
the companionship of other Mormon sisters in the nearby
village and their interest in women's suffrage. Brother Flake is
her husband, John her son.*

### February 1896

*Saturday 29th.* This morning conference commences. I went to
two meetings and had lots of company. This is leap year and
tonight the girls have a leap year dance. After my evenings work
was done I went with two other sisters to call on Sister Oakley.
Afterwards went to the dance a little while then came home,
made two beds, and went to bed but did not get much sleep. The
wind blew hard all night...

### March 1896

*Monday 2nd.* The wind blows all the time days and part of the
time nights and I feel nearly sick.
*Tuesday 14th.* The wind it blows night and day. It is just fearful.
The sand drifts like snow.... It seems lonely and dreary when
the wind blows.
*Wednesday 15th.* The wind blew hard all night and all day.
Brother Flake and John started for Holebrook this morning for
freight. I spent most of this day over to Sister Whipples knitting
on my chair cushion. Ate dinner there.

*Friday 17th.* It snowed a little last night. The wind blew all night but it don't blow quite as hard as it did yesterday but is dreadful cold.

*Satuday 18th.* Brother Flake and John came home this morning. The wind was so bad Thursday they laid up all day and could not travel. The wind blows very little today which is so nice. I cleaned up all the rooms and had a bath and am going to town to hear a lady from Kansas [Mrs. Johns] who is going to give up a few lectures on woman suffrage. I went this afternoon. Then came home, ate supper.... Her speech was nice and the reception was very good.

*Monday 20th.* This morning Brother Flake and John started for Apache. I went to town to hear Mrs. Johns lecture. She done nice and organized a club. 71 members joined. After meeting we took Mrs. Johns to our Hall. She was so pleased with it. Mrs. Johns bade me goodby and gave me a nice sweet kiss. Then I came home.

*Wednesday 22nd.* Today the wind is worse than yesterday.

*Monday 27th.* It blows hard and is dreadful cold. I spent most time reading.

*Wednesday 29th.* We are all well. The wind still blows.

*Thursday 30th.* All well. The wind still blows. Brother Flake is plowing the garden today. I have been cutting out quilt blocks. Read a sermon of Brother Woodruffs. This ends this month and I don't believe there has been one day that the wind did not blow. It has damaged the crops and covered them with sand, filled up the ditches, and made it very unpleasant. [Only] our Heavenly Father knows what this wind is for.

*Friday 15th.* Well, the folks are off for Flagstaff and the wind blows fearful. The sand almost blinds one. The children can't go out to play.

*Saturday 16th.* I will just write my morning chores. Get up turn out my chickens, draw a pail of water, take it over to Brother Whipple's chickens, let them out, then draw water, water hot beds, make a fire, put potatoes to cook, then brush and sweep half inch of dust off floor...feed three litters of chickens, then mix biscuits, get breakfast, milk, besides work in the house, and this morning had to go half mile after calves. This is the way of life on the farm.

## September 1898

*Friday 16th.* Brother Flake moved the girls to town today so they could get straightened up and fixed for school.... I washed, cleaned the cupboard, cleaned the cellar and worked hard all day. That is one of my failings, to work too hard.

*Saturday 17th.* Ironed, churned six pound butter, mended, cleaned my room and quit with a headache. Done too much work.

*Monday 19th.* Churned eight pound butter, done up my work, picked some beans and wrote to Osmer and read some. Brother Flake went to Pinedale for a load of lumber. A nice day. Milked eight cows.

*Wednesday 21st.* Churned ten pounds butter. Mended and chored.

*Thursday 22th.* I washed and picked a nice lot of hops off the vines.

*Friday 23rd.* Ironed, mended, and read some. Brother Flake went to Pinedale yesterday to buy some calves. The weather is lovely. I help milk all the time. John and me do the milking. We milk nine cows but the churning is the hardest work.

*Saturday 24th.* Churned ten pounds, cleaned windows and floor, cleaned up the front room, made cake, done up all my work and had my bath. Five o'clock I went to town to take tithing. Took one dozen eggs, ten pound of butter, forty pound of cheese. The Primary Fair came off today. I forgot it with all my cares and labor. I got a sack of sugar this evening. The first whole sack I ever had.

*Monday 26th.* We churned, made preserves out of peaches we bought from Sister Owens for cheese. Done up my work and prepared more peaches for preserves and was very busy. John started to school.

*Tuesday 27th.* Went to town, took butter and cheese to the store to sell. Roberta came home last night and she came back with me. The baby and her have gained in flesh. They both look better. Made preserves and mended some. After she went home I churned. I feel pretty well but have to be on my feet too much.

*Friday 30th.* The wind blows cold and disagreeable. I went to town. Came right home, made preserves.

## October 1898

*Saturday 1st.* All well but the wind blows very hard. John helped me churn. We made ten pounds of butter and sold one dollar and seventy five cents worth today. We are making a nice lot of butter. We made a fire in the fire place this evening, first time this fall. It is quite cloudy and looks like a storm.

*Sunday 2nd.* This is our fast day. John and me went to Sunday School. After it was out we went to Sunday School Teachers' Meeting. When it was out, I went to Officers' prayer meeting. When that was out we went to the general meeting. I was in meeting and school six hours constantly. We ate supper with the girls.

*Tuesday, 4th.* I churned eight pounds of butter, made pies, cooked dinner. I have to turn and rub my cheese every day. The wind still blows. I read and knit some.

*Thursday 6th.* Ironed. Went to town after dinner. Went to Sisters' Meeting. We quilted and all bore their Testimony. Had a very good time. Came home, helped milk and prepare some green tomatoes and onions for French pickle.

*Friday 7th.* Done up my work. Made my pickle. Churned. The wind blows. It is cloudy and looks like rain. I have been choring around all day. I have made 27 pounds of butter this week from nine cows.

*Saturday 15th.* We churned ten pounds butter and done up the work. John went after wood. Brother Flake shucked corn all day. I went out and saved husks to put in a bed. The wind blew very hard and it was dreadful nasty and disagreeable.

*Tuesday 18th.* Brother Flake has gone up to Scots to take some sheep for James. I ironed and churned, mended and worked very hard. There is so many chores to do and no one to help do anything. I am alone day after day but not lonesome. I filled my shuck tick with shucks last night. It is so nice.

*Sunday 30th.* John and me went to Sunday School. Brother Flake has gone on a missionary trip to Juniper. I came home to see to things.

*Monday 31st.* The wind is blowing very hard and the dust most blinding. I done up my work, sewed some, read some. Brother Flake got home one o'clock. After dinner him and me went out to the barn and shucked corn till night.

**November 1898**

*Tuesday 1st.* I washed, made yeast, baked pie. Brother Flake husked corn all day. I went out and husked about an hour. When John came home from school he churned for me. I feel very thankful for this days work.

*Saturday 5th.* Am dreadful tired this morning. I worked too hard yesterday. Milo Webb came for me to go to his house. His wife was sick. I was churning. I went. Was gone till seven at night. Phoebe Webb had a baby girl born a little after six. Came home. John churned. I had the butter to salt, dishes to wash, supper to fix.

*Tuesday 8th.* I washed, skimmed 26 pans of milk and cleaned the pans.

*Saturday 12th.* Primary conference convened this morning. It was my place to preside. Apostal Woodruff came. He was alone. We asked him to speak to the Primary. He did so in a beautiful way, so simple and good. Our parts were performed very nicely. We asked President Smith to speak. He did very good to the children. It was Sisters' conference this afternoon. Brother Woodruff spoke again.

## When You Come, We Die

*Chiparopai, leader of a small group of Mohave, was over a hundred years old when she talked to Natalie Curtis in 1905. Her people were about to be removed from their ancestral lands to less fertile land across the Colorado River so that white settlers could take over the richer farmland.*

Sickness comes with you [the white race] and hundreds of us die. Where is our strength?... In the old times we were strong. We used to hunt and fish. We raised our little crop of corn and melons and ate the mesquite beans. Now all is changed. We eat the white man's food, and it makes us soft; we wear the white man's heavy clothing and it makes us weak. Each day in the old times in summer and in winter we came down to the river banks to bathe. This strengthened and toughened our firm skin. But white settlers were shocked to see the naked Indians, so now we keep away. In old days we wore the breechcloth, and aprons made of bark and reeds. We worked all winter in the wind—bare arms, bare legs, and never felt the cold. But now, when the wind blows down from the mountains it makes us cough. Yes—we know that when you come, *we die.*

# FIVE:
# Less Corn, More Hell!
## Women and Rural Reform

AGRARIAN REFORM BEGAN EARLY in American history. By the late eighteenth century, wealthy landowners had begun to discuss ways of bringing about change in agricultural methods. They hoped to increase profits, thus making more money

available to families to invest in material goods and also to increase domestic production so that the new nation could become more economically independent of Europe. Farm families, these landowners hoped, would provide a market for American-made goods and a surplus of farm produce for merchants to export. Early reformers organized all-male agricultural societies to promote new farming techniques, circulating books and journals to explain the needed changes. These affluent farmers, often part of the political and financial elite, offered little criticism of American society; they wanted only to improve the quality and quantity of farm products. Susan B.

THE GOVERNOR SENDS AID TO PIXLEY 24 DEPUTY SHERIFFS 11 HIGHWAY PATROLMEN

WE WANT FOOD!

Anthony's speech to the New York farmers,[1] though aimed at women and sympathetic to small landowners, came out of this early tradition of urging farm families to produce more and better crops.

While this type of agrarian reform continued after the Civil War, it was overshadowed by an entirely new type of social protest and mass organizing. The new movements originated among less affluent middle-class farmers, who now competed in a national and world market glutted by agricultural produce. These farm reformers argued that raising more and better crops could not solve their problems; getting their products to market cheaply and receiving a fair return for their labor were more important. Reformers also began to give more attention to bettering the poor social conditions of farm families. For the first time, large numbers of women joined farm protests—speaking, writing, organizing, and exercising local and national leadership. This section portrays women caught up in the rural reform movements that arose in the United States in the period from 1870 to 1940.

The most visible type of reform activity in which women engaged during the seventy years from 1870 to 1940 involved working with farm men in social and political groups to provide mutual aid and to bring about political reform. In the last three decades of the nineteenth century, perhaps as many as half a million farm women participated in the Grange, the Farmer's Alliances, and the Populist Party. After the turn of the century, thousands more joined the Farm Union and the Socialist Party, particularly in Kansas, Texas, and Oklahoma. The late nineteenth and early twentieth centuries were also periods of mass organization of women into separate women's organizations: clubs, suffrage groups, and temperance unions. Some farm women supported both suffrage and temperance. Many joined the National American Woman's Suffrage Association and the Woman's Christian Temperance Union to work for women's votes and for prohibition, as well as joining farm organizations. But it was the work in farm groups that gave women an opportunity to join men in grappling with economic and social issues and to share political activity with men on a scale unprecedented in American history.[2]

The receptivity of the various farm groups to women was probably due in part to the continuing economic importance of women on the farm in a period when large numbers of women were anxious to organize publicly, and when farm organizations needed the strength in numbers that women could lend to their groups. The Grange and the Alliances were unique among male-dominated organizations of the time in allowing women to become members, to hold office, and to act as representatives at regional and national conventions. The Populist Party welcomed women as organizers, lecturers, political writers, party delegates, and public office holders. These organizations provided a forum within which large numbers of women could practice and advocate women's rights.

The Granges, which began to flourish in the 1870s and 1880s along the Missouri River, were the first organizational manifestation of discontent in farm areas. As mutual aid and social organizations, Granges provided a structure for regional cooperation among white middle-class farm families. Until the 1870s, most farm women had been able to trade their wares and to purchase groceries and other consumer items at local country stores and rural village market centers. After the Civil War, however, a national system of transportation and credit bypassed these local rural institutions, replacing them with a cash marketing structure that brought family farms into the national and international markets as both producers and consumers. Thus, farm families became dependent upon "middlemen" at a time when families wanted more education, more social contact, and more consumer items, but could not afford to pay for them.[3] The Granges met specific needs of women by providing buying cooperatives (sewing machines were one important item they purchased), opposing the manufacture of butter substitutes like oleomargarine that competed with the farm women's homemade butter, and by championing political rights for women. The refusal of the Granges to move beyond opposition of the manufacture of oleomargarine to other political issues like high transportation rates, however, caused a decline in the Granges in the Midwest and South where they had first flourished.[4]

Like the Grange, the Alliances spread in the Midwest and the South, but the core membership moved farther west, to the

Plains of Kansas and Texas, where newly settled farm families faced drought conditions as well as depressed prices and competition. The high cost of paying a middleman, both for selling their products and in buying consumer items, brought these families into angry cooperation against the eastern bankers and politicians whom they saw as the enemies responsible for their plight. Like the Grange, the Alliances attracted members through cooperative buying as well as marketing schemes. The Alliances also spread to the more politically conservative areas of the South, where they had a special significance for women. Even where state Alliances refused to support women's suffrage, as in North Carolina, for example, they raised the hopes of women by giving them a new place in the Alliance. Alliance women were far more active in Texas than elsewhere in the South, claiming there that the Alliance would redeem women from their enslaved conditions through equality with their brothers, and arguing that women should work for change because they had a direct interest in economic reform. In a South where women still did not speak publicly until the 1890s and had no feminist tradition upon which to build, any open discussion of women's relation to politics was new and dramatic.[5]

Numerous Midwestern women drew on the earlier Northeastern feminist tradition in becoming active public lecturers and writers on agrarian issues. Mary Elizabeth Lease, whose 1891 speech before a meeting of the Woman's Christian Temperance Union is reprinted here, was perhaps the best known. An Irish Catholic who had grown up on a Pennsylvania farm during the period of farm ferment over anti-oleomargarine laws, Lease became a well known speaker. In Kansas alone during 1890, she gave 160 speeches before taking her message to Missouri, the Far West, and the South. As a suffragist and women's rights advocate, she lectured on the need of women to be politically active on economic issues.[6]

The Populist Party, for which Mary Elizabeth Lease became an ardent champion, was a national third party formed of Alliance members and other reformers disgruntled with the indifference of major parties to reform issues. Strongest in the areas where Alliances had swept up farm families into political activity, the Populist Party advocated many public policies considered radical at the time, including national control of railroads and public utilities. Lease and other Populists claimed that capitalism had become "legalized robbery" as a result of the control of the country by Eastern industrialists and financiers. Only national control of crucial public services, they felt, could insure the survival of the system.

Populists experimented with two radical political reforms— bringing women and Black farm people into their party.[7] Both reforms provoked virulent attacks that ultimately splintered the party by setting member against member. While the national convention of the Populist Party never officially endorsed women's suffrage, it did recommend that state conventions endorse it. The Populists achieved women's suffrage in Colorado and Idaho in the 1890s. In two other states, California and Kansas, the countryside voted overwhelmingly for women's suffrage during the last decade of the century, only to have urban voters defeat the measures.

Farm families that attempted to be politically active in the South suffered the severest defeat in attempting racial and sexual political reforms. The Alliances had encouraged Black farm owners to form their own groups, and Blacks moved into the Populist Party, preparing to cooperate with white Populists. White vigilante groups backed by politicians already in power terrorized both Black and white Populists, forcing hundreds of Black families to leave their communities and intimidating white farmers into silence. To defeat the Populist movement, Southern politicians imposed poll taxes that ended what suffrage there had been for poor whites and Black males and, through vigorous anti-feminist campaigns, left the South so firmly opposed to women's suffrage that only Tennessee, Kentucky, and Texas were to ratify the women's suffrage amendment twenty-five years later.[8]

After 1896, when the Populist Party fused with the Democratic Party, the momentum for political activism among some farm families died. In Texas and Kansas, where the Populist Party had been strongest, however, many rural areas supported the Farm Union Party and the Socialist Party. Farm communities in Arkansas and Oklahoma also continued the militant Populist tradition in their support for socialist demands for greater government control over the economy. In other areas, as the demand for farm products increased in the early twentieth century and the farm depression of the 1890s ended, militant farm organizations had to compete with a new type of more moderate agrarian reform called the Country Life Movement.

The Country Life Movement was the rural component of what historians call the progressive movement. Primarily an effort of middle-class, white Protestant professional groups to moderate conflict between workers and capitalists, progressives saw rural farm life as ideal, if only it could be upgraded to match urban economic and cultural levels. Although prices of farm products rose in the twentieth century, farm family incomes remained miserably low, and their material life, by urban standards, was impoverished. Progressive leaders saw dire consequences in the poor living conditions of farm families because, like early nineteenth-century reformers, they believed agriculture to be the basis for urban prosperity, and because they considered a disaffected rural populace dangerous to the nation's political stability. Reformers were concerned that the agricultural ladder was breaking down, leaving segments of the rural population in danger of becoming permanent tenants. A few leaders, like Theodore Roosevelt, also worried that the native-born white middle-class population was on its way to extinction because of low fertility rates in urban areas. They saw the continuation of large farm families as a way to balance the increased immigration from South and Central Europe which threatened to engulf the older Euro-American population. Indeed, in the cities— where children became an economic burden not offset by the work they could do on farms—middle-class and upper-class white Protestant women had dramatically lowered their fertility by the late nineteenth century, primarily through sexual abstinence.[9]

Country Life Movement reformers, drawn mainly from agricultural colleges and state and federal departments of agriculture established in most states during the last decades of the nineteenth century, assumed leadership in identifying farm problems during the period from approximately 1900 to 1920. These reformers saw the primary problem of farm families as poor management that led to low incomes, too much work, and cultural isolation. The solution they envisioned was application of good business principles to farm management. The family farm should be run as an efficient business, operating as an economic unit of both home and field, engaged in production and consumption involving the work of all family members. With "scientific management," learned from experts who had studied agricultural and home economics in college, the farm family could abandon its outmoded use of tradition or direct experience in running the farm.

   Because two goals of the reformers were to keep farm families "down on the farm" and to encourage middle-class folk to go "back to the land," women's condition on the farm became a major focus. In the eyes of the reformers, who were predominantly from urban backgrounds, the farm woman was bound to a treadmill of constant hard work, with few rewards. They saw her performing heavy work, inefficiently, without labor-saving devices, and on servantless farms. The hired girl was gradually disappearing from the farm, along with large numbers of farm children who sought employment in the city. Although the rural birth rate had dropped steadily during the nineteenth century in response to rising costs of farm land and mechanization of the farm, the rural birth rate was still higher than urban birth rates. Thus rural women had great demands put upon their time and energy for household duties as well as for traditional farm tasks. Urban reformers felt training in scientific household management—or "home economics," as it came to be called—could make the tasks of farm women easier and farm children healthier, happier, and more likely to remain on the farm. Because few of these farm women would ever reach college, and most poor women would not even attend high school, reformers envisioned rural elementary schools as centers for the transformation of rural communities through the dissemination of the ideas of scientific household management. After the Department of Agriculture established its Bureau of Home Economics in 1913, the farm woman became the subject of even more detailed study, and state agencies followed suit. Part of a study published in 1919 by the New York Extension Service, reprinted here, shows the immense amount of work still performed by farm women. The women reformers who published the report hinted that a strike might be the only way for farm women to improve their conditions.

Local schools were one institution reformers believed they could change to improve the lives of rural women. By the beginning of the twentieth century, women had replaced men as elementary school teachers in most of the country; and by 1910, women in twenty-one states had also successfully gained the right to vote on school issues and to run for school boards. Women seemed ready to move from their homes into politics via the institution over which they had most political control. Many of the reforms engineered by rural school teachers may, in retrospect, appear to have encouraged a strict sexual division of labor on the farm. In the South, for example, white teachers organized almost 100,000 students into Corn and Canning Clubs where young men learned how to grow corn, a field crop, while young women learned how to grow tomatoes, a garden crop, and how to process and sell their produce. But the efforts of rural school teachers, both white and Black, to provide better education through organizing rural women and training young women to process food cannot be dismissed as simply reinforcing a subordinate and separate status for women. Reformers considered a separate sphere in the home as one way to expand women's freedom. To take responsibility for the home, and to organize to change social conditions that hindered women's control over their lives at home, some early twentieth century feminists thought, was one way of increasing their political influence. Organizing around education, as the selection by educator Mabel Carney shows, could also give women an expanded role as local community leaders.

The educational reform aspect of the Country Life Movement spread to Black as well as white women in the South. In 1907, Anna Jeanes, a Quaker heiress, left a million dollars to be spent on rural Black schools. Virginia Randolph's report on work as a Jeanes teacher, excerpted below, reflects the incredibly poor conditions these teachers labored to improve. Randolph's mother, freed from slavery by the Civil War, had taken in washing in Virginia to put her children in a school set up by Yankee schoolmarms and Black people to educate children kept illiterate by law under slavery. Randolph taught for sixteen years before becoming the first Jeanes teacher in 1908. She had organized a community School Improvement League to plant sod and trees, recruited mothers to care for sick women in the neighborhood, visited homes, and established a Sunday school. Her work and the work of other women who became Jeanes teachers and traveled by foot and by buggy around rural counties to institute similar reforms became a foundation for leadership among Black women teachers.[10]

Meanwhile, other women reformers in the Children's Bureau, established in 1912 with the support of feminists, had undertaken studies of rural maternal and infant care. The revelations were shocking. Rural health care, always poor in areas where there were no trained midwives, had declined still further as old country doctors died and young college-educated doctors clustered in cities. Through the nineteenth century women had practiced medicine on the frontier, and most country doctors had trained some rural women through the apprentice system. When medical practice became more urban and professional, rural women found it difficult to obtain training. State health authorities seldom encouraged retraining older granny midwives, who were often Black in the South, nor did they offer training for younger women. In some rural areas, neither doctors nor midwives were available for obstetric care; and Kentucky alone pioneered a nurse-midwife program that served the needs of rural women. Maternal and infant mortality rates remained much higher in rural areas than in cities. The letter reprinted in this section from a Georgia farm woman to the Children's Bureau was typical of letters received from isolated farm women. Even though the Children's Bureau attempted to assist women with advice and campaigned for a system of rural health clinics, the problems of rural women remained rooted in conditions that the Children's Bureau could not change. Rural women were too poor to pay for adequate health care themselves, and the political structure remained resistant to attempts by organized urban women to obtain federally funded health care for all women.[11]

World War I brought a shift from institutional reforms focused on rural health and education to a focus on individual farm families through social welfare work. During this changing period, women continued to work on the land. In the Far West, they managed nurseries, fruit farms, cattle and sheep ranches, and continued to homestead wherever public land was available. In some southern states, over 55 per cent of the white farm women living on their land, and all tenant women, Black and white, worked in the fields. In World War I, urban women formed "land armies" to help take in the crops. Some urban women succeeded in moving back to the land during the early twentieth century. In all, by 1920, census takers found half a million farm women self-employed on their farms.[12] Yet after World War I, the nostalgic, optimistic tone of the Country Life Movement had been challenged by a more pessimistic and tragic view of farm life that was reflected both in imaginative literature and in the new approach to agrarian reform through social welfare agencies and social workers.

Two selections document this shift in tone: one, a short story written by Susan Glaspel in 1917, "A Jury of Her Peers," the other, advice to rural social workers by Josephine Brown. Glaspel portrays the emotional realities of the social conditions that Brown describes in her writings. Both identify the rural patri- archal family as trapping women. Glaspel, a feminist, hoped to raise the reader's consciousness of the brutish male domination she described. The Iowa farm women in her story show that women can become conscious of their common condition and act in solidarity against it. Brown wrote out of a tradition of reform that saw women as peculiarly able to help other women through social welfare activities. This tradition, based in nine- teenth-century women's philanthropic groups, and advanced by the progressive movement, had become institutionalized in professional social work. The social worker was most often a member of the urban middle-class; white; liberal in belief; and trained in urban universities that had achieved a monopoly over social work education. In the absence of urban institutions like juvenile courts, truancy officers, probation officers, welfare organizations, and even hospitals, the rural social worker herself became an institution. She continually had to balance client's rights with community traditions and her own professional standards. The establishment of New Deal national welfare agencies during the Depression of the 1930s increased the amount of rural relief and the number of social workers.

However, although nearly one-half of all rural counties had social workers by the late 1930s, high case loads and local political opposition to New Deal agencies often meant social workers did little more than deliver welfare checks to the farm women. Money, like the food given to Native Americans on the frontier generations earlier, provided temporary relief, but did not provide the political and social institutions women needed to survive in the countryside.[13]

Between the two wars, from 1920 to 1940, urban culture carried mixed messages to farm people. In a time of urban prosperity and high employment during the 1920s, popular writers portrayed farm families as contemptible: young men were characterized as bumpkins, hicks, yokels, hayseeds, and clodhoppers, while farmer's daughters jokes, implying both ignorance and sexual promiscuity, denigrated young women. Liberal reformers often saw rural culture as the source of reactionary movements such as prohibition, the Ku Klux Klan, and religious fundamentalism. Conservatives saw the rural populace as a potentially dangerous force which, like the peasants in Russia, might join with urban workers to overturn the established political system. While American farmers and urban workers had never successfully bridged their differences, fear that these two groups might join in militant labor strikes seemed to increase among politicians, businessmen, and large landowners during these years.[14]

The Farm Bureau, a private organization composed primarily of owners of large, successful farms, came into being in 1919 in response to these early fears about radical rural movements. It continued to operate as a bulwark against militant rural organizing during the 1930s. During the twenty-year farm depression that began in 1920, the Bureau lobbied for greater federal support for middle-sized family farms. It also continued to be a white male bastion, in which the main need of farm women was seen as learning to become better homemakers. However, the more militant farm organizations that formed and disintegrated during these years seemed to meet the real needs of farm women no better. Neither the Non-Partisan League, which spread through North Dakota and Minnesota after 1915, nor the farm organizations best known for their militance during the

1930s—the Farmer's Holiday Association of Iowa and the Southern Farm Tenant's Union of Arkansas—dealt specifically with women's issues. Although radical women exercised limited leadership among male-dominated organizations, thus keeping alive the idea that women could be active in rural reform, they failed to translate their vision into terms that farm women found relevant, nor did they succeed in organizing farm women.[15]

Farm women, then, dealt with their day-to-day problems primarily by themselves. Particularly, they were alone in coping with the patriarchal family. This section ends with accounts by women who employed various methods of dealing with male domination. Mary Green chose an act of physical violence to defy familial oppression. The Misses Hodges chose not to live with men at all. While these choices appear to be purely personal, they contain the seeds of political rebellion. Without organizing, or giving speeches, or writing about their condition, Mary Green and the Misses Hodges joined the ranks of women protesters in these seventy years of agrarian reform.

## Mary Elizabeth Lease

*Mary Elizabeth Lease was the first woman to become a major speaker for a political party. She gave hundreds of campaign speeches in Kansas in 1890, and in 1892 toured the South speaking with the presidential candidate for the Populist Party, General James Baird Weaver. While she may never have advised farmers to "raise less corn and more hell," she roused many to political action. In this speech before the Woman's Christian Temperance Union, she reviewed the work of women in the populist crusade.*

**M**adame President and Fellow Citizens: —If God were to give me my choice to live in any age of the world that has flown, or in any age of the world yet to be, I would say, O God, let me live here and now, in this day and age of the world's history.

For we are living in a grand and wonderful time—a time when old ideas, traditions and customs have broken loose from their moorings and are hopelessly adrift on the great shoreless, boundless sea of human thought—a time when the gray old world begins to dimly comprehend that there is no difference between the brain of an intelligent woman and the brain of an intelligent man; no difference between the soul-power or brain-power that nerved the arm of Charlotte Corday* to deeds of heroic patriotism and the soul-power or brain-power that swayed old John Brown behind his death dealing barricade at Ossawattomie. We are living in an age of thought. The mighty dynamite of thought is upheaving the social and political structure and stirring the hearts of men from centre to circumference. Men, women and children are in commotion, discussing the mighty problems of the day. The agricultural classes, loyal and patriotic, slow to act and slow to think, are to-day thinking for themselves; and their thought has crystallized into action. Organization is the key-note to a mighty movement among the masses which is the protest of the patient burden-bearers of the nation against years of economic and political superstition.

The mightiest movement the world has known in two thousand years...is sending out the gladdest message to oppressed humanity that the world has heard since John the Baptist came preaching in the wilderness that the world's Redeemer was coming to relieve the world's misery. We witness today the most stupendous and wonderful uprising of the common people that the world has known since Peter the Hermit led the armies of the East to battle against the Saracens in the Holy Land.

The movement among the masses today is an echo of the life of Jesus of Nazareth, an honest endeavor on the part of the people to put into practical operation the basic principles of Christianity: "Whatsoever ye would that men should do unto you, do ye even so unto them."

---

*Charlotte Corday:* Assassin of the French revolutionary Jean Paul Marat. Corday, who was of the moderate, middle-class revolutionary faction, identified with the provinces rather than with Paris; it was perhaps for this reason that Lease invoked her name.

In an organization founded upon the eternal principles of truth and right, based upon the broad and philanthropic principle, "Injury to one is the concern of all," having for its motto, "Exact justice to all, special privileges to none," —the farmers and laborers could not well exclude their mothers, wives and daughters, the patient burden bearers of the home, who had been their faithful companions, their tried friends and trusted counselors through long, weary years of poverty and toil. Hence the doors of the Farmers' Alliance were thrown open wide to the women of the land. They were invited into full membership, with all the privileges of promotion; actually recognized and treated as human beings. And not only the mothers, wives and daughters, but "the sisters, the cousins and the aunts," availed themselves of their newly offered liberties, till we find at the present time upward of a half-million woman in the Alliance, who, because of their loyalty to home and loved ones and their intuitive and inherent sense of justice, are investigating the condition of the country, studying the great social, economic and political problems, fully realizing that the political arena is the only place where the mighty problems of to-day and to-morrow can be satisfactorily fought and settled, and amply qualified to go hand-in-hand with fathers, husbands, sons and brothers to the polls and register their opinion against legalized robbery and corporate wrong.

George Eliot tells us that "much that we are and have is due to the unhistoric acts of those who in life were ungarlanded and in death sleep in unvisited tombs." So to the women of the Alliance, who bravely trudged twice a week to the bleak country schoolhouse, literally burning midnight oil as they studied with their loved ones the economic and political problems, and helped them devise methods by which the shackels of industrial slavery might be broken, and the authors of the nation's liberties, the creators of the nation's wealth and greatness, might be made free and prosperous—to these women, unknown and uncrowned, belongs the honor of defeating for reelection to the United States Senate that man who for eighteen years has signally failed to represent his constituents, and who during that time has never once identified himself with any legislation for the oppressed and overburdened people.

Three years ago this man Ingalls* made a speech on woman suffrage at Abilene, Kan., in which he took occasion to speak in the most ignorant and vicious manner of women, declaring that "a woman could not and should not vote because she was a woman." Why? She was a woman, and that was enough; the subject was too delicate for further discussion.

But we treasured up these things in our hearts, and then his famous, or rather, infamous interview in a New York paper appeared, in which he declared that:"It is lawful to hire Hessians to kill, to mutilate, to destroy. Success is the object to be attained; the decalogue and the golden rule have no place in a political campaign; the world has outgrown its Christ and needs a new one." This man, said the law-abiding God fearing women, must no longer be permitted to misrepresent us. So we worked and waited for his defeat. And the cyclone, the political Johnstown, that overtook the enemies of the people's rights last November, proves what a mighty factor the women of the Alliance have been in the political affairs of the nation.

I overheard yesterday morning at the hotel breakfast table a conversation between two gentlemen in regard to Ingalls. "I consider his defeat," said the first speaker, "to be a national calamity." "Your reasons," said the second. "Why, he is such a brilliantly smart man," he replied. "True," said the other; "but he must needs be a smart man to be the consummate rascal he has proven himself to be." And I thought as I heard the remarks, "Our opinion is also shared by men." You wonder, perhaps, at the zeal and enthusiasm of the Western women in this reform movement. Let me tell you why they are interested. Turn to your old school-maps and books of a quarter of a century ago, and you will find that what is now the teeming and fruitful West was then known as the Treeless Plain, the Great American Desert. To this sterile and remote region, infested by savage beasts and still more savage men, the women of the New England States, the women of the cultured East, came with husbands, sons and

*Ingalls: John James Ingalls, Republican Senator from Kansas, 1872–1891, was defeated by populist opposition in his bid for reelection in 1890. Ingalls was hated by farmers for his connection with financial firms that held mortgages on farms and for his claim that legislation wanted by farmers could not relieve agricultural distress.

brothers to help them build up a home upon the broad and vernal prairies of the West. We came with the roses of health on our cheek, the light of hope in our eyes, the fires of youth and hope burning in our hearts. We left the old familiar paths, the associations of home and the friends of childhood. We left schools and churches—all that made life dear—and turned our faces toward the setting sun. We endured hardships, dangers and privations; hours of loneliness, fear and sorrow; our little babes were born upon these wide, unsheltered prairies; and there, upon the sweeping prairies beneath the cedar trees our hands have planted to mark the sacred place, our little ones lie buried. We toiled in the cabin and in the field; we planted trees and orchards; we helped our loved ones to make the prairie blossom as the rose. The neat cottage took the place of the sod shanty, the log-cabin and the humble dug-out.

Yet, after all our years of toil and privation, dangers and hardships upon the Western frontier, monopoly is taking our homes from us by an infamous system of mortgage foreclosure, the most infamous that has ever disgraced the statutes of a civilized nation. It takes from us at the rate of five hundred a month the homes that represent the best years of our life, our toil, our hopes, our happiness. How did it happen? The government, at the bid of Wall Street, repudiated its contracts with the people; the circulating medium was contracted in the interest of Shylock from $54 per capita to less than $8 per capita; or, as Senator Plumb* tells us, "Our debts were increased, while the means to pay them was decreased;" or as grand Senator Stewart† puts it, "For twenty years the market value of the dollar has gone up and the market value of labor has gone down, till to-day the American laborer, in bitterness and wrath, asks which is the worst—the black slavery that has gone or the white slavery that has come?"

Do you wonder the women are joining the Alliance? I wonder if

*Senator Plumb: Preston B. Plumb, Republican Senator from Kansas, 1877–1891, was able to avoid the wrath of farmers, and died in office.
†Senator Stewart: William Morris Stewart, Republican Senator from Nevada, 1863–1875 and 1887–1905, a supporter of the free coinage of silver.

there is a woman in all this broad land who can afford to stay out of the Alliance. Our loyal, white-ribbon women should be heart and hand in this Farmers' Alliance movement, for the men whom we have sent to represent us are the only men in the councils of this nation who have not been elected on a liquor platform; and I want to say here, with exultant pride, that the five farmer Congressmen and the United States Senator we have sent up from Kansas—the liquor traffic, Wall Street, "nor the gates of hell shall not prevail against them."

[At this point many women in the audience were severely shocked, and the orator explained that the phrase "gates of hell" was a quotation from the Bible.]

It would sound boastful were I to detail to you the active, earnest part the Kansas women took in the recent campaign. A Republican majority of 82,000 was reduced to less than 8,000 when we elected 97 representatives, 5 out of 7 Congressmen, and a United States Senator, for to the women of Kansas belongs the credit of defeating John J. Ingalls. He is feeling badly about it yet, too, for he said to-day that "women and Indians were the only class that would scalp a dead man." I rejoice that he realises that he is politically dead.

I might weary you to tell you in detail how the Alliance women found time from cares of home and children to prepare the tempting, generous viands for the Alliance picnic dinners; where hungry thousands and tens of thousands gathered in the forests and groves to listen to the words of impassioned oratory, ofttimes from woman's lips, that nerved the men of Kansas to forget their party prejudice and vote for "Mollie and the babies." And not only did they find their way to the voters' hearts, through their stomachs, but they sang their way as well. I hold here a book of Alliance songs, composed and set to music by an Alliance woman, Mrs. Florence Olmstead of Butler County, Kan., that did much toward moulding public sentiment. Alliance Glee Clubs composed of women, gave us such stirring melodies as the nation has not heard since the Tippecanoe and Tyler campaign of 1840. And while I am individualizing, let me call your attention to a book written also by an Alliance woman. I wish a copy of it could be placed in the hands of every woman in this

land. "The Fate of a Fool" is written by Mrs. Emma G. Curtis of
Colorado. This book in the hands of women would teach them to
be just and generous toward women, and help them to forgive
and condone in each other the sins so sweetly forgiven when
committed by men.

[Here the gavel announced that the time was up, but the
speaker begged for and received a short extension.]

Let no one for a moment believe that this uprising and
federation of the people is but a passing episode in politics. It is a
religious as well as a political movement, for we seek to put into
practical operation the teachings and precepts of Jesus of
Nazareth. We seek to enact justice and equity between man and
man. We seek to bring the nation back to the constitutional
liberties guaranteed us by our forefathers. The voice that is
coming up to day from the mystic chords of the American heart
is the same voice that Lincoln heard blending with the guns of
Fort Sumter and the Wilderness, and it is breaking into a clarion
cry to-day that will be heard around the world.

Crowns will fall, thrones will tremble, kingdoms will dis-
appear, the divine right of kings and the divine right of capital
will fade away like the mists of the morning when the Angel of
Liberty shall kindle the fires of justice in the hearts of men.
"Exact justice to all, special privileges to none." No more
millionaires, and no more paupers; no more gold kings, silver
kings and oil kings, and no more little waifs of humanity
starving for a crust of bread. No more gaunt faced, hollow-eyed
girls in the factories, and no more little boys reared in poverty
and crime for the penitentiaries and the gallows. But we shall
have the golden age of which Isaiah sang and the prophets have
so long foretold; when the farmers shall be prosperous and
happy, dwelling under their own vine and fig tree; when the
laborer shall have that for which he toils; when occupancy and
use shall be the only title to land, and every one shall obey the
divine injunction, "In the sweat of thy face shalt thou eat bread."
When men shall be just and generous, little less than gods, and
women shall be just and charitable toward each other, little less
than angels; when we shall have not a government of the people
by capitalists, but a government of the people, by the people.

Ladies and gentlemen, I thank you.

# A Strike for
# Farm Housewives

*As a part of the Country Life Movement, the Extension Department of the New York State College of Agriculture at Ithaca, New York, established correspondence courses for farm women. Readings offered in these courses instructed women on how to raise poultry, squabs, and bees, as well as how to prevent contamination of milk, how to lighten their housework, and how to work with rural schools.*

*After gathering information from 1400 New York farm women, the Extension Department released the report that follows. Although the report was dated 1919, it serves as an accurate introduction to the living and working conditions of farm women described throughout this section.*

Her morning begins at five or six o'clock. She starts the kitchen-range, which heats the kitchen in winter and in summer. She draws the water for breakfast, not from a convenient faucet, but from a well or a cistern which is likely to have no pump. She carries this water from five to fifty feet, in some cases even two hundred feet, to tea-kettle, stove-reservoir, wash-basin, or dish-pan. This is just the beginning of the day as disclosed by the answers written by farm-women in a survey taken by the United States Department of Agriculture with the cooperation of the State extension service.

On Mondays she rises a little earlier and draws more water to wash the clothes, but she does not wash with an electrically operated washing machine, wringer, and mangle. She uses heavy tubs or a washing machine which she runs by hand—the only laundry equipment recorded in the returns except in rare cases (two in two hundred) in which electric machines are used, altho the washing is an inevitable part of the routine. Not only is there a lack of laundry equipment, but the farm-woman, unless she is an invalid, does the washing without help. The ironing occupies her spare moments throughout the week....

By the time breakfast is almost ready, she calls the rest of the family. All too seldom are there children to be helped dress for school or vacation days; for these records suggest that race suicide seems to be oprating in the rural population of the State, or else the majority of New York farms are inhabited by older folk whose children have left the farm. According to the State College these conditions call for work to get better money returns for the farmers and to educate children for, instead of away from, life on the farm. Junior projects, nature study, agricultural high schools, and extension activities, should be so directed as to increase social and material benefits in the country, lest in another generation rural sections of the State be occupied by tenant farmers.

However, at present most of the farms studied are worked by their owners. Thus, in twenty-five farms there were twenty worked by their owners and four rented or worked on shares. Among twenty-five in another county, seventeen were farmed by their owners.

After the family has been speeded on its way for the morning, the farm-woman feeds the chickens, takes care of the eggs, and on market day dresses poultry. She washes the milk-pails despite the primitive water-supply. Recent reports of the dairymen's league regarding milk spoiled in transit prove that a water system for the dairy farm is a good business proposition as well as a convenience.

After the dairy or poultry duties are done, the farm-woman must take a trip to the garden, tend it, and gather its fruits for feeding the family, or in winter she must get from storage in the cellar the day's food-supply. Then there are always beds to be made and lamps to be cleaned and filled (in forty among fifty homes), and mending to be done. Near the week-end, with the ironing done, there are the baking and the sweeping and dusting. And these farmhouses are generally large, from eight to fourteen rooms, some of them being closed in winter. Then there is the weekly or monthly shopping-list to make, of foods which the farm does not produce and of other things that the family needs. The farm-woman is from two to five miles from town, and she must order with foresight in contrast with the city woman who can call for deliveries of a spool of thread or a collar-button.

Next there is dinner to get for the grown-ups, the children having taken luncheon to school except where hot school-lunches not only have improved the children's health, but also have taken one chore out of the tired farm mother's day. The farm-woman must see to 1,095 meals a year with such help as the family can give, for one hired girl to one hundred homes is typical. Too often the intimacy of the family's association at table is destroyed by the presence of from one to three hired men (from five to ten at harvesting), who may be not only uncongenial but an actual menace because of the deterioration in the character of available farm-labor.

After the dinner-dishes are done there is that omnipresent mending, and the farm-woman sits down to sew while she is resting! She buys some of the clothes for the family, but makes many in order to save money. One household convenience is practically universal—the sewing-machine....

The farm-woman may see in the weekly home paper an invitation for all farm-women to attend meetings of the home bureau, the Cornell study club, the grange, and a farmers' picnic. But the horses, or the men who drive the car, are busy, she lives too far away to walk, and, besides, she must be at home to get supper, to help about the milking, or to feed the chickens. Yet, by her own testimony, she stays at home almost every day in the year except for occasional trips to town to buy or sell.

Her day ends from fourteen to eighteen hours after it begins (some women wrote "Never" in the space for recording the end of the day's work). What would happen if a labor-union of farm-house-wives should strike for an eight-hour day and double pay for overtime? She gets no pay at all in most of the cases studied—except the board and keep to which "Little Orphant Annies" are entitled. She is unacquainted with cash. Her men handle the money. Sometimes she personally markets the eggs or the butter or the garden stuff she has helped to produce, but in thirty-seven among forty-five homes the egg- or butter-money goes into general household expenses; in one home it is "used by the man of the house," while in seven it is the farm-woman's own to use as she pleases. There were but seven farm and home bureau members in this group.*

*Farm and home bureau members: The Extension Department encouraged families to join the Farm Bureau (see p. 153), which in New York separated members into the two categories of "farm" and "home."

The farm is farther from the shopping center, the church, and the doctor than from the district school, which varies from "just across the street" to two miles. . . . The doctor is from one-half to six miles away. This may explain the interest the farm-women have taken in the health projects of the home bureau and in learning how to feed the family in sickness and in health. In about a third of the homes there is no telephone, and illness needs first aid while the horse is being saddled, the car started, or the lantern trimmed, for a summons of the nearest doctor.

The farm-woman is also incidentally a nurse. The records of family sickness cover total days of illness in bed for as many as 276, but more typically about thirty, days in a year. Many records show no illness, which might seem to indicate good sanitary conditions such as an adequate water-supply, screens, plenty of milk, eggs, and vegetables in the diet, lack of overwork; but, on the contrary, all efforts to relate prevalence of illness to lack of screens or water are fruitless. The conclusion seems to be that there has been a survival of those fit to survive and adapt themselves to living conditions which would kill off Robert Louis Stevensons before they ever wrote a line.

In most cases no contacts with regular extension-service agencies are indicated. The space for recording the source of most help is either empty or filled with the home paper: The Farm Journal, The American Agriculturist, The National Stockman, The Rural New-Yorker, and Farm and Fireside. Some records mention bulletins from the college. This would seem to indicate that the printed word—especially in the mediums they read, such as the home papers which print a great deal of material from the college—is the chief source of information. Relatively few farm-women confess to a knowledge of the home bureaus, which are complimented by occasional words of approval, but not by an actual membership in more than ten per cent of the homes.

The record on labor-saving devices reveal that many farm-women are doing the housework with the equipment their grandmothers had; whereas capital has been invested on these same farms in modern machinery to save labor outside the house. . . .

The time has evidently come when farm capital should be

invested in the farm home for labor-saving devices and methods. Live-stock is infinitely less important than children. Moreover, "buying more land to raise more corn to feed more hogs to buy more land" will always be less important in the long run than an abundant life for the human family on the farm.

# Country Life and
# the Country School

*Mabel Carney, perhaps the best known of the women advocates of the Country Life Movement, was among those who argued that proper education could make rural life more attractive spiritually as well as economically and socially. In a study published in 1912, she described the role she envisioned for the rural school teacher.*

A chief characteristic of country life is its isolation or openness, and one of the effects of this openness is a scarcity of leaders. In this respect the rural community is essentially different from the town or city. The city is composed of men and women of all professions and occupations. This affords many leaders of diverse and varying points of view. There are lawyers, teachers, business men, ministers, and editors, all eager and capable of leadership and able to render good public service of this kind. The country community, on the other hand, is composed almost entirely of people of one pursuit. This naturally develops a common point of view and causes farmers to fail to appreciate many opportunities not directly related to their own line of work and thought.

Most of the slow growth and retardation of country life can be traced to this want of good active leaders. It is not because farmers are intellectually inferior in any sense or even because desire is lacking that progressive movements mature so slowly in the country. Country people often neglect to begin a measure that they well know will add to the convenience and welfare of their lives. The consolidation of schools is a typical instance. Many communities appreciate the advantage of such a change but fail to act simply because there is "nobody to start it." One of the worst features of the local jealousy so often found in a farm neighborhood lies in the fact that capable men who might develop the power of good leadership refrain from action through fear of incurring the displeasure of public opinion.

Right here lies the country teacher's opportunity. For, in the first place, the position of the teacher as a director of children requires that she be at least something of a leader; the more developed her powers of leadership, the greater her influence both within and without the schoolroom. Moreover, people turn to the school as a center of authority, and look to the teacher, without jealousy or criticism, as one who has the right to lead. She is in close and varied contact with them and on the same level. She also embodies a new point of view with often a larger perspective than any one else, and is sensitive to community needs and conditions. Furthermore, the teacher is the director of the one community institution in the neighborhood, the only all-inclusive community institution society affords, and in many instances in the open, where granges, farmers' clubs, and even churches are sometimes wanting, the only social-service institution of any kind. She is also the guardian of the educational interests of the community and may easily enlarge her office to include adult instruction and thus introduce ideas of progress relating to all phases of farm living, social, economic, and scientific. The fact that she usually comes from outside the neighborhood and has no pecuniary interests to promote also adds to her power. To these advantages may be added the further argument that country teachers of all rural social workers are most easily trained for leadership. This is true because as a group they already possess the proper attitude and are at present better able than others to obtain special training for rural leadership....

By this leadership of the country teacher I do not mean something exalted, indefinite, and impossible. I mean only an increase and expansion of the good work now going on in scores of communities at the present time. I mean a movement quiet, humble, unassuming, and of small beginnings. I mean a leadership that first occupies itself with its legitimate task of teaching a good school, for no teacher can gain or hold the confidence of any community who is not first of all a good teacher. I mean a leadership, as I have tried to indicate throughout, that begins by leading dirt, double desks,* and unsightly stoves out of the schoolroom and by leading soap and water, ventilation, and better teaching into it. I mean also a type of leadership that learns from others, is never unwilling to take the smallest suggestion from the simplest soul, and that leads for the service and comfort it may give rather than for commendation before the eyes of men. Such leadership will be what has been termed true leadership because it will be a work of quiet, social direction, which sincerely seeks to stimulate and develop the ability of others rather than to exploit its own good parts....

There is almost no virtue or ability not listed in the category of a good country teacher's accomplishments. She must possess a fair degree of all-round scholarship; be something of an artist, carpenter, cook, musician, and gardener; know just what ails a smoky stove, a rattling window, or a dull boy; be able to bandage wounds, pull teeth, start fires, drive a fractious horse, conduct a Sunday school, or fish lost boots from the muddy depths of the public highway. And all this for the royal sum of forty or fifty dollars a month!

# The Jeanes Teachers

*The Jeanes Teachers were Black teachers who acted primarily as supervisors, but also instructed other Black teachers on how to improve their work. Virginia Randolph's report on her first term as a Jeanes teacher, excerpted here, was sternly restrained and businesslike. In the careful listing of each penny collected and disbursed during her efforts to reform*

---

*Double desks:* An extra-wide desk and a bench shared by two students. These came to be identified with outmoded school equipment, to be replaced whenever possible with single-student desks.

*rural Black schools may be seen, in microcosm, the struggles*
*of Black teachers to advance their students and themselves.*
*This struggle would continue until it joined with the larger*
*Civil Rights Movement that arose in the 1950s.*

**A Brief Report**
**of the Manual Training Work**
**Done in the Colored Schools**
**of Henrico County, Va.**
**For Session, 1908–1909**

**H**aving taught Manual Training in Mountain Road School
for sixteen sessions, I was recommended by the Supt. of
Henrico Co. as Supervisor of the work for the entire county. My
work began Oct. 26, 1908, under the auspices of the "Negro Rural
School Fund," Dr. James H. Dillard of New Orleans, La. President.
This work should begin in the primary grades and continue as
long as the children remain in school. The destiny of our race
depends, largely, upon the training the children receive in the
schoolroom, and how careful we should be. The great majority of
the children in the country schools will never reach a high
school, therefore we must meet the demands of the schools in
the Rural Districts by introducing this phase of training in
every schoolroom.

It must be impressed upon the minds of the pupils that "Clean-
liness is next to Godliness," and when this law of Hygiene is
obeyed, they have conquered a great giant. They must also see
that their schoolroom is neat and attractive with curtains at
their windows, pictures on the walls, stoves kept neatly polished, and the grounds neat and clean, have a book on the "Laws
of Health" hung in the schoolroom and each child be made to
make himself familiar with it. The teacher should also give
instructions along these lines which will be of great benefit
because the teachers are models for the school-room.

My first step was to organize School Improvement Leagues.
The constitution says that the grounds must be beautified and
everything done to make an attractive school. Each scholar is
expected to pay the sum of five cents per month and from time to

time, give entertainments to strengthen the treasury but they must have a tendency to elevate the community morally and educationally.

During the term Mr. Wood gave me one thousand plants of hedge and twenty shade trees which I have distributed in each District. Hon. John Lamb of Washington, D.C., sent seeds for the school garden. Mr. Horace Peterson of Glen Allen, gave shucks to five schools for mats.

The schools are progressing nicely and with a few recommendations for next term, I will give a report from each school. I recommend:

I. The time given for Manual Training be six hours a week instead of three, and that time divided in periods to suit the teacher.

II. That the schools furnish their cooking materials and that the community may feel that they can order bread, cakes, etc. to be cooked at school and the proceeds made, go into the school treasury.

## Improvements Made at Each School

*Brookland District, Barton Heights School, Principal, Mary M. Scott.* Fenced in the yard, granolithic walk, set out hedges, trees, and rosebushes, white washed the trees and fence, taught sewing, needlework, carpentry, and shuck mats. Amount collected during the term, $50.05, Expended, $10.95. Balance in the treasury for next term to fit up kitchen, $39.10. . . .

*[Brookland District], Pole Road School, Principal, Emma J. Washington.* Set out hedge, built a large pavilion, white washed the trees, planted flowers, taught domestic science, sewing, fancy work, laundry work, paper cutting, mats and carpentry. Much interest is being manifested in the school garden. Amount collected, $25.00, Expended, $10.00. Balance in treasury, $15.00. . . .

*Fairfield District, Woodville School, Principal, Ernestine Christian.* Set out hedge, white washed fence, planted trees, taught sewing, making mats, bead work and carpentry. Have a

stove and cooking utensils ready for a kitchen. Amount collected, $7.85, Expended, $2.85. Balance in treasury, $5.00....

*[Fairfield District], Boa Swamp School, Teacher, Annie M.
Whiting.* Planted trees and flowers, taught sewing and making
baskets. Amount collected, $3.00, Expended, $1.00. Balance in
treasury, $2.00....

*Tuckahoe District, Zion Town School, Teacher, Amanda
Brown.* Cleaned up an acre of ground and turned it into a lawn,
taught domestic science, sewing and needlework. Much interest
is being manifested in the school garden. Amount collected,
$29.47, Expended, $16.69. Balance in treasury, $12.78.

*[Tuckahoe District], Carbon Hill School, Teacher, Mabel. v.
Harris.* Plowed up ground and made a twenty ft. walk, planted
trees, rooted up stumps, taught domestic science and sewing.
Amount collected, $14.18, Expended, $4.00. Balance in treasury,
$10.18....

*Varina District, Sydney School, Teacher, Martha Ross.* The
Chairman of Varina Board, Mr. S.C. Freeman, knowing how hard
the teacher and patrons were working to build up their school,
sent a good many workmen that he employed at Curls Neck
Farm, to the school and fenced in the yard, put up belfry and bell,
graveled the walk, built a porch, made benches and set out
hedges; free of charge. He also assisted many of the other schools
whenever called upon. Taught sewing and needlework. Amount
collected, $5.30, Expended, $1.50. Balance in treasury, $3.80....

No. of schools, 22.
No. of visits during term, 190.
Amount collected, $331.49.
Amount expended, $108.81.
Balance in the different treas. to date for stoves and cooking
utensils next term, $222.68.
I am indeed proud of the interest manifested by each teacher in
carrying on the Manual Training work. Every school without
any exception took hold of the work willingly and cheerfully,
one can but admire the energetic efforts put forth by each

teacher to carry out every suggestion that pertained to the advancement of the work. I hope by the beginning of next term, kitchens will be built in all the schools.

Respectfully submitted
Virginia Estelle Randolph

# I Am Quarlsome
# When Tired and Fatigued

*When the Children's Bureau was established in 1912, it sent out a notice that it would provide help for mothers and expectant mothers. The response documented the isolation and medical ignorance of many women, both urban and rural. In the South, midwives were being gradually legislated out of existence, and rural women were left with almost no health care. The following letter, written by Mrs. H.B. Rogers of Winterville, Georgia, in 1920, eloquently describes the condition of these Southern rural women. The reply, from a Children's Bureau physician, was probably not helpful to Rogers; but concerned women did lobby through the Sheppard-Towner Act, which helped offset the deteriorating health conditions through the establishment of pre-natal clinics.\* In 1927, Congress refused to fund the Act. Thereafter, conditions continued to decline for poor rural Southern women—white and Black.*

**D**ear Madame:
I need advice. I am a farmers wife. Do my household duties and a regular field hand too. The mother of 9 children and in family way again. I am quarlsome when tired and fatigued. When

---

\**Sheppard-Towner Maternity and Infancy Act:* Passed by Congress in 1921, the Act provided grants to states to develop infant and maternity service, including midwife education projects. The American Medical Association opposed the Act, which lapsed in 1929.

I come out of the field to prepare dinner my husband and all the children gets in my way. I quarrel at them for being in my way. I tell them I will build them a fire if they are cold. I also threaten to move the stove out on the porch. What shall I do? My husband wont sympathise with me one bit but talks rough to me. If I get tired and sick of my daily food and crave some simple article, should I have it. I have helped make the living for 20 years. Should I benied [sic] of a few simple articles or money either.

Does it make a mother unvirtuous for a man physician to wait on her during confinement; is it safe for me to go through it without aid from anyone? Please give me some advise. There isn't any midwives near us now. I am not friendless but going to you for advise to keep down gossip. Yours,...

*The response to this letter came from Grace Meigs, Director, Division of Hygiene, the Children's Bureau. Dr. Meigs wrote:*

I think probably the reason you are so tired and cross is because you are doing too much work. Would it not be possible for you to at least leave off working in the field while you are pregnant and for quite a long time after your baby is born? It is customary all over the United States for men physicians to attend women at confinement. It would be very unwise for you to run the risk of permanent injury to yourself and baby by not having a properly qualified attendant when the baby is born and I should strongly urge you to put yourself under the care of a physician at once.

# A Jury of Her Peers

*Born and raised in Iowa, Susan Keating Glaspell began her writing career as a journalist but turned in 1901 to writing short stories, novels, and eventually plays. "A Jury of Her Peers," first published in 1917, portrays prairie women searching for their own inner strength as they discover with*

*horror the life a neighbor has lived for twenty years. The*
*story begins with Martha Hale and Mrs. Peters, the sheriff's*
*wife, accompanying their husbands to the home of Minnie*
*Foster, who has just been arrested for the murder of her*
*husband, John Wright.*


**M**r. Henderson said, coming out, that what was needed
for the case was a motive. Something to show anger—or
sudden feeling."

"Well, I don't see any signs of anger around here," said Mrs.
Hale. "I don't—"

She stopped. It was as if her mind tripped on something. Her
eye was caught by a dish-towel in the middle of the kitchen table.
Slowly she moved toward the table. One half of it was wiped
clean, the other half messy. Her eyes made a slow, almost
unwilling turn to the bucket of sugar and the half empty bag
beside it. Things begun—and not finished.

After a moment she stepped back, and said, in that manner of
releasing herself:

"Wonder how they're finding things upstairs? I hope she had it
a little more red up there. You know," —she paused, and feeling
gathered, —"it seems kind of *sneaking:* locking her up in town
and coming out here to get her own house to turn against her!"

"But, Mrs. Hale," said the sheriff's wife, "the law is the law."

"I s'pose 'tis," answered Mrs. Hale shortly.

She turned to the stove, saying something about that fire not
being much to brag of. She worked with it a minute, and when
she straightened up she said aggressively:

"The law is the law—and a bad stove is a bad stove. How'd you
like to cook on this?" —pointing with the poker to the broken
lining. She opened the oven door and started to express her
opinion of the oven; but she was swept into her own thoughts,
thinking of what it would mean, year after year, to have that
stove to wrestle with. The thought of Minnie Foster trying to
bake in that oven—and the thought of her never going over to
see Minnie Foster—.

She was startled by hearing Mrs. Peters, say: "A person gets
discouraged—and loses heart."

The sheriff's wife had looked from the stove to the sink—to the pail of water which had been carried in from outside. The two women stood there silent, above them the footsteps of the men who were looking for evidence against the woman who had worked in that kitchen. That look of seeing into things, of seeing through a thing to something else, was in the eyes of the sheriff's wife now. When Mrs. Hale next spoke to her, it was gently:

"Better loosen up your things, Mrs. Peters. We'll not feel them when we go out."

Mrs. Peters went to the back of the room to hang up the fur tippet she was wearing. A moment later she exclaimed, "Why, she was piecing a quilt," and held up a large sewing basket piled high with quilt pieces.

Mrs. Hale spread some of the blocks out on the table. "It's log-cabin pattern," she said, putting several of them together. "Pretty, isn't it?"

They were so engaged with the quilt that they did not hear the footsteps on the stairs. Just as the stair door opened Mrs. Hale was saying:

"Do you suppose she was going to quilt it or just knot it?"

The sheriff threw up his hands.

"They wonder whether she was going to quilt it or just knot it!"

There was a laugh for the ways of women, a warming of hands over the stove, and then the county attorney said briskly:

"Well, let's go right out to the barn and get that cleared up."

"I don't see as there's anything so strange," Mrs. Hale said resentfully, after the outside door had closed on the three men—"our taking up our time with little things while we're waiting for them to get the evidence. I don't see as it's anything to laugh about."

"Of course they've got awful important things on their minds," said the sheriff's wife apologetically.

They returned to an inspection of the block for the quilt. Mrs. Hale was looking at the fine, even sewing, and preoccupied with thoughts of the woman who had done that sewing, when she heard the sheriff's wife say, in a queer tone:

"Why, look at this one."

She turned to take the block held out to her.

"The sewing," said Mrs. Peters, in a troubled way. "All the rest of them have been so nice and even—but—this one. Why it looks as if she didn't know what she was about!"

Their eyes met—something flashed to life, passed between them; then, as if with an effort, they seemed to pull away from each other. A moment Mrs. Hale sat there, her hands folded over that sewing which was so unlike all the rest of the sewing. Then she had pulled a knot and drawn the threads.

"Oh, what are you doing, Mrs. Hale?" asked the sheriff's wife, startled.

"Just pulling out a stitch or two that's not sewed very good," said Mrs. Hale mildly.

"I don't think we ought to touch things," Mrs. Peters said, a little helplessly.

"I'll just finish up this end," answered Mrs. Hale, still in that mild, matter-of-fact fashion.

She threaded a needle and started to replace bad sewing with good. For a little while she sewed in silence. Then, in that thin, timid voice, she heard:

"Mrs. Hale!"

"Yes, Mrs. Peters?"

"What do you suppose she was so—nervous about?"

"Oh, I don't know," said Mrs. Hale, as if dismissing a thing not important enough to spend much time on. "I don't know as she was—nervous. I sew awful queer sometimes when I'm just tired."

She cut a thread, and out of the corner of her eye looked up at Mrs. Peters. The small, lean face of the sheriff's wife seemed to have tightened up. Her eyes had that look of peering into something. But next moment she moved, and said in her thin, indecisive way:

"Well, I must get those clothes wrapped. They may be through sooner than we think. I wonder where I could find a piece of paper—and string."

"In that cupboard, maybe," suggested Mrs. Hale, after a glance around.

One piece of the crazy sewing remained unripped. Mrs. Peters' back turned, Martha Hale now scrutinized that piece, compared with the dainty, accurate sewing of the other blocks. The difference was startling. Holding this block made her feel queer, as if the distracted thoughts of the woman who had perhaps turned to it to try and quiet herself were communicating themselves to her.

Mrs. Peters' voice roused her.

"Here's a bird-cage," she said. "Did she have a bird, Mrs. Hale?"

"Why, I don't know whether she did or not." She turned to look at the cage Mrs. Peters was holding up. "I've not been here in so long." She sighed. "There was a man round last year selling canaries cheap—but I don't know as she took one. Maybe she did. She used to sing real pretty herself."

Mrs. Peters looked around the kitchen.

"Seems kind of funny to think of a bird here." She half laughed—an attempt to put up a barrier. "But she must have had one—or why would she have a cage? I wonder what happened to it."

"I suppose maybe the cat got it," suggested Mrs. Hale, resuming her sewing.

"No; she didn't have a cat. She's got that feeling some people have about cats—being afraid of them. When they brought her to our house yesterday, my cat got in the room and she was real upset and asked me to take it out."

"My sister Bessie was like that," laughed Mrs. Hale.

The sheriff's wife did not reply. The silence made Mrs. Hale turn around. Mrs. Peters was examining the bird-cage.

"Look at this door," she said slowly. "It's broke. One hinge has been pulled apart."

Mrs. Hale came nearer.

"Looks as if someone must have been—rough with it."

Again their eyes met—startled, questioning, apprehensive. For a moment neither spoke nor stirred. Then Mrs. Hale, turning away, said brusquely:

"If they're going to find any evidence, I wish they'd be about it. I don't like this place."

"But I'm awful glad you came with me, Mrs. Hale." Mrs. Peters put the bird-cage on the table and sat down. "It would be lonesome for me—sitting here alone."

"Yes, it would, wouldn't it?" agreed Mrs. Hale, a certain determined naturalness in her voice. She had picked up the sewing, but now it dropped in her lap, and she murmured in a different voice: "But I tell you what I *do* wish, Mrs. Peters. I wish I had come over sometimes when she was here. I wish—I had."

"But of course you were awful busy, Mrs. Hale. Your house— your children."

"I could've come," retorted Mrs. Hale shortly. "I stayed away because it weren't cheerful—and that's why I ought to have come. I"—she looked around—"I've never liked this place. Maybe because it's down in a hollow and you don't see the road. I don't know what it is, but it's a lonesome place, and always was. I wish I had come over to see Minnie Foster sometimes. I can see now—"

She did not put it into words.

"Well, you mustn't reproach yourself," counseled Mrs. Peters. "Somehow, we just don't see how it is with other folks till— something comes up."

"Not having children makes less work," mused Mrs. Hale, after a silence, "but it makes a quiet house—and Wright out to work all day—and no company when he did come in. Did you know John Wright, Mrs. Peters?"

"Not to know him. I've seen him in town. They say he was a good man.

"Yes—good," conceded John Wright's neighbor grimly. "He didn't drink, and kept his word as well as most, I guess, and paid his debts. But he was a hard man, Mrs. Peters. Just to pass the time of day with him—." She stopped, shivered a little. "Like a raw wind that gets to the bone." Her eye fell upon the cage on the table before her, and she added, almost bitterly: "I should think she would've wanted a bird!"

Suddenly she leaned forward, looking intently at the cage. "But what do you s'pose went wrong with it?"

"I don't know," returned Mrs. Peters; "unless it got sick and died."

But after she said it she reached over and swung the broken door. Both women watched it as if somehow held by it.

"You didn't know—her?" Mrs. Hale asked, a gentler note in her voice.

"Not till they brought her yesterday," said the sheriff's wife.

"She—come to think of it, she was kind of like a bird herself. Real sweet and pretty, but kind of timid and—fluttery. How— she—did—change."

That held her for a long time. Finally, as if struck with a happy thought and relieved to get back to everyday things, she exclaimed:

"Tell you what, Mrs. Peters, why don't you take the quilt in with you? It might take up her mind."

"Why, I think that's a real nice idea, Mrs. Hale," agreed the sheriff's wife, as if she too were glad to come into the atmosphere of a simple kindness. "There couldn't possibly be any objection to that, could there? Now, just what will I take? I wonder if her patches are in here—and her things."

They turned to the sewing basket.

"Here's some red," said Mrs. Hale, bringing out a roll of cloth. Underneath that was a box. "Here, maybe her scissors are in here—and her things." She held it up. "What a pretty box! I'll warrant that was something she had a long time ago—when she was a girl."

She held it in her hand a moment; then, with a little sigh, opened it.

Instantly her hand went to her nose.

"Why—!"

Mrs. Peters drew nearer—then turned away.

"There's something wrapped up in this piece of silk," faltered Mrs. Hale.

"This isn't her scissors," said Mrs. Peters, in a shrinking voice.

Her hand not steady, Mrs. Hale raised the piece of silk. "Oh, Mrs. Peters!" she cried. "It's—"

Mrs. Peters bent closer.

"It's the bird," she whispered.

"But, Mrs. Peters!" cried Mrs. Hale. "*Look* at it! Its *neck*—look at its neck! It's all—other side to."

She held the box away from her.

The sheriff's wife again bent closer.

"Somebody wrung its neck," said she, in a voice that was slow and deep.

And then again the eyes of the two women met—this time clung together in a look of dawning comprehension, of growing horror. Mrs. Peters looked from the dead bird to the broken door of the cage. Again their eyes met. And just then there was a sound at the outside door.

Mrs. Hale slipped the box under the quilt pieces in the basket, and sank into the chair before it. Mrs. Peters stood holding to the table. The county attorney and the sheriff came in from outside....

The sheriff came up to the table.

"Did you want to see what Mrs. Peters was going to take in?"

The county attorney picked up the apron. He laughed.

"Oh, I guess they're not very dangerous things the ladies have picked out."

Mrs. Hale's hand was on the sewing basket in which the box was concealed. She felt that she ought to take her hand off the basket. She did not seem able to. He picked up one of the quilt blocks which she had piled on to cover the box. Her eyes felt like fire. She had a feeling that if he took up the basket she would snatch it from him.

But he did not take it up. With another little laugh, he turned away, saying:

"No; Mrs. Peters doesn't need supervising. For that matter, a sheriff's wife is married to the law. Ever think of it that way, Mrs. Peters?"

Mrs. Peters was standing beside the table. Mrs. Hale shot a look up at her; but she could not see her face. Mrs. Peters had turned away. When she spoke, her voice was muffled.

"Not—just that way," she said.

"Married to the law!" chuckled Mrs. Peters' husband. He moved toward the door into the front room, and said to the county attorney:

"I just want you to come in here a minute, George. We ought to take a look at these windows."

"Oh—windows," said the county attorney scoffingly.

"We'll be right out, Mr. Hale," said the sheriff to the farmer, who was still waiting by the door.

Hale went to look after the horses. The sheriff followed the county attorney into the other room. Again—for one final moment—the two women were alone in that kitchen.

Martha Hale sprang up, her hands tight together, looking at that other woman, with whom it rested. At first she could not see her eyes, for the sheriff's wife had not turned back since she turned away at that suggestion of being married to the law. But now Mrs. Hale made her turn back. Her eyes made her turn back. Slowly, unwillingly, Mrs. Peters turned her head until her eyes met the eyes of the other woman. There was a moment when they held each other in a steady, burning look in which there was no evasion nor flinching. Then Martha Hale's eyes pointed the way to the basket in which was hidden the thing that would make certain the conviction of the other woman—that woman who was not there and yet who had been there with them all through that hour.

For a moment Mrs. Peters did not move. And then she did it. With a rush forward, she threw back the quilt pieces, got the box, tried to put it in her handbag. It was too big. Desperately she opened it, started to take the bird out. But there she broke—she could not touch the bird. She stood there helpless, foolish.

There was the sound of a knob turning in the inner door. Martha Hale snatched the box from the sheriff's wife, and got it in the pocket of her big coat just as the sheriff and the county attorney came back into kitchen.

"Well, Henry," said the county attorney facetiously, "at least we found out that she was not going to quilt it. She was going to—what is it you call it, ladies?"

Mrs. Hale's hand was against the pocket of her coat.

"We call it—knot it, Mr. Henderson."


## The Rural Social Worker

*Josephine Brown, like Mabel Carney, saw women as central to rural reform but as social workers rather than as teachers. In 1933 she described the ideal social worker and the "patriarchal" farm family. Her comments on the latter show no substantial changes in the conditions which had inspired Susan Glaspell's short story nearly two decades earlier.*

**M**any of the social workers who may be available for the position in the agency will be young women who have always lived in a city and who have received their preparation for social work in a city organization. When a social worker whose background is wholly urban is employed in a rural county, certain adjustments must be made by her on the one hand and by the county people on the other if the two are to work together effectively. These adjustments are necessary not because of any inherent differences between urban and rural people, but because the widely different conditions under which they live have inevitably influenced their methods of thought and action. While it must be admitted that in a number of instances such adjustments have been found difficult and sometimes impossible, there is also abundant evidence of the wholehearted acceptance by country people of social workers who have had no previous experience with rural life, and of mutual understanding and adaptability which have made it possible for them to work together in the finest kind of partnership. Such satisfactory results have been due to the ability and willingness of the social workers to adjust themselves to ways and conditions of living which are new and unaccustomed to them, and to the efforts of country people who have made this adjustment easier by their understanding and sympathy. Ability to adjust to new conditions may, therefore, be considered an essential qualification in a social worker who is to come into a rural community with no previous experience of rural life. . . .

There are factors in rural work which point to the need for special emphasis on some if not all of these qualifications. The rural case worker must usually carry executive responsibility. She is sometimes the first and often the only social worker in the county. Her contact with people in a rural community is much closer than it is in a city. The people among whom she works will seek first to know her as a person and unless they accept her they will probably not accept the work she stands for, no matter how well qualified she is professionally.

For these reasons not only the highest type of training but the most exacting personal qualifications are desirable for rural work. It presents the difficulties and also the challenge of a pioneer field. The opportunities it offers for work in partnership with rural people of insight and vision are such as to appeal strongly to social workers of the highest caliber.

Love of the country for its own sake is perhaps the most important of all qualifications.

The rural social worker should be a friendly person, willing to drop all formality; able to identify herself with the people with whom she works, and to become a part of the community in which she lives. This involves freedom from prejudice, the ability to make constant adjustments and the willingness to modify her personal habits to conform with local standards. If she is self-reliant, she will be better able to put up with the inevitable loneliness which results from separation from others who have the same professional interests.

Case work in the average rural county must be done without the help of specialized social agencies and other resources which are usually available in a city. The rural worker, therefore, should have initiative and ingenuity in developing resources, and in recognizing and using whatever facilities may be at hand.

If she is to work in a satisfactory partnership with the people in the county she should be willing to efface herself and to let others take credit for accomplishments in which she has had a share.

Since she must deal directly with all types of human problems and will not have older and more experienced social workers to share her responsibilities, it is important that she have sufficient maturity to command confidence, both in her general community contacts and in case work.

Executive ability of a high order, good judgment, and vision are essential if she is to assume a position of leadership in the community program. She must be able to see clearly the interrelationship and relative importance of varied community problems. She should be able to look far ahead to possibilities in the development of the community program and at the same time be willing to go slowly in suggesting new plans.

Experience with rural life is of undoubted value. This background, however, has been found unnecessary by workers of special adaptability and imaginative powers who have made up for the lack by study, reading, and observation.

The farmer's family is apt to be patriarchal in type. The father, who manages the farm, generally dominates the home life. If his wife is inclined to be submissive, she may not challenge this domination but find her compensation in seeking sympathy. If she has a strong personality and is proud, friction is likely to result. If she is more competent than he is there may be nagging. If she is a woman of high ideals she may try to satisfy her suppressed longings by winning opportunities for the education of an unusual son. The social worker will discover that the girls of the family often grow up with a feeling of inferiority to the boys and often stay at home working without wages while the boys are educated. The husband generally maintains the traditions of his father's family, while his wife, who has perhaps been reared in another type of farm family, often brings another viewpoint to the home.

# I Just Up and Bashed Him Good

*White North Carolina farm tenant Mary Green described herself in 1939 to writer Adyleen G. Merrick as "tired, wore out, and ready for the joys of heaven." Here she tells what she did when her husband sold the calf she had raised.*

I ain't had no new dress nor nothin' else new since I married Pap, but them no count boys is always togged out and always goin' some'ers like big rich. They take all and give nothin'. Just like the time when Pap sold my heifer calf. Man come by one day and he says, "That's a right nice little calf thar. If you're aimin' to part with her I'll buy. I can make out to give you three dollars now if you'll sell." I weren't right anxious to part with my calf, she was a likely little thing, gentle and nice, but I wanted the three dollars so bad. I knowed it would buy us some meetin' clothes and a pair o' shoes, so I let Pap sell.

Sister, I never got nary cent of that there money! Me and him and the two boys stood about while the trade was bein' made. After the stranger paid for the calf and went on his way, Pap hands each of them boys a dollar and put the other in his pocket. When I seed what he done, it looked like more then I could swaller, it bein' my calf. I says to Pap, "How come you part with my cash money to them boys?" and he says, "Men has to have a little spendin' money on 'em in case of need." I says, "Well, if they do what about t'other dollar? Don't I get none?" He says, "I reckon not, you ain't got no need for cash money." I stood thar a-lookin' at him in wonder. Mind, he'd done and sold *my* calf and he weren't aimin' to give me ary penny from the trade. Thar we stood, Pap looked at me and I at him. Thoughts was just a-flyin' through my mind. My throat hurt, I was so outdone about losin' the money. I reckon if Pap had stopped to reason with me instead of just walkin' off like he done I wouldn't a acted so ugly, but when he santered 'round the house with no more to say I just flew mad all over. I run in the house and grabbed a gallon jar. I put it in a tow sack right quick and ran through the house to the kitchen door. Right thar I met Pap fair, and I just up and bashed him good over the head with that jar. When he drapped I got my dollar and went on to the fields to my hoein'. I truly never aimed to do him so much hurt. Pap were a long time gettin' over them cuts he got from that broke jar. He wouldn't speak to me for days after that and from then on we have fit a heap, off and on, mostly 'bout them two triflin' son o' his'n and him never givin' me no cash money.

## The Misses Hodges

*In 1939, Bernice Harris made the rounds with a rural social worker to meet and interview farm women like the Misses Hodges, three white women who lived together in North Carolina. One sister, eighty-four year old Aunt Sarah, had recently died after picking out a spot on the farm where she wanted to be buried. The second sister, seventy-eight year old Aunt Sue, had just bobbed her hair, and threatened to get a permanent, but vowed never to wear a corset. Aunt Sue and*

*her niece Tommie told Harris about their lives and about the
ways the three women took care of one another.*

L ivin' way back off the road with woods on both sides of
us don't worry us, for not hardly a day passes that
somebody in the neighborhood don't send over here to find
out how we are and if we need anything. If we was to take bad off
way in the night— Well, maybe we'll have sense enough to wait
till day. Some of the women has offered to let their boys come
here and sleep at night, but it's been just three women in the
house so long we don't feel the need of a man. If one of us had
married, a husband would've come in handy now we're old. I
loved a man one time and was thinkin' about gettin' married. His
name was Hodges, though he wa'n't no kin to us. Here's a tin type
picture of him. Le'me dust it off so you can see how he looked. I
thought enough of him to keep his picture hangin' here all these
years. We didn't get married, because he fooled me—not that he
wouldn't marry me, but— Well, he done somethin' bad, and I
couldn't forgive him. Held my hand? Law, no, 'twa'n't that! Kissed
me? No, 'twa'n't that! Cussed a oath in my presence? No, 'twa'n't
that! Stoop over here, and I'll whisper it: He took up with a bad
woman. Here's a tin type of Sarah when she was young. We've
got a good picture of her, but a woman come by and got it to
enlarge, and it ha'n't come back yet.

"My pappy moved here a long time ago from down about
Lasker and bought this little farm, where we've been livin' ever
since we could remember. Till late years, Sarah always said she
wanted to be taken back to Lasker where Mammy and Pappy was
buried, but she decided before she died she'd rather stay here.
After Pappy died me and Sarah stayed on here and farmed long as
we was able. We done the hoe work, cut our own wood, planted
our crop and garden, and worked just like men folks. When our
brother died and left a little baby girl, we took and raised her—
Tommie there. I don't know what we'd done without her. As we
begin to age, she took holt o' the farm and run it long as she could.
I used to stay round with my kinfolks a right smart to help 'em
nu'se their younguns, while Sarah and Tommie carried on the
business here.

"We've got ten acres in our little farm, though most of it has growed up now. We've been rentin' it out, what was fittin', and that little rent was what we've had to live on. This year we couldn't rent it, and we'd been flat if it hadn't been for the old age pension; I get $7.50 a month, and that keeps us. Our livin' don't cost us much; me and Tommie both has to buy medicine and our flour, sugar, coffee, and such. But we got pretty chickens, plenty o' eggs and meat, and till this year we always had all the collards and dried peas we could use; we failed on 'em this time, but we can get greens from our neighbors often as we want 'em. Right lately our hens has gone back on us, refusin' to lay a single egg; we didn't even have one to stir us up a cake for Christmas, but that didn't matter when the neighbors keeps us in cake and milk and somethin' all the time. We threatened to sell our hens, but we think too much of 'em to part with any more'n we have to. We don't eat but twice a day, and while I'm hearty Tommie don't eat enough to work on. If folks would raise their somethin' t'eat at home, they'd live all right. We never had no money, but we ha'n't suffered none. We never owned nothin' but this little unpainted shack, but it's been home."

"We couldn't rent the land," Miss Tommie reminds her aunt, "but the taxes had to be paid just the same, $3.60 a year. We owe doctors' bills, and while they told us not to worry over them I can't forget my debts. When Aunt Sarah was buried, I told the undertaker I'd pay the burial expenses along as I could. He said I'd never hear from him about it, and I ha'n't, not these five years. When money gives out, we sell a hen and do along on that little change till Aunt Sue's check comes in. We get along real good on that $7.50 a month. It'll be nine years before I can get the old age pension, for I ain't but fifty-six. Some has told me to say I'm sixty-five, but I rather do without than to get anything wrong.

"Like Aunt Sue said, I've been the man here. Little as I am, I've picked up Aunt Sarah in my arms and toted her from one bed to the other, as heavy as she was compared to me. Looked like God gave me strength. When I was younger, I used to put on overalls and go to the woods to split firewood, though we have to hire it done now. I still knock up rotten stumps for kindlin', and I penned them little piles o' stove wood there by the dairy. My health is bad now, and I've had to slow down on hard work. I have fallin' out spells; with out no warnin', I suddenly go blank, and when I wake up there I'm lyin' on the floor or ground wherever I happen to be. I've always had these spells from a girl on, but they come more frequent now as I get older. Bad kidney trouble is what ails me.

"We never think about bein' afraid here by ourselves. I keep a pistol lyin' close to my bed, and if anything messes around here I'll shoot. A while back somebody stole some chickens, and the other night I heard 'em makin' a fuss like somethin' was botherin' out there. I raised the window and shot in the direction the fuss come from. Everything was quiet after that. Another night somebody come to the door there and tried to get in. It was a man, or he had a man's voice. The light was out, for we had gone to bed and was near 'bout asleep when he knocked. I asked who was there.

" 'It's Smith,' he said.

" 'Smith who?' I asked.

" 'R.L. Smith.'

" 'The only R.L. Smith I ever heard of is dead. Who are you, and what do you want here?'

" 'I want to come in and get warm by your fire. I'm cold.'

" 'I can't open the door. We've done gone to bed.'

" 'You needn't mind me. I ain't but sixteen.'

" 'I don't care where you're sixteen or sixty. We done gone to bed.'

" 'But I'm freezin'. Le'me come in and warm. I'll cut you some wood.'

" 'We got a plenty wood cut.'

" 'Just le'me warm. I won't hurt you.'

" 'If you don't go on away from that door, I'll hurt you. Aunt Sue, hand me that pistol.'

"I reckon he went away. We didn't hear no more from him. At the time I didn't have no kind o' weapon in the house, but after that the Masseys brought a pistol here for me to use. Folks is all time after me to get me a man, but I've done along these fifty-six years without one, and I won't risk it now. I'm afraid to marry— not afraid I wouldn't be good to a husband, but afraid he wouldn't be good to me. Lots of different ones has courted me, but I never cared for nobody much as I did Aunt Sarah and Aunt Sue."

# SIX:
# The Uncertain Harvest

## Women Who Don't Give Up

THE DEPRESSION OF THE 1930S accelerated a long-term trend, the movement of people off the land. Throughout the nineteenth century, the fertility of farm women had remained higher than

that of urban women, and the rural areas continued to grow in population. But the farm economy could no longer absorb farm offspring as the century progressed to its close. From 1910 to 1940, the farm population stabilized at about thirty million. During the years from 1929 to 1965, another thirty million farm people moved off the land. By the 1950s, one million were leaving annually. These three-and-a-half decades of internal migration brought a larger number of people to the city than the entire foreign immigration of 1840 to 1960 brought to the United States. By 1970, the farm population had declined to ten million; the old majority had become a new minority. The

189

political influence of this new minority would last until the early 1960s through over-representation, and then collapse as the Supreme Court mandated reapportionment of state and federal representation.[1]

The selections in this chapter show how farm women have fared in the period of exodus to the cities, from the 1930s to the present. The exodus has left on the land some who are wealthy, some who are middle class, and some who are poor. Off-farm income, from city jobs, allows many women to remain living on land that cannot support them.[2] Among the poor are a disproportionate number of Black, Hispanic, Asian, and Native American women, through whom the tradition of protest and organized social action has been carried forward. In this final section, these women, as well as the urban descendants of farm women, describe their feelings, their memories, and their hopes. This section also includes documents by women engaged in new communal experiments that allow them to remain on the land. In their various ways, the women presented here have not given up their ties to the land.

Some farm women survived the farm depression of the 1920s and 1930s. Judy Van der Veer, who owned a large ranch near San Diego, was one such woman. This section opens with Van der Veer's description of a poorer neighbor's delight in buying and raising a heifer. Thousands of other farm women got by during these hard times: they bartered, worked harder, cut corners, and managed to hang on to their land.[3]

Many women, however, found farm life increasingly inconvenient and isolated in a time when urban women appeared to be gaining greater mobility and freedom. Though these advantages may have been illusory—some scholars have argued that city women spent even more time on housework than their country sisters in the 1920s and 1930s—farm women were not always satisfied, even when they were farm owners.[4] Farm women's discontent may have stemmed, in part, from the increasing emphasis on housework on the farm. Margaret Hagood found, as the selection here reprinted shows, that women in the tobacco lands preferred field work to housework, when they had a choice. Farm women, when not overworked because of poverty, often enjoyed the work that weathered and wrinkled their faces.

New Deal reforms offered little occupationally for these farm women. One answer of New Deal reformers to farm women's complaints was to furnish canning instructions, equipment, and training as a way to increase farm family income. While farm women did increase the amount of food processed and thereby decrease expenses, household production could bring in only a limited amount of cash in an economy where food processing itself was becoming rationalized and mechanized. Reformers could not solve the farm problem by urging women to return to an earlier type of production. Women's hand labor simply could not compete with modern industrialized processes. Budgeting and canning could, in some cases, allow families to hang on, but they could not keep people on the farm when urban jobs became available.[5]

As the farm depression of the 1920s merged with the general depression of the 1930s, farm tenancy increased among the white population in the South. Here, among the seven million white and non-white sharecroppers of the cotton South, rural life reached its lowest economic level. Not just work but the precariousness of life itself, sheer survival, made the lives of these sharecroppers ones of desperation. Between 1935 and 1937, in the wake of New Deal farm reform, 300,000 sharecroppers fled the Southern Plains states of Arkansas, Missouri, Oklahoma, and Texas. It was not drought that drove these sharecroppers out; it was the evictions of landlords who used their Agricultural Adjustment Act allotment checks to buy tractors and replace their permanent labor force. The migrants headed West. Many of them ended up in California, competing with Mexican and Mexican-American laborers. The Southern white migrants of the 1930s, seeking permanent homes, refused to remain migratory. As permanent residents, they were entitled to health services, schools, and relief. Most of these families remained in the urban West, eventually being absorbed by the wartime expansion of Pacific Coast industries.[6]

The economic boom of World War II drew into the cities many thousands of additional rural people. During this period, families that had lived in subsistence farming areas, such as those in the hill country of Kentucky and Arkansas, joined the earlier streams from the cotton belt. Women who could still provide ample food for their children on subsistence farms followed their husbands to industrial cities where the men could find jobs. In an excerpt printed in this section, novelist Harriette Arnow describes the emotions of one such woman, Gertie Nevels, transported to the alien environment of wartime Detroit. Not all women suffered as keenly as Gertie, but Arnow's account grasps the familial tensions, confusion, and pain that often accompanied these wartime relocations.

Black women also swelled the exodus to the city. During the early days of the Depression many southern Blacks returned to live with their sharecropper parents. Farm sons and daughters stayed home. Then, as millions of farm tenants lost their homes because of crop limitation under the Agricultural Adjustment Act and farm mechanization, they sought employment in other rural areas or on government work projects. Older farm people were sometimes able to keep their homes and survived precariously on their garden produce and relief. When the economy improved in 1936 and jobs once again became available, the exodus continued. And, during World War II, rural Black women sought city jobs as household workers, while urban Black women began to move into jobs in business and industry.[7]

After the war, hard work in the country looked even less inviting to the young. In a selection reprinted here from *Coming of Age in Mississippi*, Anne Moody recalls the hard work of her parents and their continuing attachment to the land. For their daughter Anne, however, as for thousands of other young southern Blacks, liberation lay in the cities. Many of these young Black southerners from rural areas flooded into Black colleges during the 1950s, and from there launched a drive that gave organized support and youthful militance to the civil rights movement. The civil rights movement, though often fought on city streets, had its roots in the Black rural neighborhoods where the Black farm family had been entrapped by tenancy, the company store, and rural white social control. In some of these rural communities, Blacks began to demand better schools for their children; and from these islands of rural protest, the larger movement gained strength. Out of the struggles for voter registration and the efforts to organize rural communities, many young Black women and men, Anne Moody among them, emerged to dedicate their lives to social change.[8]

In the decades after World War II, so many Black women left farms for the cities that almost 75 percent were urban by 1970. Nevertheless, in that year, over 900,000 people, 25 percent of the total farm population, was Black. Although about 100,000 Black farms existed, they covered less than six million acres, three-tenths of one percent of all privately held land. By 1974, another one-half million acres had passed from Black to white ownership.

Among Black reformers, there has been a growing concern over the loss of this land, acquired through hard labor and usually against opposition from the white population. A "Black Manifesto," issued in 1969, called for a southern land bank and cooperative farms to halt the loss of the remaining land. Private donors enabled the establishment of the Emergency Land Fund to assist Black farmers, but government policies continued to favor programs for middle and upper income farmers and to ignore Black land grant colleges in the awarding of grant monies. The Rural Development Act of 1972 was passed by Congress without the loan program advocated by Blacks. Against the background of Black land loss, deteriorating urban life seemed even more threatening to Black people. Many sent money home to help parents hold on to their remaining land. Some even sent their children home to be raised by grandmothers still living on the land.[9]

As the farm tenants left the land for better jobs in the cities, landlords mechanized and depended more on migratory labor, some native-born Black and white farm families, but primarily on Mexican immigrants. Large-scale Mexican immigration began in the 1920s. Usually isolated in labor camps, the families worked as a unit for miserably low wages, with the oldest male often collecting pay for the whole family. Thus women were economically tied to the family in a way that urban women— especially young single women—were not in the city. Owners might bring in farm laborers from Mexico, desperately in need of work, using them as tenants to compete against native-born families, or more often, simply as day laborers. By 1929, Mexican workers had replaced German and Russian immigrants in the beet fields of Colorado which supplied the Great Western Sugar Company, as well as in the cotton fields of Texas, and the vegetable farms of California.[10]

Hispanic women joined union organizing efforts when the Depression brought cuts in the already low wages being paid. Two such women were killed during a King Country strike in the new cotton fields of California's Central Valley. During the late 1930s, many Mexicans were deported or voluntarily repatriated to Mexico; and under the bracero program of World War II, males came from Mexico to work alone in the fields.[11] Following the war, families came once more, and *campesinas* continued to migrate and work in the fields.

Hispanic women who remained in the fields faced continuing discrimination, both as women and as migrant workers. In the canneries, owners discriminated against them, reserving the easiest and highest paying work for the native-born Euro-American women. In the fields, when owners paid women separately for their work, women often received lower wages. Through the 1960s, for example, women working in tomato fields were paid a lower wage than men performing similar labor. Growers also barred women from the better-paying skilled field jobs such as cutting lettuce.

Gradually, most Hispanic women left the land for less seasonal jobs and lost their rural identity almost entirely. Over 90 percent of women of Hispanic heritage are already in urban centers, large numbers in Los Angeles, Chicago, Phoenix, San Antonio, and New York. Chicanas can still hear stories of the experiences of *campesinas* from their grandmothers, but the land which was once in the care of Hispanic farm families has mostly passed into other hands. A high percentage of Chicanas are working in clothing factories or as household and clerical workers. For those who remain on the land, the United Farm Workers is one last attempt to oppose a world of mechanization and corporate control.

Four selections here represent the involvement of Hispanic women in field work and in organizing efforts. A *campesina* describes her migration from Mexico to Texas to work in the fields and her present commitment to helping younger farm workers organize. Dolores Huerta, whose ancestors lived in New

Mexico for hundreds of years, also describes how she became involved in organizing farm workers in California. A powerful leader of the United Farm Workers of America, Huerta explains why organizing is important for Chicanas still in the fields. Two farm women active in the United Farm Workers tell about the oppression they encountered in California as they began to organize.[12] Finally, Isabel Flores, who grew up in the fields, but who has now joined her Hispanic sisters in the city, recalls field work and the words of her father, "*Trabaja, muchacha—trabaha*": Work, little girl—work.

Like Black and Hispanic women, Asian women moved off the land in increasing numbers during the twentieth century. The Chinese moved to urban areas in the wake of violent anti-Chinese riots along the West Coast during the late nineteenth century. The Japanese who arrived in Hawaii and along the West Coast in the period of agricultural expansion during the early decades of the twentieth century found their labor in the fields welcomed. Korean, Filipinos, and East Indians also settled in rural areas along the Pacific Coast. By far the largest number of Asian-American women to work in the fields were Japanese, who after the 1930s faced mechanization as well as anti-Asian sentiment. World War II, bringing unjustified fears on the West Coast about the loyalty of Japanese residents, violently disrupted the farm life of Japanese women. Forced to leave their farms for detention in concentration camps, uprooted and sent to other parts of the country, most never went back to the land. In Hawaii, labor needs dictated that Japanese remain on the land in World War II. Soon after, however, large corporations in Hawaii became mechanized; and farm families there also migrated toward city jobs.[13] Thus most Asian daughters must search for their roots through the memories of grandmothers who have worked on the land. Gail Miyasaki, in the selection *Obāchan*, describes her grandmother, who worked in the cane fields of Hawaii during the early twentieth century.

Mothers, whether married or widowed, have more often stayed on the land than their daughters. Even when they owned only a small plot of land like Mita, the Puerto Rican woman whose comments are reprinted here, they might dream of their daughters returning with sons-in-law to help work the land. Other mothers similarly waited, holding the land in the hope that daughters or sons would return. Nina Gilson, the "Ranch Widow" whom Blanche Irving captures so concisely in a few lines of poetry, waited until 1978, when she was seventy-five, before finally selling her ranch.

While World War II and the economic expansion following it provided millions of new urban jobs, continued mechanization on the farm allowed fewer farm families to produce more food. The number of farms in the United States dropped from a peak of 6.8 million in 1935 to 2 million in 1970. The family farm and power from horses disappeared together. By 1970, three million family workers and one million hired workers farmed one billion acres of American farmland. By then, the United States Department of Agriculture had ceased to census horses. Horsepower now meant engine capacity, not the number of horses. By 1970, four million farm workers with a vast array of mechanical equipment could feed the country and still produce a surplus.

Poor women continue to live on marginal farms. Many of them are old, and most of the elderly married women and widows tend to cluster in rural villages. Typically, poor farm women no longer support themselves or contribute major support to their families through work done on the farm. Black, Hispanic and Native American women have taken low-paying service and industrial jobs. Farm women also work in non-unionized clothing factories near small towns or commute many miles to better-paying clerical jobs in town. The wage work of these women allows the family to remain on the farm and maintain a way of life they still value.

Wealthy women, like the commuting farm women, are also usually removed from day-to-day farm labor. Living on large commercial farms whose thousands of acres and hired workers exemplify what is commonly called "agribusiness," these women enjoy a comfortable suburban life style. Women who live on these 24 percent of farms that took 70 percent of the net farm income in 1972 are likely to fly to such centers as Denver or Houston to do their shopping.

Economically located between the agribusiness families and the families who work in town to support farms, are the middle-class farm women. They cannot afford to participate in the leisure world of their wealthier neighbors, nor are they willing to work away from the farm at poorly paid fulltime jobs. Only fulltime work on the farm makes their survival on the land possible.[14] Unionization of farm workers and increased federal regulations seem to threaten this survival on one side, while the encroaching monopoly of food processing and growing corporate conglomerates press in from the other. After the price freeze and consumer boycotts of 1973, these women began to organize groups such as Women Involved in Farm Economics, American Agri-Women, and Women for the Survival of Agriculture. Jacqueline Furber and other members of WSA speak in the following pages for women on these small-scale farms, describing the anger and frustration they feel as they see themselves striving to live on totally farm-derived incomes. These women on middle-income farms keep farm accounts, handle specialized farm production, drive tractors and trucks, and provide management skills. For their daughters (and for city daughters), the contemporary women's movement has helped open up Future Farmers of America, agricultural education, and the vision of becoming fulltime owners and partners.[15]

Today, as in the past, Native American women remain the most rural of all American women: three of every four are living away from urban areas. They have endured poverty, high mortality rates, and continual discrimination in their long struggle to remain on the land and to keep their cultural traditions. More recently, they have become militant in their opposition to conditions that keep them from living in dignity and in harmony with the land. They have fought both government and corporate infringement on their lives in a new struggle growing out of a resurgent community tradition. One of these women, Emma Yazzie, explains in a selection below how she faced down coal companies to retain her land.[16]

Out of an attempt to revive and recreate traditions has also come a new communal back-to-the-land movement among the daughters of mothers who, like my own, ran away from the farm to the city during the great exodus. The energies of many women have powered this movement, and women have been among those most successful in relearning old hand labor skills, adapting urban machine technology to rural needs, and experimenting with new human relationships. The farm economy, however, has not yielded easily to such attempts at self-sufficiency; and for many women, communal experiments have ended with a journey back to the city and the search for a job to support themselves and their children.[17]

The painfully acquired experience of these communal pioneers led to a few stable communities where women kept alive the belief that they could still live on the land outside the economic constraints of large commercialized farms. In northern California, many communes succeeded, as women developed successful rural home industries and exchanged survival skills through the magazine *Country Women*. There, too, separatist communal experiments of the type Jeanne Tetrault describes have been able to exist in a benign physical and social climate.[18]

The rural communes and communities drew thousands—no one yet knows how many—young middle-class women into them, and thousands more passed through. Twin Oaks, successful and long lived (it began in 1967 and continues to the present day) owed much of its success to changed conceptions of work functions for men and women. While many communes encouraged or enforced traditional roles for women, Twin Oaks attempted to eliminate sexism in daily life. Through a labor credit system which encouraged non-traditional ways of dividing work, and an apprenticeship system giving women an opportunity to use tools and acquire skills usually reserved for men, Twin Oaks offered an alternative for the women able to settle there. Self-criticism, feedback, and encounter groups all helped members solve interpersonal conflicts. And observers agree that Kathleen Kinkade, who worked tirelessly to provide drive and continuity for the commune, was one of the crucial elements in the success of Twin Oaks. In an early interview, excerpted here, she describes the first stages of the communal experiment.[19]

Alternative communities provided a choice for only a few women. Today, in towns and cities, the attachment of women to the land lingers in token vegetable patches or herb gardens, in a pot of flowers blooming on a tenement windowsill. For most of us, the closest we will come to the land will be the household plants or urban backyard gardens that we tend. Out of these activities, which Marge Piercy captures so well in the concluding poem in this collection, "Kneeling Here," may come the vision of rebirth and change that, after all, touches our own lives as it did the lives of our foremothers who once worked the land.

# Brown Hills

*In Southern California, the hills turn brown in summer and green with the fall and winter rains. Judy Van der Veer, who ran a ranch near San Diego in the 1930s, writes of her experiences during one dry summer.*

I began thinking about the brown hills and wondering about all the things that may come to pass before our hills turn green again. For a long time the world I know will be half asleep under the summer sun. No wild green grass will grow, only a few hardy flowers will last, the landscape will seem unchanging until fall comes with rain and frost. But things will be happening, even back in the lifeless looking hills. Coyotes will hunt and call at night and hawks will circle over the canyons by day. Before the rains come buzzards will be watchful for cattle and horses grown weak with hunger in barren hill pastures. Deer will come to lick salt put out for cattle and to drink by wind mills; and quail and brush rabbits will hide away from hawks.

Down in our valley the summer days will go on, seemingly uneventful, but each day will be unlike the one before it or the one after. People will love and hate, be born and die; and much the same thing will happen to the animals. Before the hills turn green again birth and death will have visited our own ranch. I shall have cared for sick cows and injured horses, there will be sorrow and there will be laughter. Things will be pleasant and things will be unpleasant—who dares think of all that will happen before the brown is gone from our hills?...

"I've most got Wilbur talked into the notion of lettin' me buy a cow," said Amelia hopefully to me one day.

She was a huge drab woman and the only time I ever saw her big honest face light up was when she talked of cows. Often she came in my corral at milking time to buy a jug of warm milk. She always stayed to admire the cows, the fat heifers and calves. She was like a cow herself, a great full-bellied woman, placid and wise. Plainly she remembered the lush meadows of her father's farm "back East," she could shut her eyes and see the string of spotted cattle coming home at milking time.

And now here she was in this arid land where one had to pour gallons of water on the earth and loosen it with a hoe so it wouldn't dry like cement, where one felt guilty of robbing vegetables of water in order to keep a few flowers bright around the dooryard. On their land she and Wilbur had vegetable gardens and fruit trees and a little vineyard; their live stock consisted of pigs and poultry. Amelia would be satisfied if she could only have a cow. If you had a good cow there would be milk for the turkeys and ducks and cream for butter, and maybe enough to raise a calf that would grow into money.

"Wilbur thinks it would cost too much to feed a cow. But in summer I could raise a little patch of field corn and sudan grass and beets; and in winter there's green grass a-plenty around our place. Why I'd work my fingers to the bone to feed a cow. She'd pay for herself in no time, anyway."

Amelia would watch my slow milking with disdain. "Let me pump that cow awhile," she'd exclaim, and I'd relinquish stool and pail to watch her beautiful mannish hands stroke thick streams of milk from William's udder.

The cows and calves loved her for her quiet understanding. Even Fawn, William's high-bred nervous heifer would nose around her affectionately, and Amelia would run her hands over each one, gloatingly, telling me of their fine points.

"Look at that there nice long tail and straight back. Did you ever see anything as big as this heifer's eyes! And look what long tits she's got. She'll make a fine cow for sure. Wish't she was mine."

I wished so, too. But I knew that heifer was worth far more than

Amelia could afford to pay. How I longed to be rich enough to give it to her or sell it to her cheaply.

One day when I was riding down by the river I saw old Henery riding along on his mule, "bunching up" his little herd of cattle. Henery's cows never do well. They look gaunt and moth-eaten, and his calves are always pot-bellied and lousy. He can never find enough good pasture for them and he hasn't any money with which to buy hay.

"Got a heifer I orta sell," shouted Henery, "she lost her calf and I ain't got another one to put on her. Might let her go cheap if 'twas cash. I need a few dollars."

I thought about Amelia. For a long time she had been saving egg money and doing without things for herself.

Her face was bright when I hurried home and told her about the bargain.

"Don't get your hopes too high," I cautioned. "I didn't see the heifer, she's probably an awful scrub, and maybe your husband won't think she's worth buying."

"Well, it's my money I've saved," said Amelia. "I've sewed for the neighbors till I most put my eyes out; I've made underwear for myself and the kids out of feed sacks; I've chased the hens around after eggs; and if that heifer looks at all good to me, I'm a-gonna buy her. If Wilbur don't like it he can jest go take a jump somewheres."

A few days later when I rode past Amelia's place she came out and hailed me. "Come in and see Rosie," she cried, "I bought her jest like I said I was gonna do!"

When I looked at Rosie I saw a stunted, dull-eyed, scrawny, red heifer. She looked to be half Hereford and half Jersey, and I wondered if she would give as much milk as a goat. Rosie was eating cornstalks as if she had never tasted anything so delicious in all her two years, and probably she hadn't.

But while Amelia petted the heifer's rough coat and talked about her I began to see what Amelia was seeing—the Rosie of the future. Red coat shining from much brushing, sides sticking out with fatness and pregnancy, eyes clear with good health, bag swollen with milk, curved horns and neat hoofs polished, and a beautiful red curl on the end of Rosie's tail. Suddenly I saw it all just as Amelia did, and together Amelia and I waxed poetical over that gaunt red heifer.

And would you believe it, in a few months Rosie began to resemble the picture of her future self! Amelia lavished care on that little cow and Rosie responded by growing fatter and "coming up on her milk." Her eyes were bright now, and they burned with affection when they were turned toward Amelia. She would stretch out her tongue to lick at Amelia's dress or arm, she mooed with joy whenever she saw her. She was bred again, too. Amelia had saved up five dollars to pay the breeding fee on a fine Jersey bull.

"Yes, sir," said Amelia, "jest wait until she comes fresh. She'll give as much good milk as any cow in this here valley. Feed a cow good and take care of her right and dry her up at least two months before it's time for the calf, and she'll give a lot of milk. And when she's had a couple of more calves and is in her prime some dairy man will be just achin' to buy her. But I won't sell, no sir-ee. I'm sacrificin' to make a fine cow out of her and I'm a-gonna keep her for myself."

## Mothers of the South

*Margaret Hagood, who was born in Georgia, taught in a rural school before receiving her doctorate degree in sociology. Known for her careful statistical analyses, she also produced a classic study of poor white southern tenant farm women, from which this selection is taken. Later, she toured the South with Dorothea Lange and Marion Post Wolcott as they documented the work of these women in photographs.*

One might imagine that these mothers of large families would be so occupied with childbearing and caring, with cooking, washing, sewing, and cleaning, that they would of necessity have their activities circumscribed by the four walls of home—or at most by the boundaries of yard, garden, and outhouse. This is not at all true. While the women yield to their husbands the prerogative of planning and managing the farm, of assigning tasks and directing the family's labor on it, of selling the crop at their own discretion and pocketing the proceeds, they nevertheless have an active interest in the farms and crops often exceeding that in the home. Their knowledge of farming matters is surprising and pertains not only to the immediate condition of the current crop but to details of renting, credit, the sequence of operations, and to the basic data for making an estimate of how they will "come out this year."

So universal is this interest in farming that the topic offered a handy escape in interviewing impasses. Recourse to "crops" as a subject on which the mother felt safe and at home alleviated timidity in the early stages and embarrassment after very intimate revelations in the later. The mother of a feebleminded child was at first unwilling to talk of her children but warmed cordially on the subject of tobacco as she proudly told of being the only one in the family who could grade it right. On later visits the greeting, "How are you getting along?" sometimes brought forth a history of health since the last visit but more often a review of specific and general farm conditions: that they turned out one hundred and twenty-five barrels of corn at their shucking last week, that cotton prices had dropped so low and theirs was so scattered it was hardly worth picking over again, that the hail had ruined the best leaves of their tobacco, or that tobacco was bringing better prices now than they had hoped for.

The sort of farm information offered by different mothers may be illustrated by the following typical bits: that the rain had drowned out six and a half of their ten acres of tobacco; that they had got thirty-five hundred pounds from a small cotton patch the first time over; that they had planted forty thousand hills of tobacco, five thousand hills to the acre—although this mother could not do the necessary division to calculate the number of acres; a lucid and detailed description of each process in producing a tobacco crop up to the marketing stage—she had never been to a sale; an account of the ravages of the boll weeveil, which would cut the yield from five acres of cotton to half a bale; a listing of all the different renting arrangements in the neighborhood according to the fractions of each crop paid and the variations in supplying fertilizer and team; an exposition of a complicated system of cane syrup division whereby the man who owns the syrup mill gets the first three gallons for "setting down," then of every five in addition he gets one, the landowner one, and the tenants three.

There were a few women who professed no interest in or knowledge about such matters. One woman, desirous of identifying herself with the "town" women of a small village four miles away, insisted that she knew nothing of what went on outside of the house, which was her domain, that she had no idea of how her husband ran his business (farm), that she would be utterly helpless about farming if her husband should die, and that she felt women should devote all their time to homemaking. She gave herself away a little later when another visitor arrived by saying that he would have caught her in the striphouse if the men hadn't been measuring up corn today, by reporting that her husband had gotten $100 more than he expected from his tobacco last week, and finally by bragging on her daughter for having done all the cooking for the family last fall while she herself worked at getting the crop in the barn....

The most completely farm-centered interests were manifested by a hunched but hale woman of sixty with a wrinkled and weathered face, only two teeth and those snuff covered, but with clear blue eyes which twinkled as she shrewdly surmised as to how "these here foreign wars" make cotton go down because they can't ship it, or confided her suspicions that "the government just don't know what to do to help the farmers even though they mean well." Her concern over the death of her husband's father in another part of the State was great because it meant loss of the husband's working time for nearly a week in the busiest season. It had kept them from getting the fodder off the cane and the leaves had carried the frost right down to the heart of the stalk and ruined it. This woman was quite willing to give information about her children and her home, but the intensity of her interest in the farm never let her stay away from that subject for long. The esteem in which she held the visitor fell when she was unable to give the latest cotton quotation after admitting she had seen a morning paper....

A few of the women had done something during the year to "bring in a little extry." The most common means of doing this was the stringing of tobacco sacks, which has been described above but which exists no longer. This was one of the ways in which an energetic mother of thirteen earned money during her spare time after caring for her children, cooking, cleaning, sewing, and washing for a family of twelve, working in the field and tobacco barn, hiring out to grade for others when her own crop is stripped, and taking in sewing for nearby owners. Another way is the selling of garden or dairy products, although only one takes her wares regularly to a curb market. One woman says she doesn't like selling in crowds and would rather either sell "straight" or give her extra produce to neighbors. Between stripping barns of their own crop, or after it is finished, a few mothers strip tobacco for other farmers—usually owner-operators who need some extra hands. Or in cotton areas, a few reported hiring out to pick for a few days in the rush season. In any one neighborhood, however, the farms have their rush periods simultaneously and since a tenant usually "tends" as much land as his family can work, the hiring out of women to other farmers is not frequent in this group. One woman and her children hire out as regularly as they can get work now since the husband has pellagra and can no longer farm. Children contributed to the income in about ten percent of the cases. Some few live at home and work in town at mills, restaurants, or ten cent stores. Others get seasonal jobs of the types listed for the fathers or mothers. Jobs are scarce in rural areas, however, and after children leave home to work and live in town, little money is sent back to the farm....

In the matter of work preference, an overwhelming majority—seven-eighths—of the mothers like field work (including work in tobacco barns) better than housework. Here again in many instances the statement of preference was annotated with, "I was brought up to it," or "I've always done it." These general statements were sometimes elaborated by descriptions of their bringing up—"We was most all girls and had to do field work just like boys," or contrariwise, "I was the only girl and worked just like a boy with my brothers." There is a great deal of pride in the ability to work like a man, which is evidenced in a boast frequently heard, "My papa said he lost his best hand when I got married." Older women like to reminisce about their former strength. One with pellagra who cannot do field work now because dew or moisture makes her skin crack, bragged of how she had plowed, cut and mauled wood, harrowed, and done everything a man could do before her sons were old enough to work.

The matter of preference was not always so simple. Considering the triple role of childbearing and caring, homemaking, and field work, several shared a twenty-year-old mother's view that "If you've got to be taking care of children, too, housework is easier." Her two children give her more trouble in the field than in the house and she has to stop at the end of almost every row to nurse the baby. If it weren't for worrying over them, though, she would rather be working outdoors any time, "because I was brought up that way." Another comment explaining preference occurred so regularly that it could almost be predicted. This was, "In the house you never get through," or a variant, "In the field there's just one thing and you can finish it up; but here in the house there's cooking, cleaning, washing, milking, churning, mending, sewing, canning, and always the children—and you don't know what to turn to next."

# Gertie

*Appalled by the effect of war on farm women migrating to urban centers, Harriette Arnow wrote a novel on the subject titled* The Dollmaker. *In this excerpt, she describes the homesickness and frustration of Gertie Nevels, a self-sufficient farm woman who had raised all her own food in*

*Kentucky, confronted with life in a crowded government housing development in World War II Detroit.*

**A**s usual, the alarm had gone off at six o'clock so that Clovis could be at work by seven. Six o'clock, she understood now, was four back home; too early for getting up in winter. Clovis, never eating enough at breakfast, seemed like, to keep a working man alive, went away in the dark with a bottle of coffee, sandwiches, a piece of pie, and beans in his lunch box. Six-thirty to seven-thirty was pure dark still, like the middle of the night. It was a lonesome in-between time when her hands remembered the warm feel of a cow's teats or the hardness of a churn handle...the taste of spring water, the smell of good air, clean air, earth under her feet....

Gertie took change from the high shelf. She gave milk money, TB money, a can of pork and beans to Clytie, a can of tomatoes to Reuben for the food drive. Each child kissed her with a quick dabbing as it went out the door, hurriedly....

Gertie closed both doors on Reuben, the last as always. She looked down at her hand. One nickel was left over....

She remembered now, looking down at the nickel, that she had forgotten potatoes. The buying of potatoes was a part of the never ending strangeness. Back home, no matter what the season, she had always raised enough to carry her from one potato-digging time to the next. Now she would either have to go to one of the small stores near the project...or buy from the man she had seen in the alley, selling stuff from a truck. He was maybe cheaper....

Strange, she hadn't noticed the rain on the window until now. Back home she would have known it: a spring rain blown in on a red, windy dawn with thunder growling far across the ridges, the pines crying out the warning, and the sugar tree flowers blowing down the hillside, all when the poplar blooms were like yellow lilies unfolding. But better than anything had been the sound of the rain on the roof shingles when the early potatoes and peas and lettuce showed, and the early cabbage was set....

A train blew. She shivered...her body pressed against the door, her hands pressed hard against her eyes. She was able at last to look again at the window, gray white under the moving sheets of rain. Seemed like the last time she had looked, the window had been a square of quivering red light. It was daylight now—another night was through—and now another day.

# Coming of Age
# in Mississippi

*Although their land was rented and their mule was ancient, Anne Moody's family loved farming. Growing up in the 1940s, young Anne also felt the pull of the land—but acquainted with the backbreaking labor and uncertainties of farming, she was determined to leave it. When she left the farm for college, however, Moody did not forsake her background. She went on to an active part in the civil rights movement and continuing contributions to the advancement of Black people. In the selection that follows, from her autobiography,* Coming of Age in Mississippi, *she recalls the torments of hoeing cotton.*

**S**chool ended and I sadly said good-bye to Mrs. Claiborne. Raymond had said that on Monday morning, my first week out of school, we would start chopping cotton. I was angry because I didn't expect to quit Mrs. Claiborne until it was time to *pick* the cotton. I didn't even know anything about chopping. All I thought you had to do to cotton once it was up was pick it.

That weekend Mama and Raymond both prepared for the chopping. Mama went into town and bought a whole lot of food and a straw hat for each of us, and Raymond stocked up on hoes. All day Sunday he sat out under the pecan tree sharpening the hoes. He called me and Adline out and had us make believe we were hoeing so he could cut handles the right length for us. As I watched Adline pretend to hoe, I thought, "Lord have mercy! Little Adline hoeing!"

That night as I went to bed, I thought of how hot it had been all day. I was sure the temperature was over a hundred degrees. I knew that it would be just as hot the next day and I could see myself standing out there sweating over a hoe. I fell asleep worrying about hoeing in that boiling hot sun, and I had a terrible dream.

In my dream a whole group of us were out in the cotton field, up on the hill where there was only that one tree that Raymond had left for shade. We were hoeing slowly down the hill when the sun came up so big that it seemed to fill up the whole sky. It came so close to us, it looked like a big mouth about to swallow us. The whole sky and everything around us was red. I was getting terribly hot and great big drops of sweat were dripping all over me. I looked at that little tree that was up on the hill and it was drying, bending, wizzling up to nothing. I looked around in the far distance and the trees were on fire, the whole forest was burning, the trees were just flapping down. I looked around for everybody else in the cotton field, for Raymond and all of them, and they were all dead, lying between the rows. I was leaning on my hoe and I was rocking and the sun came down even closer. I was the last one standing and I knew it was coming for me. I quickly glanced at all the dead bodies evaporating around me. And I felt myself crumbling under the heat of the sun. And then I woke up.

When I got out of bed that morning I was sweating and shaking like someone with palsy. I couldn't touch my breakfast. Mama kept asking me what was wrong, but I was too scared to tell her about the dream, so I just mumbled that I wasn't feeling well. I hoped that she would tell me to stay home but instead she handed me a couple of aspirins and sent me off to the cotton field with the rest.

Raymond took along Adline, Alberta, and me for the chopping and Junior and James as waterboys. . . .

Raymond and Alberta were the only ones who knew how to chop cotton, so they walked up and down the rows and showed us how to do it. The cotton was heavily planted. We had to thin it out so it would have enough earth and air to grow freely. Darlene and I caught on fast and we were soon hoeing by ourselves. Raymond and Alberta lagged behind, helping Adline and Cherie.

I got all wrapped up in trying to outhoe Darlene. I finished three or four rows quickly, way ahead of her. Every now and then I looked back to see how far she was behind me. When she was one whole row behind, I stopped to shake my arms out. I could feel the sweat running down under them.

I was scared to look up at the sky because I knew the sun had come up. My heart began to beat like a loud drum. I shook all over. I could almost feel the sun rising in the sky. I stood there for a while, giving Darlene a chance to catch up with me. Then I hoed along slowly for a couple of hours pretending that the sun didn't even exist. Every now and then James or Junior brought someone water. I didn't want to look at them because I knew it was getting hotter and each trip they made reminded me of the sun.

Along about ten-thirty or eleven I could feel my shirt clinging to my body, like a big, wet crab. I was soaked to my waist. I didn't look up, but I knew that sun was up there just like it had been in my dream. Water was running down my face from under my hat. And big drops of sweat were dripping off my arms. It was getting harder and harder for me to hoe. Every time I reached out to chop some cotton, the row seemed to move away from me, like a big wiggling snake. I looked around at everybody else in the field and they were wiggling like the row in front of me. They looked like they were falling, just like in my dream. I didn't want to look at them. I looked up at the sun and for a moment I was completely blinded. Then I knew the others were dead. I could see the sun again. My eyes got fixed on it. I felt myself reeling and rocking on my hoe.

"Hey, Junior! Come over here, boy! Bring that water! This gal out here 'bout to faint or something'!" Raymond yelled.

Next thing I knew I was sitting on the ground and Raymond was trying to force me to drink some water. Everybody else had stopped hoeing and now they were all standing around me.

Raymond told me to rest awhile under the little tree. Thinking about how that tree shriveled up in the sun, I was afraid to go near it. I thought if I did, I would really die. When Raymond told me that we would be going home for lunch in about half an hour, I rested for a few minutes, picked up my hoe, and went back to hoeing with the rest of them. After eating lunch I felt much better, and when we went back to the field, the sun didn't seem very hot.

After a couple of days and didn't anybody die, my dream began to fade. Soon I even began to like the work. I'd pull off my shoes and let the hot earth fall over my feet as I was hoeing. It sent a warm feeling over my whole body. Even the burning of the hot sun no longer frightened me, but seemed to give me energy. Then when I went home there were those good hot meals Mama made. During the first few days of chopping cotton, we ate better than we had in our whole life. Mama was doing everything she could to keep us going. That first day she made a feast. She cooked at least five chickens, two big pones of bread, lots of rice and string beans, and even a couple of big coconut cakes. When we came in from the field, we found the picnic table out under the pecan tree loaded down with food.

I had never seen Raymond so happy as when he was sitting up at that table running over with food, surrounded by all his "workers," laughing and eating and listening to Mama's nasty jokes. While we sat at the table we didn't even think about the field. And when we went back, we felt like we were just beginning the day. It went on like that for days, until all the money was gone from the little loan Raymond had made from the bank. After that we went back to our usual beans and bread.

Finally we finished chopping the cotton for Raymond. Then Alberta, Darlene, and I took our hoes and went to chop cotton at two dollars a day for big-time farmers in the area, including some who were Raymond's relatives. They were among the few Negroes who had worked over the years to build up successful farms. When it came time to scrape the cotton a couple of weeks later, we returned to our field. We had to remove the weeds that had grown up among the cotton stalks. Then the cotton could grow freely until picking time.

In addition to the cotton for market, Raymond planted corn and potatoes for our own use. Within a couple of months I could really handle a hoe. When I wasn't chopping or scraping cotton, I was chopping corn or helping Mama in the garden. I had learned a lot about farming, but the more I learned, the surer I was that I would never become a farmer. I couldn't see myself becoming totally dependent upon the rain, sun, and earth like most farmers. I used to look at Raymond and Mama running around the house praying all the time and think that they were crazy. Farming was a fever they couldn't get rid of. When they first planted the cotton they prayed for rain. Once the cotton came up they didn't need rain any more, so they prayed for sun, so the cotton bolls would open. Then after the bolls opened, they worried about the boll weevils, and spent a lot of money on poison to kill them. When the poison didn't work, they started praying again. It was always something.

Mama and Raymond had been hooked to the soil since they were children, and I got the feeling, especially from Mama, that they were now trying to hook me. Sometimes I'd help Mama hoe in the garden and she'd be telling me how she used to pick so much cotton and how she used to do this and used to do that. Then she'd be pitty pattin' around the soil, barefooted, bragging about her collard greens and how "old Mother Nature" took care of things. "Looka these mustard greens here! Gol-lee, wasn't nothin' but a seed a few weeks ago. Now they ready to eat." She would kick her foot into the soil and say, "Boy, you c'n put *any* kinda seed in this garden—'fore you know it you got somethin' to eat." I saw how happy she was in her garden and most of what she said was true. She did have the most beautiful garden I'd even seen. The whole thing fascinated me—planting seeds, growing your own food, using the rain and the sun and the earth, and even the idea of making a living from it. But it was the hardest way I knew of making a living.

So whenever Mama started one of her long lectures on the pleasures of farming, I would drown her out with my thoughts of Mrs. Claiborne and all the traveling she had done and the people she had met. Mrs. Claiborne had told me how smart I was and how much I could do if I just had a chance. I knew if I got involved in farming, I'd be just like Mama and the rest of them, and that I would never have that chance.

After the cotton season was over I was surer than ever that I would never be a farmer. Out of all that work we had put into the cotton, we didn't even make enough money to buy school clothes. We had one good picking and that was it. The land was just no good. If Raymond hadn't planted corn and sweet potatoes,

and Mama's garden hadn't been so good, we would have starved
to death that winter.

## Una Campesina de Texas

*Maria Salas interviewed this farm worker who came to the
United States from Mexico in 1940.* La campesina *explains
what it was like to work in those days in the fields; her
reasons for joining the Texas farm worker's union when it
began organizing in the late 1960s; and the importance of
"la causa." The interview is given first in the original Spanish,
followed by an English translation.*

Yo he sido campesina desde la edad que yo me acuerdo. Soy
nacida en México y tengo como, no me acuerdo, pero como
58 años. Yo me vine de México en 1940, desde ese tiempo he
trabajado en las labores, en el algodón, el chile, en el frijol, en el
maíz, elote, cortando espiga, limpiando repello, zanahoria,
lechuga...bueno, todo...todo lo de la labor...

En ese tiempo se ganaba, a veces, un peso, en veces, dos por día
y corríamos todo el día y no ganábamos nada. Se miraban los
algodonales, labores muy grandes, pero cuando el algodón está
en el capullo se suelta todo y se mira grande, parece que es
mucho pero no hay nada y nos pasábamos corrí, corrí todo el día.

No, nomás aquí en Texas he pasado muchos años duros en la
labor, pero como ahora ya no puedo, no puedo más que seguir la
lucha, digo puedo despacio andar con la bandera en la mano, es el
trabajo más duro andar en la marcha. Es más duro que el trabajo
porque anda andi, andi, andi, y cuando se puede no hay ayudas
ningunas. Si tiene uno un pedazo de tortilla la lleva para comer; si
no la tiene, la lucha es lucha, y tiene uno que pasar a veces en
ayunas, a veces con agua, a veces sin nada. Se trata de demostrar
la lucha para que más se levante para ver cual es el que tiene
conciencia y cual no tiene.

Yo siempre me he criado trabajando en la labor.... Es un trabajo muy duro, es una carga muy pesada. Tengo hijos y por eso ando en esta lucha. Yo no lo veré, pero si estoy luchando para el bien de mis hijos; mis hijos tendrán hijos y para que ellos no tengan que trabajar tan duro.

Hago lo que se necesite allí: hacer banderas, llevantar peticiones, visitar las colonias, casa a casa pidiendo el apoyo para la causa, andar en los files con la bandera, hablando con la gente. Pienso que la paciencia es la primera, y que tengan valor y cortesía para hablar con la gente con buenas palabras.

I have been a *campesina* ever since I can remember. I was born in Mexico and I'm around—I don't remember—but about fifty-eight years old. I came from Mexico in 1940. Since that time, I've worked as a farm laborer in cotton, chile, beans, cutting corn, thinning cabbage, carrots, lettuce—everything that has to do with farm labor.... When I came there were no laws and if there were, the growers didn't say anything to us about them. We weren't aware of any benefits. Those of us who were in farm labor would literally drink from dirty puddles, for there was no water. Sometimes we would carry a little thermos of water, but because we would work all day, we would run out.

In 1940 we would sometimes earn a peso, other times two pesos per day and we would be on the move all day and sometimes earn nothing. You could see the big cotton fields. It looked like a lot of work but when the cotton bolls are open it seems like a lot but there is nothing. We would spend the day running from field to field.

I have worked only here in Texas. I spent many hard years as a farm worker but now that I can't do it any longer I can support the cause. I can walk slow with the union flag in my hand. It's harder than work because you keep walking and walking and walking and when you can't go on any longer, there's no one around to help. If you have a piece of tortilla you take it with you to eat; if you don't have anything, that's life. Sometimes you have to go without food, sometimes without water, sometimes without anything. You try to show your fighting spirit so that others will see you.

I grew up working at farm labor... It is very hard work; a

very heavy load. I have children and that's why I am involved in this struggle. If I am struggling for the welfare of my children, my children's children will not have to work so hard.

I do whatever is needed here. I make flags, circulate petitions, go house to house in the camps asking for support for the cause. I walk in the rows with the flag talking with the people. I think that patience is the main quality organizers should have. They should have the courage and the courtesy to talk calmly with people.

## Dolores Huerta:
## Un Soldado del Movimiento

*As a child, Dolores Huerta did not work in the fields, although she is the daughter of farm parents. In a pattern that is the reverse of Anne Moody's, Dolores Huerta was an adult before she rediscovered the life of farm workers through politics. Today Huerta is vice-president of the United Farm Workers of America, the union she helped to found with Cesar Chavez. Here she describes her political development and her way of life as a woman farm union activist. "My mother was a very active woman," Huerta says, "and I just followed her...she always got the prizes for registering the most voters."*

**M**y family goes way back to the 1600s in New Mexico. My father was a migrant worker who used to travel from New Mexico to Wyoming, following the work, living in little shacks. My mother was a very ambitious woman. She got a little lunch counter together, then she got a bigger restaurant, and when the war came she got a hotel. That's how I was able to go to school and how I got a more affluent background than the other kids.

When my dad and my mom divorced, he stayed in New Mexico and she came to California. I would beg my mother to let me go to the fields when I was little, but she would not let me. My brothers used to go pick tomatoes in Stockton, but my mother wasn't going to let her daughter go work in any field. So when I was fourteen, I went to work in the packing sheds instead, which were just as bad.

I was a little bit luckier than most Chicanos because I was raised in an integrated neighborhood. All the Chicanos who went to school where I did are all making it. We grew up in Stockton but we weren't in a ghetto. In our school, there was Mexican, Black, White, Indian, Italian; we were all thrown in together. We had all of the old guard teachers who treated everybody very mean. But they didn't hate each other. We didn't have a whole bunch of hang-ups, like hating Anglos, or hating Blacks.

When I got into high school, then it was really segregated. There was the real rich and the real poor. We were poor too, and I got hit with a lot of racial discrimination. My four years in high school hit me very hard and it took me a long time to get over it.

When I was in high school I got straight A's in all of my compositions. I can't write any more, but I used to be able to write really nice, poetry and everything. But the teacher told me at the end of the year that she couldn't give me an A because she knew that somebody was writing my papers for me. That really discouraged me, because I used to stay up all night and think, and try to make every paper different, and try to put words in there that I thought were nice. Well, it just kind of crushed me.

I couldn't be active in college though, because it was just too early. I was the only Chicano at Stockton Junior College. At that time, there was just a handful of us that you might call liberals.

I was frustrated. I had a fantastic complex because I seemed to be out of step with everybody and everything. You're trying to go to school and yet you see all of these injustices. It was just such a complex!

Then my mother took me to Mexico City when I was about seventeen. She had never been there either. It was our first trip. But that opened my eyes to the fact that there was nothing wrong with Chicanos. I felt inside that everybody was wrong and I was right. They were wrong in beating the people up in the streets and all of the things they did to people. I felt I had all of these frustrations inside of me, so I started joining different Chicano organizations—El Comité Honorífico, Women's Club, all of these organizations that didn't do anything but give dances and celebrate the Fiestas Patrias.

By the time I was twenty-five years old, I had been married and gotten a divorce. I was still living in Stockton when Fred Ross came into town and he started telling us about forming this organization, the Community Services Organization (CSO). And he told us about how in Los Angeles they had sent these policemen to San Quentin for beating up a Mexican. At that time, I didn't even talk about things like that publicly. Everybody knew that the cops did it, but you just accepted it. Now these two cops were sent to San Quentin and Fred had organized it.

When Fred started telling us that if we got together we could register voters, elect Spanish-speaking representatives, and turn everything around, I just didn't believe it. He showed us how they had gotten these clinics in San Jose and he told us about Cesar Chavez. He showed me all these pictures of big meetings with 100 to 200 people together. Well, I thought he was telling me a fairy tale....

I was actually in the organization for two years before I got to talk to Cesar [Chavez]. I met him once, but he was very shy. He wouldn't talk to anybody except the people he was organizing. But I heard him speak one time at a board meeting and I was really impressed. Well, after a big voter registration drive in 1960 where we registered 150,000 people, Cesar got this bright idea to send me to Sacramento.

So I went to Sacramento and we got all these bills passed. I headed up the legislative program in 1961 when we fought for the old-age pension for the non-citizens, for *los viejitos.* I lobbied the welfare bill through so that the parents could stay in the home. Cesar and I and the rest of us worked to get the right to register voters door to door, and the right for people to take their driver's license exams in Spanish, and disability insurance for farm workers, and the right for people to get surplus commodities. And, of course, we were the ones that ended the Bracero Program. I have a lot of experience in legislation, and I guess I've become sort of a trouble-shooter in the union.

I guess because I'm articulate, I came to the forefront. A lot of people who do a lot of hard work in the union are not mentioned anywhere. *Son los soldados razos del movimiento.** And that's what I consider myself—just a person working at what I'm supposed to be doing. The fact that I get publicity is sort of a by-product of the union. But there's an awful lot of people who have worked continuously since the union started, a lot of women, for example, who nobody even knows.

There's been no reaction from the farm workers to my role as a woman within the union. They will appreciate anybody who will come in to help them. In terms of the leadership itself I get very little friction from anybody, really. Anyone who can do the job is welcome to come in and share the suffering.

There are a lot of other women in the union besides me and they share some of my problems. But I think it's mostly a personal conflict and it depends how much you let it hang you up in terms of what you're doing. If you let it bug you when people say that you're not being a good mother because you're not with your kids twenty-four hours a day, well then of course it will deter you from what you're doing. In the union, you know, everybody cooperates to take care of your kids.

The idea of the communal family is not new and progressive. It's really kind of old fashioned. Remember when you were little you always had your uncles, your aunts, your grandmother and your *comadres*† around. As a child in the Mexican culture you identified with a lot of people, not just your mother and father like they do in the middle-class homes. When people are poor their main interest is family relationships. A baptism or a wedding are a big thing. In middle-class homes you start getting away from that and people become more materialistic. When you have relatives come to visit it's a nuisance instead of great big occasion.

While I was in jail some of my kids came down to Delano to see me, but my little girl, Angela, didn't come. She wrote me a little note which said, "Dear Mom, I love you very much, but I can't come because the people need me. I've got to go door-knocking

*Son los soldados razos del movimiento:* They are the real soldiers of the movement.
†*Comadres:* godmothers.

this weekend and I can't leave my job." I think that's really great because she put her priorities on the work she has to do instead of coming down to see me.

The time I spend with my kids is very limited. This year I was in Washington, D.C. for almost two months, then I was in Arizona for another six weeks, then I was in Los Angeles working on the McGovern campaign for another two weeks. So this year I've spent very little time with my children. Since August the 27th I've seen them twice for visits for about an hour.

Sure, it's a hardship for me, but I know that my kids are all working in the union itself. They have to grow up with the responsibility of their work, but they have fun too. Probably the problems they have is like the kind of schools that they go to which are very reactionary.

I think it's important for the children to be fed and clothed, which they are. When I first started working with Cesar I had this problem worrying about whether my kids were going to eat or not, because at the time I started working for the union I was making pretty good money and I knew I was going to start working without any money, and I wondered how I could do it. But the kids have never gone hungry. We've had some rough times, particularly in Delano during the strike because my kids went without fresh milk for two years. They just had powdered milk we got through donations. It's made them understand what hardship is, and this is good because you can't really relate to suffering unless you've had a little bit of it yourself. But the main thing is that they have their dignity and identity.

My family used to criticize me a lot. They thought that I was a traitor to my Raza, to my family and to everybody else. But I think they finally realized that what I'm doing is important and they're starting to appreciate it now....

...You could expect that I would get a lot of criticisms from the farm workers themselves, but it mostly comes from middle-class people. They're more hung-up about these things than the poor people are, because the poor people have to haul their kids around from school to school, and the women have to go out and work and they've got to either leave their kids or take them out to the fields with them. So they sympathize a lot more with my problem in terms of my children.... Giving kids clothes and food is one thing, you know, but it's much more important to teach them that other people besides themselves are important, and that the best thing they can do with their lives is to use them in the service of other people....

...All the women in the union have similar problems. They don't have to leave their families for as long as I do. But everybody shares everything, we share the work.

The way we do the work is we do whatever is needed regardless of what we'd really like to do. You have a problem when you develop into a kind of personality like Cesar because that really takes you away from the work that has to be done with the farm workers in education and development of leadership. That's what I'd really like to do. I'd just like to keep working down there with the ranch committees and the farm workers themselves because they have to take over the union. I can put my experience there. Cesar would much rather be organizing than anything. He loves to organize because it's really creative. But he can't do it because right now he has to go around speaking, as I am doing also. I'd rather be working on the strike.

# We Got through Together

*In the early 1970s, as increasing numbers of Chicano farm workers joined the United Farm Workers, they often found themselves evicted, arrested, or harassed in more indirect ways. Here two women—"Sister T and Sister V"—describe the reprisals of employers against farm workers when they began organizing the union in the strawberry fields of Salinas, California.*

**Sister T:** Three years ago we moved to California. We heard a radio announcement from the Pic n' Pac company saying that, in their fields in California, everyone could work, from the biggest to the smallest.

We found out that only the adults could work. There was no childcare and both my husband and I were picking strawberries. The older children took turns staying home from school to take care of the younger ones. We lived in La Posada Trailer Camp in Salinas. The company provided the trailer camp and took the rent out of our paychecks weekly.

When we joined the union [United Farmworkers of America] we got our rents cut. It was soon after that and some other union actions that the company told us that the trailer camp was sold and we would have to move. The company claim that the camp was sold to become an old-age center was a lie.

The Government Labor Office told us that if we were going to be evicted, we should leave California and go to Washington. But all the families decided to stay here together and resist eviction.

We never knew the exact day. When the police did come, with orders for us to get out, most of the men were at work.

I had angry words with a Mexican-American cop. I said, "Why are you armed? I'm only a woman. I won't fight." He said, "You talk too much," and he tried to put me in the police van. But the people inside the trailer camp and the crowd of people outside watching wouldn't let him take me away.

They got my youngest son. My husband was in the fields when he heard our boy was taken. He came running. The cop went to hit him. My man moved out of the way and the cop hit another cop in the face. We were evicted but we decided to stay in Salinas near our work. We parked our cars and lived in them by the side of the road. We confronted everything with strength. Everyone was equal.

**Sister V:** My family and I are from Texas. My husband was born in Mexico. I have ten children, eight of them were born in Texas and two were born here in the state of California. We came to Salinas six years ago. At that time we were signed up by a contractor that worked for the strawberry company and we've settled here since them. The problems we've had at the job began when the contractor would fire people over unjustified reasons.

He accused them of not doing their work, of being lazy. The families that he fired were the ones that began the movement. We followed them because they had done so much for us too.

We were given eviction notices at La Posada....

The police and company guards came to take us out. They harrassed and shoved people around. The families hurried as fast as they could to remove their things from the trailers, but it was never fast enough to please them. My daughter was almost arrested. The police claimed that she had refused to leave. She and her little boys were already in the police car. I pleaded with them to wait. I told them that I had gotten consent from one of the guards to allow her to move her things out while she waited for her husband to get back from the fields. I insisted that she hadn't begun to move because she was alone and didn't have help. I pleaded for them to let her go. What harm could she do? All her children were so little. They finally let her go, but we had to move out her belongings onto the sidewalk because her husband was still at work with the car. It was a hard day to get through for everyone but we got through it together.

# I Remember

*For the children of migrant farm workers, the memory of fields and hard work is still vivid. Isabel Flores recalls the cotton fields where her parents worked.**

I remember
riding on my mother's
sacka
as she picked
cotton

*Translations of Spanish words and phrases in the order of their occurence are as follows: *sacka,* sack; *surcos,* furrows or rows; *lonches,* lunches; *terremote,* whirlwind or "dust devil"; *las risas,* laughs; *gritos,* shouts; *lavor,* work; *el algodon,* the cotton; *esposa de moro,* wife of Moro; *"la chula,"* "the cutie"; *bote de agua,* water jug; *apúrate, muchacha,* hurry up, girl; *trabaja,* work.

in the middle of two
surcos

lonches
tortillas y frijoles
in an opened field
with the dust
and the Wind

terremote
fights in the fields
with the other kids
las risas y gritos
in the middle
of the lavor

I remember
watching a cloud
slowly covering the sun
and giving thanks for the minutes
of shade

don Felipe
leather straps
around his knees
to kneel
as he picked
el algodon

lupe, esposa de moro
in the field
with
all her twelve
children

remember
hearing the whistling
of Ramiro
as he worked

Gloria
"la chula"
powdering her face
in the middle
of the lavor

the taste
of fresh water
from the bote de agua
in the truck
at noon
when the sun
was
burning up the world

a fifty pound
sack of cotton

I remember my father
saying
"Apúrate, muchacha, apúrate
you dream
of crazy things.
¡Trabaja, muchacha—
Trabaja!"

## Obāchan

*Gail Miyasaki's grandmother, "Obāchan," was an early Issei (first generation) immigrant to Hawaii. Like many of the Japanese women who migrated to Hawaii and mainland United States in the first decades of the twentieth century, Obāchan had been a picture bride, her marriage pre-arranged by her family. These pioneers from the East usually joined farm worker husbands and worked in the fields, as well as at such household tasks as washing, cleaning, sewing, and child care, Young Gail Miyasaki adored her hardworking grandmother, the strong and fascinating figure whom she here recalls.*

**H**er hands are now rough and gnarled from working in the canefields. But they are still quick and lively as she sews the "futon" cover. And she would sit like that for hours Japanese-style with legs under her, on the floor steadily sewing.

She came to Hawaii as a "picture-bride." In one of her rare self-reflecting moments, she told me in her broken English-Japanese that her mother had told her that the streets of Honolulu in Hawaii were paved with gold coins, and so encouraged her to go to Hawaii to marry a strange man she had never seen. Shaking her head slowly in amusement, she smiled as she recalled her shocked reaction on seeing "Ojitchan's" (grandfather's) ill-kept room with only lauhala mats as bedding. She grew silent after that, and her eyes had a faraway look.

She took her place, along with the other picture brides from Japan, beside her husband on the plantation's canefields along the Hamakua coast on the island of Hawaii. The Hawaiian sun had tanned her deep brown. But the sun had been cruel too. It helped age her. Deep wrinkles lined her face and made her skin look tough, dry, and leathery. Her bright eyes peered out from narrow slits, as if she were constantly squinting into the sun. Her brown arms, though, were strong and firm, like those of a much younger woman, and so different from the soft, white, and plump-dangling arms of so many old teachers I had had. And those arms of hers were always moving—scrubbing clothes on a wooden washboard with neat even strokes, cutting vegetables with the big knife I was never supposed to touch, or pulling the minute weeds of her garden.

I remember her best in her working days, coming home from the canefields at "pauhana" time.* She wore a pair of faded blue jeans and an equally faded navy-blue and white checked work shirt. A Japanese towel was wrapped carefully around her head, and a large straw "papale" or hat covered that. Her sickle and

*Pauhana: literally, "drudgery"; i.e., season when field hands must be continually at work.

other tools, and her "bentobako" or lunchbox were carried in a khaki bag she had made on her back.

I would be sitting, waiting for her, on the back steps of her plantation owned home, with my elbows on my knees. Upon seeing me, she would smile and say, "Tadaima" (I came home) and I would smile and say in return, "Okaeri" (Welcome home). Somehow I always felt as if she waited for that. Then I would watch her in silent fascination, as she scraped the thick red dirt off her heavy black rubber boots. Once, when no one was around, I had put those boots on, and deliberately flopped around in a mud puddle, just so I could scrape off the mud on the back steps too.

Having retired from the plantation, she now wore only dresses. She called them "makule-men doresu," Hawaiian for old person's dress. They were always gray or navy-blue with buttons down the front and a belt at the waistline. Her hair, which once must have been long and black like mine, was now streaked with grey and cut short and permanent-waved.

The only time she wore a kimono was for the "Bon" dance. She looked so much older in a kimono and almost foreign. It seemed as if she were going somewhere, all dressed up. I often felt very far away from her when we all walked together to the Bon dance, even if I too was wearing a kimono. She seemed almost a stranger to me, with her bent figure and her short pigeon-toed steps. She appeared so distantly Japanese. All of a sudden, I would notice her age; there seemed something so old in being Japanese.

Whenever I see an old Oriental woman bent with age and walking with short steps, whenever I hear a child being talked to in broken English-Japanese, I think of her. She is my grandmother. I call her "Obāchan."

## Mita y Yo

*In search of her roots, city granddaughter Rosa Gonzalez recorded the comments of her grandmother Mita, excerpted below. Mita was born in 1898, the year the United States*

*invaded her native island of Puerto Rico. She lived all her
years in two small towns on the western side of the island.
When her four daughters went to New York during the
1950s, Mita refused to migrate. She hoped that her daughters
would return with their families, build houses, plant crops
together, and live on the land. Here she describes the variety
of work done by "the women of before."*

The women of before were farm workers; fetching water,
roasting coffee, grinding corn, tending the fire, cooking,
washing, making "pavas," embroidering handkerchiefs....* I
used to be fond of making a lot of things, that's why I could
support myself. On Saturdays I'd walk barefoot into town to sell
the "pavas" for a quarter and carbon for a quarter a sack. After
selling these I'd buy tobacco, sugar, cheese, bread, and "bacalao."
Then I'd split for home to cook and while I cooked I'd make more
"pavas." In fact I would make "pavas" all day pausing only to cook,
fetch water and wood.

I used to plant rice, corn, "gandules" (pigeon peas), beans,
"yuca" (manioc), sweet peppers, "yautia," "name" (two root
vegetables), coffee, oranges, lemons.... I'd tend to these and
search the fields, cutting those bananas that were ripe and
anything else that was ready to eat.

When "he" was sick for six months I used to cut wood, haul it
over to the house and get an oven together. Like I tell you, the
women of the past would tie a cloth around their head and go out
to work all day long but the people of today are lazy.

# Ranch Widow

*Nina Gilson was born in 1904 in a mining camp in western
New Mexico. She grew up on a ranch, rode horses most of
her life, and continued to ranch after her husband died.*

*Pava: a broad brimmed straw hat.

*Blanche Irving, a neighbor, wrote this poem in 1973 when Nina Gilson was seventy. Five years later, Gilson finally sold the ranch and joined her family in migration to the city.*

The wrinkles are
hand-tooled
in the worn leather of her face.
Seventy,
she can pull a calf, brand, ride all day
with
leathered grace.

## The Militant Middle

*Formed in 1972, Women for the Survival of Agriculture in Michigan reported on its activities at the annual meeting of the Michigan State Horticultural Society in 1973. In the reports which follow, Laura Heuser, Millie Schultz, Jacqueline Furber, and Connie Canfield transmit the energy and excitement they had found in working with other farm women on political issues relating to the sale of fruit from middle-sized farms. Jacqueline Furber's account of the western New York women brings to mind the Jennies, Minnies, and Lizzies whom Susan B. Anthony had urged to shift to fruit growing over one hundred years before. Now, their descendants were fighting to change a system that no longer worked.*

**Laura Heuser, Hartford, Michigan:** It's really been a great year. I've been angry, furious, irritated, astounded, curious, amazed, and dead tired—sort of in rotation—the whole time. It's great for your circulation. But most of all I've been indignant. Indignant that the most efficient, vital and hard working people in the country should take so much abuse from so many sources. We are exploited by everybody from the handlers that buy our products, to legislators, to social organizations of every description. I am also very indignant at us. We farmers pull some very dumb stunts.

One of the things that has *sustained* me this whole year has been the women themselves. They are an amazing bunch of people. I really believe farm women *have* to be. They are a delight to know. Their talents are endless. Their courage is boundless. And most of them have an earthy robust sense of humor—it's probably necessary to survive.

**Millie Schultz, Michigan:** When we heard about the Women for Agriculture in Oregon we decided to contact them, determine what we had in common, and to establish channels of communication between the groups to form a loose federation to coordinate efforts for mutual support on national issues and to form sister groups in other states.

A meeting was set for women from here to go meet them, live in their homes and get acquainted.

Arriving in Portland we were welcomed with open arms. Those folks are just like you—Wonderful People. Seventy percent of the population of Oregon live in the valley where we were staying. Women for Agriculture was formed three years ago and they are fighting diligently for their cause. Mary Holzapfel, founder of their group... knew they had more than one problem when she heard city people say: "We don't need farmers, we can buy all the food we need in the store."

They also share a number of other problems with us though; namely, finding markets for their products and getting hand labor. They are in the process of giving up strawberries because the only help that they are able to get is high school children and not even enough of them. They are also concerned, as we are, about land use—farms being subdivided for other uses. These problems exist not only in Salem, their "fruit belt," but all over the state.

Some of their problems, however, are of a different scope; having to do with ecology. They grow grass seed in the

Willamette Valley on farms considerably larger than we have here, from 500 to 3,000 acres each. It's necessary to burn the fields of straw after harvest to stop [crop] disease, and there is no market for straw. The smoke from these fires goes down the valley to Eugene and the people there are complaining. Their Governor McCall is all for ecology. In fact, thirty-seven legislative bills have been passed directly affecting it. These women have been given until 1975 to find an answer to the smoke problem.

**Jacqueline Furber, Wolcott, New York:** Are farmers taken for granted? You bet we are! We have not told our story. Until now, we have stood back and silently taken our lumps. This silence has come to a screeching halt. WSAM has put on the brakes! These women are out spreading the word on the farmers' true situation and they are being heard far and wide and getting startling results.

[In late September 1972], a major New York processor announced a price on processing apples essentially unchanged from last year's low, low price and 50¢ lower than their announced price in Pennsylvania. We knew our apples were worth *much* more this year and our growers realized that their very existence was on the line.

Western New York growers, like all northeastern growers, were in serious financial trouble. Last year nearly 5½ million bushels of apples were abandoned in the eastern United States, and of that total, 3 million were western New York apples!

The Farm Bureau Apple Operations Committee held an emergency meeting on this disastrous price and decided to send out an SOS. When my husband called from that meeting and asked me to begin calling other women to organize a picket line, I thought he had lost his mind! *My* neighbors on a picket line! *Never!*

I started calling—didn't dare mention *picket line*—just asked the women to come to a meeting to see what we could do.... When the meeting was over the question was not, "Do we picket?" It was, "What time do we start?"

Bright and early Monday morning, the women appeared at the

plants in Hamlin and Williamson armed with queasy stomachs and protest posters. As the apple-laden trucks arrived, they were blockaded by the fruit growers' wives who then proceeded to convince the drivers to take their apples home and hold them until the bargaining group could attempt to achieve a realistic price. We cheered the departing loaded trucks all day! They not only went home, they stayed home!

By the next day a 24-hour picket schedule had been established to insure that no apples would get through—day or night. As the stockpile of apples in the plant yard diminished, the women's determination grew.

We were bolstered and encouraged by the interest and concern shown by our entire communities. We were joined at our posts by our families, community leaders, local and state legislators, agri-businessmen, bankers, dairymens' wives, teachers, students, farm bureau leaders, ministers, and many other concerned citizens. Probably those who cheered our cause most were growers who had been forced out of farming in past years.

Our cause and methods caught the fancy of the news media and coverage rapidly spread to a national scale. We gave special, on-the-scene, up-to-the-minute radio bulletins; we were in the papers; in living color on many TV channels; and we even made the *New York Times!* What had started as a picket line became a Survival Line.

While the women fought the battle and held the line on the processing plant field, another phase of the applesauce war was being won by the Farm Bureau Marketing negotiating team at the bargaining table. By the end of the week, a total 50¢ price increase was gained and was accepted by the growers. Our efforts earned over two million dollars for western New York growers on processing fruit alone.

The women of the Survival Line in New York are now organized as "Women for the Survival of Agriculture" and are committed to help bring change to a system that no longer works. We realize that picketing is not the most desirable way to conduct business. We need strong legislation that will allow us to bargain for fair prices on equal terms and our group is now working to get that legislation.

We have come a long way in New York this year. Our county and state Farm Bureaus now support marketing and bargaining legislation, including compulsory arbitration. Our growers' attitudes have become more optimistic. Farmers and their wives are becoming better informed. They are finally realizing that there is strength in unity, and only disaster in accidental profit.

But none of this would have ever happened if "Women for the Survival of Agriculture in Michigan" had not reached out to New York State and struck the spark that lit the whole fire under us.

**Connie Canfield, Decatur, Michigan:** Last year a man said that all we women were going to do was raise a lot of hell and that would be the end of it. Well, I guess we've done just that but, believe me, this isn't the end of it.... We learned that we share some of the same problems. We are not afraid to tell each other what is happening on our farm, or to call someone and ask if they ever had a similar thing happen to them. The grapevine has been set up! I think we have alerted the farmers to an important realization, that although a minority (this nation's smallest minority), we still have each other and we still control a product that is highly valuable. Watch out, buyers!

# A Woman Who Won't

*Navajo women were the backbone of the Coalition for Navajo Liberation (CNL), a group that formed in 1974 to protest economic conditions and racist treatment. With a tradition of strong female deities, a matrilineal culture, an economy based on sheep herding and weaving, and a heritage of political equality as chiefs and medicine people, the Navajo women had good reason to protest the conditions of the male-oriented non-Indian culture that surrounded them. Emma Yazzie was sixty-eight at the time of this 1977 newspaper feature story by Beth Wood, and an active participant in the CNL's organizing campaigns. This account tells of Yazzie's individual acts of resistance, also indicative of the growing militance of Navaho women.*

**E**mma Yazzie spoke out when the coal companies came to her Chapter House to buy the land of her family and community. That was in 1948, she remembers, when the people really didn't understand the impact of energy development and the false promises of the white man.

Despite her solitary protests, the coal companies took the land and the people got a few hundred dollars. Emma refused to move and, now, almost thirty years later, she still lives adjacent to the mammoth Four Corners Power Plant in the hogan on the land of her birth. By her presence and by her words, she is continuing her protest against the giveaway of the Navajo land and skies.

At dawn, after only a few hours of sleep, Emma wakes up "tight in my chest from the poisons of Four Corners." She calls her new neighbor "Smoke and Disease." "It is the worst disease we have ever known. The smoke and the ashes are killing us all," she says.

"We now have no grass. The disease has killed it all. And the sheep and goats are all sick from the smoke too. Some of the sheep won't even grow.

"My sheep are my life. Without grass, they will die. They will probably all be gone by next year. All the pretty birds have gone. The power lines killed them. Now all we have left are crows and blackbirds.

"The water kills the sheep but the tribe and the company won't give us a new well. They are bums. They gave away our land and took the money.

"I have lived here all my life. Everybody moved to the river and different places. I won't move. I like my place. If I ever die, I want to be laying right by my home."

With her staff, Emma and her sheep go past the ruins of her mother's hogan. Only the stones from the chimney remain out of that past—the four black stacks of Four Corners have now risen up to replace it.

At night, Emma walks down to the power plant where she

works the night shift as a cleaning woman tidying up the monster that is killing her and her sheep.

But Emma Yazzie is the story and the symbol—not of hopelessness—but of the endurance and the certainty of the Navajo people. She cuts the fences to reclaim stripped land; she throws pop bottles at company officials; and she speaks out publicly as a member of the Coalition for Navajo Liberation. She won't give up.

# The Next Step:
# Women-identified Collectives

*Moving out of traditional relationships and attempting new ones often clarifies the old as well as the new, allowing people to make more conscious choices about their life styles. Jeanne Tetrault describes her experiences living in a mixed rural commune in California in the 1970s and her decision to live only with women.*

**M**y friend Ryon once wrote that she wanted "to gather up all the people that she loved and live with them near the ocean forever." We tried that one. To our California farm we tempted friends we loved from all corners—Brazil, New York. We imagined we could live with anybody, so when they brought along friends, husbands and lovers, we assumed harmony and compatible life styles would evolve naturally.... We would make our family of diverse beings melt into one communal pot....

Ah, yes....

One liked the other but not the third. Two could stand only one of four. Three were fine together; five jarred. Divisions. One to one, it worked. But it was always five to one, or three to three, or two to four. It never worked. On the surface plane it sometimes flowed. Where it was rough, we made rules to live by—and this made the surface smooth again but underneath things rumbled and quaked. It all blew up eventually. Sometimes it would be piece by piece, until we were distant and alienated from one another. Sometimes there were great steaming scenes. Some retreated inward, others to Vermont. More entered. New equations, new combinations, new results.

We learned that it is really difficult to live with other people, to create and sustain honesty in relating, to work out all the things that must be worked out. Living together in a deeply sharing way means giving a great deal of energy to one another—and having a great commitment to stay at it. We always lived very closely in physical terms—sharing all of our meals, our work, our time. Even the physical realities of our living together weren't easy to work out. We struggled with different paces, different priorities, different approaches. We tried to work out all of our differences without really grasping the fundamental problems. On any deeper level, our attempts to communicate weren't serious. Not because we didn't want to but because we didn't have the tools. We moved in polite spaces, trying not to suffocate, offend, or terrify each other. We withdrew from confrontation as though it were the very demon that would bring it all tumbling down. We sometimes touched obliquely. There were times we let defenses fall and stood heart-to-heart or fear-to-fear. High times, sharing and warmth. Not enough to teach us how to really touch, though. We turned away from intensity and vulnerability and didn't understand our turning. Our politics were very slow in developing, but were to give us some of the keys—always retrospectively—to what was happening.

It was my impulse to write just about living with women, because for the last two years I've lived just with women and living with men seems remote and irrelevant. But because part of my decision to live just with women came from realizations about living with men, it seems worth a few thousand words....

We lived mostly with men who were attached to the women we wanted to live with. Not a good beginning, for sure. But we were fairly open to it—not separatists, then, at any rate. Not very feminist-conscious, though we were lesbians and certainly oppression-conscious.

From the very beginning, the women who lived on the farm took a primary part in the building, fencing, animal care, gardening and so forth. All of the multitude of skills and basic information we had to learn were taken on by anyone concerned or excited enough to take the initiative. Most of the men we lived with were seriously into writing and this (pre)occupation often limited their interest in and energy for the farm. Most of the women were very much into learning to farm.... so things were balanced in a slightly different way than in most other commune-ities we knew. Still, we managed to fall into some classic traps. For a time all of us—men and women—assumed that the women were the primary housekeepers. It took some struggling and rule-making to equalize work —and it was never wholly equalized. The men, without exception, simply didn't have a house-keeping consciousness. And (understandably) they had no desire to develop one. So while they would take turns cooking and dishwashing, and even floor-sweeping (sometimes willingly, sometimes grudgingly), the hundred-thousand other details of keeping home together and functioning for a family of five to eight fell predictably upon the women. No man ever noticed that the tomato paste was running out, canned a single jar of preserves, cleaned the toilet bowl, or took on window washing! Machines and electricity were another pitfall. If the electric pump broke, the women automatically expected the men to be able to fix it—or the men acted on that assumption, and though we were all equally ignorant, the pump was their problem. (It took living just with women and one day a broken pump to demystify that one for us). Cars—broken chainsaws—anything mechanical—we women took a cursory look and faded away.... It seems strange now to see those areas where we presumed incapability—they are so classic, it shocks me...but I'm still struggling with it in myself, forcing myself to look at it and deal with it.

Working together was sometimes a pleasure, more often a hassle. We usually worked in twos or threes or alone—group projects always felt difficult to get together and sustain. It was impossible to share skills with many of the men—they simply couldn't learn from a woman even though she knew how to do something they didn't. A good example was shingling the house—two of us (women) had learned how from an old-time carpenter friend, and had done a good part of the house ourselves. Of the three men we tried to teach our knowledge of shingling axes, measuring strings, 7" lap, etc., three went on to space shingles at every conceivable variance, work without the strings (so that the shingles careen in arcs and angles), and generally disregard everything we suggested. This was a simple case of politics—but we weren't seeing it that way then. We wondered at what was happening, realizing they would have listened to our (male) carpenter friend, and saw it as some peculiar personality problem. . . . When we worked on a building project, the men inevitably related to it in contractor-fashion. There would be a boss—a foreman who (though he be only slightly less ignorant than anyone else) would direct the workers. Building with other women was a cooperative venture—we shared our ignorance, worked together to learn—no boss, no need for one. These differences were felt but not explicit. We knew they were happening but didn't examine the whys.

Most difficult to live with was the inability to communicate emotions that sent some of the men into hostile rages, others into sullen tempers, and others just into themselves. Those men who were halves of couples related mainly with the women they were with—and mostly at her initiative. We found individually and collectively that the women were always having to force the issue of talking feelings with the men: "How are you feeling?" "What's happening with you?" "How do you think we should work this out?" Not just within couples, but within the group as a whole. For a long time we each saw this as a peronal-problem-in-relating-to-one-man. Gradually, it became clear as a pattern. The men themselves saw it too and either couldn't or wouldn't change it. The women always took it upon themselves to deal with it—or lived with the silences. The men worked together, lived together as part of a family, but rarely talked about themselves with each other and rarely touched.

When the women of the farm became part of a women's consciousness-raising group, we began to learn a new kind of communication, a new method of sharing and thinking about

238 THE UNCERTAIN HARVEST

our experiences. Woman to woman, there had always been openness—not perfect and not without distance and difficulty—but there was a mutual willingness to talk, to explore feelings, to try to reach each other. Simultaneously, a lot of love and tenderness grew. In the painfulness of our first woman-awareness, we came close to one another. We experienced the first breaking open of roles and patterns—the delight in reading "The Politics of Housework" and recognizing home, the anger of realizing "oppression" was not just a rhetorical phrase. We grew woman-high, woman-conscious.

At the same time we began to understand the politics of living with men. The hierarchical work structures, the issues of control and power that had been seething under the surface. We came to see that an inability to talk out feelings wasn't just one man's personal problem—nor was resorting to physical violence (actual, threatened, or implied). We began seeing how we all related to one another—woman to woman, woman to man, couples and singles, as a group and as individuals. All of these elements that determined how we lived day to day pivoted on the basic man/woman relationship. Personal, political, cultural psychological—very, very deep. Working them out would take more and more energy and time as we became more and more conscious of their depth and complexities. Our continuing to live with men would have to mean giving primary energy to working out these problems. We could no longer not see them, and we could no longer excuse them as personal trips. All of the time that we were still struggling through this, the men talked about beginning a group of their own—and never did. If they were pushed by the women, they would talk of it—but by themselves, they had neither the incentive nor the need. They were alternately sullen and withdrawn when we came home really high from our group—or they were supportive and encouraging. The sullenness and the fact that they never attempted to deal with their own consciousness-raising made us suspicious of the "support."

As we came to understand ourselves more and more in the relationship to the men we lived with, in our relationships to one another and to other women, we became more and more conscious that we wanted to live just with women. Wanted to live in the growth that happens among women consciously trying to free themselves. And wanted not to live with the struggle inherent in male/female relationships—a struggle culturally impressed for centuries and as real as ever in our new new "hip" counter-culture. We knew that we wanted to give our best energy to our sisters, focusing our lives on our woman-consciousness as the way to grow the most and be the strongest. And besides, it was the space we were happiest with and highest in. Loving women, living and working together in the comfortableness of deep understanding. . . sisterhood, whatever you choose to call it. . . . It gave us a new ground to grow from.

"And they lived happily ever after. . . ." Well, not exactly. We've found that living with other women is neither perfect revolution nor feminist Camelot. It is just as hard to work through compromises, priorities, idiosyncracies. It is hard to see one another's needs and strengths and failings and always respond openly. There's a lot of emotional bondage we've inherited from our heterosexual couple-oriented upbringing that is really difficult to break free of. The struggle is still real—a struggle to live honestly together, to grow and keep changing. . . . Conditioned as we are to serve others, we must have developed some supersensitivity to other's needs. This allows us to live together in a state of what I'd call loving anarchy, and what a friend rephrased "responsible anarchy." We need neither structure nor rules to live together. We find ourselves sharing the work freely, being aware of what things must be done and what can be let go for more important priorities or frivolities. . . .

Phillippe, aged seven, who comes to stay with us, looked around the kitchen one morning and asked, "How come it's only ladies here all the time?" "Women," I corrected, many flashes simultaneous in my head. After my explanation of how we like being with other women, working together and living together, he concluded, "It's not fair." A seven year old's version of "You're separatists!" For a long time that one stopped me—until I realized that yes, I am—we are—separatist. That for me, right now, separatism seems the best and most realistic way to women's freedom because separatism is the quickest and most workable way for women to unlearn limitations, to find out who they can be, to become whole....

Today I live with one other woman (and assorted creatures, plants, objects, unformed free energy). Two years ago there were four of us, and we called ourselves a "woman's collective." Now we call ourselves a "woman's farm." We imagine we will again be a women's collective or perhaps we still are. This summer there will be eight or nine women living here. The numbers seem irrelevant—we live in, take part in the creation of a woman's space. It feels good and positive—a place where we all can push our limits, a place of woman-energy and woman-imagination. A friend sent us her hand-made card last December. "Celebrate Sisterhood this Season," it said. It is still on the kitchen wall. The message is clear and simple and stays with us. I believe it.

## Twin Oaks

*Kathleen Kinkade and her daughter Josie were among the eight people who founded Twin Oaks, near Louisa, Virginia, in 1967. Because this rural experiment has endured for more than a decade, its approach to social and economic survival is of special interest. In the first months of the community's existence, Kinkaide was inteviewed by Richard Fairfield, editor of a journal on alternative communities. Here she tells him how the group organized its early collective life.*

*In the years subsequent to this interview, feminist influence brought about many changes in the community's daily habits, including language usage. The use of the male pronoun, for example, which appears throughout Kinkade's interview, was eliminated. Twin Oaks members substituted the sex-neutral term* co *to stand for* she, he, hers, his, her, *and* him.

**Dick:** Did you deliberately choose a farm that would be so far from any large city?

**Kathleen:** No. That choice was dictated by price. You can't buy a farm within reach of a large city for the money we had available....

**Dick:** Are you still accepting new members, Kathleen?

**Kathleen:** Certainly—provided they are people able to accept our crowded conditions and severe economics. We have a very serious housing shortage right now. We are going to build a large structure this fall which will contain several bedrooms, in addition to work space for our hammock industry on the first floor.

**Dick:** Tell me about those hammocks.

**Kathleen:** The hammocks are made of cotton rope and kept in comfortable shape by oak stretchers. They sell for $25 to $35 each, the price depending on the size. They come complete with the hardware for attaching them to trees or porches, and we are developing a hammock-stand for people who don't have any trees to hang them from. We don't make a big profit on them, because the materials cost a large part of the price. But it is a means of putting our labor to use on our own premises. It is much more pleasant and better for the community than going to work in the nearby towns.

**Dick:** The hammock makers seem to be having a good time, not like working in a factory, for sure.

**Kathleen:** I don't know many factory managers who would put up with that amount of joking and singing, or with the hi-fi that alternately blasts them with the Beatles and Gregorian chants. We find that most work done in compatible groups is relatively pleasant.

**Dick:** Quite often people who tell about their communities tell only the good things. It always leaves us wondering what is left unsaid. How about people getting the work done. What about interpersonal conflict?

**Kathleen:** Dick, you must realize that we are talking about a community that is less than three months old. We are still on our honeymoon. Interpersonal difficulties are minimal. So far we find a great deal more satisfaction from each other's company than we do annoyance from each other's idiosyncrasies. Of course there is the person who always spills water on the bathroom floor, and another who can never remember to clean up after herself on cooking and baking projects. But remember we have the whole outdoors and several barns to work in, so we aren't stepping on each other's feet too much in the summer months, which minimizes petty annoyances. We realize that this kind of thing can be a problem, though, and we have thought up a means of dealing with it. Along with our other managers, we appointed one called the Generalized Bastard. His job is to be officially nasty. For example, suppose that a certain member has a habit of letting his work partner do the dirty part of the work and of skipping out on the last ten minutes of cleanup on a shared job. If this happens once or twice, his work partner ignores it. If it keeps happening, his partner begins to resent it but hates to say, "Hey, how about doing a full share of this job for a change." In order to avoid a building-up of resentment, the complaining member goes to the Generalized Bastard and explains the situation. Then it is the Bastard's job to carry his complaint to the offender, which he can do in an objective way.

**Dick:** Isn't that a bit roundabout? Couldn't you just encourage people to be frank with each other? It seems like a cop-out on the whole idea of community to have people unable to confront each other face to face with a problem....

**Kathleen:** Maybe you're right ideally; but we've found the Generalized Bastard helps things to run smoothly.

**Dick:** You mentioned that managers had been appointed. That sounds like Walden Two.* What kind of system have you set up?

**Kathleen:** We spent five weeks without government. Everybody did what seemed to him appropriate for him to do, and we got along all right. Occasionally we would have a meeting and try to get consensus on something important, like spending a large amount of money on some particular item. We would still

---

*Walden Two: A utopian novel published in 1948 by psychologist B.F. Skinner. Twin Oaks was inspired by the novel, but not identical in its organization of community life. In Walden Two, a system of positive reinforcement is used to maintain the ideal society. Child care and household duties in Walden Two are performed collectively, thus leaving women free to participate to the same extent as men in all activities.

be carrying on our business in that manner except for one thing: some of us couldn't stand meetings. Some objected to what they termed "wasted time." Others always got upset because of disagreements that arose at the meetings. What happened is that we had fewer and fewer meetings because they were so unpleasant. And as a result we found that decisions were going unmade, except when one member would just do something on his own initiative. Like, one weekend, one person just went and bought some wire and wired the shop. He figured that if he waited for a meeting on the subject, it would be winter before the shop got any electricity, and the printing press that was there doesn't run on treadle power. Now we have elected a board of planners with broad powers. And the board in turn appoints managers to various areas of work. I can't tell you how well this system works because at this point it is too new. We have a hammock-making manager, community-health manager, vegetable-garden manager, visitor manager.

**Dick:** And you're the one who manages visitors?

**Kathleen:** Actually, I'm three managers. All of us are at least two. There are more jobs than people. I tell visitors where to pitch their tents and remind them to pay for their meals. I'm not required to entertain them. We can't spare the labor for that.

**Dick:** How do you divide up your labor?

**Kathleen:** Our labor credit system is very much in the experimental stages. Right now we divide the work weekly by means of a kind of card game, where everyone is dealt a hand and passes his unwanted cards to the right until he accumulates the right number of credits and the jobs he prefers.

**Dick:** Is it working out well?

**Kathleen:** It seems to be fair to everyone and there has been general good-will toward the system, but it takes a long time. We keep imagining what it would be like if we had fifty members instead of ten.

**Dick:** What would you do here if someone refused to do his share of the work?

**Kathleen:** Ask him to leave. That everyone works is a fundamental assumption at Twin Oaks. There is a lot to be done and we are not in a position to afford any loafers.

**Dick:** So you consider yourselves an experimental community in the same sense that Skinner intended a Walden Two?

**Kathleen:** Yes. Of course we aren't the avant-garde of the sexual revolution. So far we are sticking to patterns which give the feeling of free choice; and free choice for a woman could mean a one-to-one relationship that is fairly stable. We are different from society at large in that we merely practice marriage. Society at large virtually requires it. In our community the practice of lifetime marriage will endure just exactly as long as it is functional and no longer. Society at large regards it as a sacrament in itself greater and more important than the happiness or unhappiness it produces....

**Dick:** What about free love?

**Kathleen:** The community doesn't take a stand on free love. We take it for granted that couples will find each other and seek the kind of relationship that they mutually consider desirable. We foresee no reason to regulate it.

**Dick:** You seek to regulate some behaviors and not others, according to whether you feel they need regulating. Tell me, have you found certain pressures in community living that are not found in ordinary life?

**Kathleen:** Some. We have to remember to clean up after ourselves, to put tools back in their places, to do our work at a reasonable time so that other work which follows it will not be held up. Community life is not entirely free of restrictions. On the other hand, we escape a great many pressures by being here. We dress as we please; our schedule is more flexible than it would be if we worked at a city job; there are no artificial standards we have to meet, such as qualifying for a degree or earning a promotion. I personally feel very free here.

**Dick:** How many hours a day are you people working?

**Kathleen:** We average about six, but a lot of things get done outside the labor credit system. I don't think anybody got labor credits for arranging the library, for instance. I wouldn't be surprised if we were all averaging closer to seven hours a day. That should go up when emergency projects are added, such as the actual construction of the building that is now being planned.

**Dick:** What do most of the members do for fun?

**Kathleen:** In a group this small, recreational interests always vary a great deal. One member plays a clarinet, using a phonograph record for his back-up orchestra. Another is interested in ham radio. The most organized activity we have is the Repulsive Quartet. That's a group that meets whenever the mood strikes and sings hymns in four-part harmony. I imagine it will eventually develop into a good choir—given time, practice, and the addition of some more voices. But in the meantime we are out-of-tune fairly often. When we get to sounding better, maybe we will change the name.

**Dick:** So most of you just follow individual hobbies?

**Kathleen:** Yes, or sit around and talk, which is quite a recreation in itself. This summer has been great for conversational games.

**Dick:** If conversation is a common recreation, you probably are a group with a great deal in common. Would you agree?

**Kathleen:** A number of people have commented that we are a lot alike. From inside the group it doesn't seem that way. We can see our differences much more clearly than our similarities. Probably the very fact that we are here indicates something about us. Certainly we have a set of common opinions on a few subjects. We all think society is in bad shape; we all think intentional community is a reasonable way to make at least a small improvement in it.

**Dick:** How does a person become a member of twin Oaks?

**Kathleen:** First, he visits us and talks to us about it. Then he would have to move in and live here for three months. If he is acceptable after his three-month trial period, he becomes a member.

**Dick:** Does he have to give all his money to the community?

**Kathleen:** The simple answer to that question is "yes." Actually, there are some exceptions, but they aren't important enough to talk about except to individuals whom they might affect.

**Dick:** How about the personal property the member brings in? What happens to it?

**Kathleen:** It remains his.... All the sharing is voluntary....

**Dick:** What is your prognosis for the survival of Twin Oaks?

**Kathleen:** Finances look bad and the draft is a serious threat, but I still think we have a fair chance of surviving. We are on the farm and will not go hungry. There is no lack of potential members. They pour confusedly out of colleges every spring. We will not get bored and we are not likely to be intimidated easily. We are building good relations with our neighbors. Above all we are prepared to change our policies as they prove unworkable and make new ones that suit our purposes.

## Kneeling Here, I Feel Good

*Poet Marge Piercy lived in the center of cities until 1971, when her health forced her to move to the country. A political activist, she speaks here of revolution and germination as mysteries of birth.*

Sand: crystalline children
of dead mountains.
Little quartz worlds
rubbed by the wind.

Compost: rich as memory,
sediment of our pleasures,
orange rinds and roses and beef bones,
coffee and cork and dead lettuce,
trimmings of hair and lawn.

I marry you, I marry you.
In your mingling under my grubby nails
I touch the seeds of what will be.
Revolution and germination
are mysteries of birth
without which
many
are born to starve.

I am kneeling and planting.
I am making fertile.
I am putting
some of myself
back in the soil.
Soon enough
sweet black mother of our food
you will have the rest.

# A Photo Essay

## Documentary Photography
## During the Depression

Like early agricultural workers, these Mississippi women
were still cultivating the soil by hoe in 1936 when Dorothea Lange
took this photograph for the Farm Security Administration.

248

ROUGHLY TWO-THIRDS of the photographs illustrating this book were taken in the 1930s and early 1940s by photographers working with the Farm Security Administration. The timeless quality of many of the photographs provides an appropriate statement about women's work on the land in other eras than those they recorded. The photographs also offer a unique documentary record of the Depression.

The photographs were produced under the direction of Roy Stryker, an economist and former Columbia University teacher who had developed a reputation for utilizing visual aids in the classroom. With Stryker's guidance, a group of professionals that included Dorothea Lange, Walker Evans, Russell Lee, Arthur

Rothstein, Ben Shahn, and Marion Post Wolcott created a visual historical record of the United States which may never again be equaled. Most of the Farm Security Administration photographers were reformers, and the federal government used their works to further New Deal farm reform. These photographers were also experienced artists, each with an independent conception of visual beauty, and an independent style. Thus the interests of reform and art came together to create pictures that—as Lange said of the work by Evans—caught the "bitter edge" of life in the United States.[1]

Ironically, the Farm Security Administration came into being to take care of the miscalculations of the New Deal farm reforms. Under the Agricultural Adjustment Act of 1933, thousands of land owners took land out of cultivation, making the labor of tenant farmers no longer necessary. The Farm Security Administration attempted to resettle families on productive land, help marginal farmers through loans, and provide migratory camps for farm laborers. To gain support for this program, Stryker sent photographers into the fields in all parts of the country, in order to picture to the American people the great distress of the rural poor. After the summer of 1938, the Farm Security Administration asked for photographs showing the positive effects of government policies as well. In both phases, a rich representation of farm women of all ethnic groups resulted.

In the 1930s, and later, many of Dorothea Lange's photographs became famous for depicting the plight of migrant women, troubled and poverty-stricken. Often, however, Lange and other FSA photographers emphasized their subjects as workers, rather than as women helplessly cut adrift from the land and idled by unemployment. And while Lange's photos bluntly depict social injustice, her subjects also appear dignified, sympathetic, and beautiful. Many of the pictures have a portrait quality.[2]

Among the FSA photographers, Lange photographed primarily in the West, continuing to operate out of her Berkeley, California studio. Already committed to changing the conditions of the rural poor before joining the FSA, Lange saw the planned rural communities that were being set up in California as "real achievements," especially, she wrote Stryker in 1936, "after seeing the misery of the homeless people that I've been meeting and photographing." She felt that Stryker had "an instinct" for what was important in documentary photography, and a "hospitable mind," which allowed photographers to continue to work creatively even while they were attached to a Washington bureaucracy.

As Lange's letters indicate, she was able to link her social concerns effectively to those of the FSA. In February 1937, for example, she wrote to Stryker asking for permission to go into the Imperial Valley of California, where growers opposed the establishment of migrant camps because they feared the workers might use them as a base to organize. "What goes on in the Imperial Valley is beyond belief," she wrote. "The valley has a social structure all its own and partly because of its isolation in the state those in control get away with it.... Those in control are bitterly opposed [to the camp] and there is trouble ahead.... Down there if they don't like you they shoot you and give you the works...beat you up and dump you in a ditch at the county line.... In other words it's a hot spot and for R.A. [Resettlement Administration] to go in is a dramatic situation. We shall need pictures." Lange went in; and her pictures became part of the campaign which brought about decent, government-run camps for migrants throughout California.[3]

Like Lange's husband, the economist Paul Taylor, most FSA reformers came to believe that displaced farm people had to be absorbed through industrial expansion rather than crowded back onto the land, where they were already "surplus." While the FSA projects relieved distress, they did not change the rural economic structure. World War II was to provide the industries that absorbed the surplus farm population of the Depression.

In May of 1936, when Lange first went to Washington, D.C. to meet Stryker, she wrote to a friend about the photographs already collected: "The files in Washington are rich. I wish you could see them." The pictures here reproduced are selected from the 80,000 FSA prints now housed in the Library of Congress. They will allow readers to see a part of the "permanent national treasure" bequeathed to the people of the United States by the FSA photographers.

# Yesterday on the Land

**1**: Yakima Indians in the hop fields of Washington, 1904. Long before the arrival of Europeans in North America, Native Americans had established self-sufficient farming communities in which women were central to cultivation, planting, and harvesting.
**2**: In the sugar cane fields of Louisiana, 1901. Black women had a tradition of sharing field work with men and of responsibility for maintaining strong kinship ties.
**3**: Churning butter, 1897. In that day, butter provided farm families with a dependable cash income.
**4**: Feeding chickens in Buffalo County, Nebraska, 1890s. A host of chores went hand-in-hand with the opportunities on the frontier which drew many women west.

# Farm Foremothers

**1**: A rice raft, South Carolina, 1895.
**2**: In Hawaii at the turn of the century, Japanese field hands pose with hoes.
**3**: Three daughters and a son of Julius and Marie Schellenberg on a farm near Johnson, Nebraska, Nemaha County, 1897.
**4**: Mormon farm women Mrs. George Showell and Etta Lee, Utah, ca. 1898. The hard work and isolation of the frontier were offset for Mormon women by relatively high living standards in their well-organized, co-operative communities.

2

4

# Cotton
# Was King

**1**: Cotton hoer,
born a slave,
Mississippi, 1937.
Cotton dominated the
fate of thousands
of Southern
rural women before
the Civil War,
and after.
**2**: Cotton picker,
San Joaquin Valley,
California, 1936.
In more modern
times, cotton
flourished in the
far west.
**3**: Tenants on a
cotton plantation,
family earning fifty
dollars a year,
Eutaw, Alabama, 1936.
**4**: Cotton picker
dragging bag
of cotton, Lake Dick
Project, Arkansas,
1938.
**5**: Family group
picking cotton in
the South, ca. 1910.

For Farm Security
Administration:
photos 1, 2, 3 by
Dorothea Lange;
photo 4 by Russell Lee.

256

2

3

5

257

# I Have Planted and Gathered

**1**: Woman trussing up hay, ca. 1917.
**2**: Farm woman working on hay wagon, Schenectady County, New York, 1943.
**3**: Young Mexican woman cutting spinach, La Pryor, Texas, 1939
**4**: Mexican migrant tomato worker, Santa Clara County, California, 1938.
**5**: Apple pickers, n.d.

For Farm Security Administration: photo 3 by Russell Lee; photo 4 by Dorothea Lange.

3

259

# In the Heat of the Sun

**1**: Migrant woman picking hops, Pacific Coast, 1939.
**2**: Tenant farm woman, Texas Panhandle, 1937.
**3**: Black woman tending her garden near Princess Anne, Maryland, 1940.
**4**: Migrant pea picker, Nipomo, California, 1937.

For Farm Security Administration: photos 1, 2, 4 by Dorothea Lange; photo 3 by Jack Delano.

# This Earth Must Yield

**1**: Native American woman picking blueberries near Little Fork, Minnesota, 1937.
**2**: Evicted Arkansas sharecroppers resettled at Hill House, Mississippi, 1936.
**3**: Loading carrots on truck, Camden County, New Jersey, 1938. From the Italian section of Philadelphia, these women traveled to New Jersey to work on the large truck farms.
**4**: Pea picker near Calipatria, California, 1939.

For Farm Security Administration: photo 1 by Russell Lee; photos 2, 4 by Dorothea Lange; photo 3 by Arthur Rothstein.

2

4

# Hard Times Never Was a Stranger

1: Farm Security Administration borrower with inculcator in basement house, Dead Ox Flat, Oregon, 1941.
2: Young woman sharecropper planting sweet potatoes, Person County, North Carolina, 1939.
3: Woman displaying chili peppers, Concho, Arizona, 1940.
4: Women picking carrots, Camden County, New Jersey, 1938.

For Farm Security Administration: photos 1, 3 by Russell Lee; photo 2 by Dorothea Lange; photo 4 by Arthur Rothstein.

2

3

# With These Hands

**1**: Woman separating vines from potatoes, Rio Grande County, Colorado, 1939.
**2**: Florida migrant gathering onions near Accomac, Virginia, 1940.
**3**: Women picking cranberries, Burlington County, New Jersey, 1938.
**4**: "Re-pickers" who pick over the hops after original picking by portable, mechanical picker. Yakima Chief Hop Ranch, Yakima County, Washington, 1941.

For Farm Security Administration: photos 1, 3 by Arthur Rothstein; photo 2 by Jack Delano; photo 4 by Russell Lee.

2

3

4

# Sunrise to Sundown

**1:** Women picking cranberries, Burlington County, New Jersey, 1938.
**2:** Celery workers, Malheur County, Oregon, 1942.
**3:** Mexican carrot worker, near Edinburg, Texas, 1939.
**4:** Japanese-American broccoli workers, Guadalupe, California, 1937.

For Farm Security Administration: photo 1 by Arthur Rothstein; photos 2, 3 by Russell Lee; photo 4 by Dorothea Lange.

2

4

# A Woman Works Everywhere

**1**: Potato picker, Monmouth County, New Jersey, 1938.
**2**: Polish immigrant husking corn, Greenfield, Connecticut, 1941.
**3**: Enos Royer farm, Lancaster County, Pennsylvania, 1938 [?].
**4**: West Texas tenant farm woman, 1937.

For Farm Security Administration: photo 1 by Arthur Rothstein; photo 2 by John Collier; photo 3 by Sheldon Dick; photo 4 by Dorothea Lange.

2

3

# We Farmed Long As We Was Able

**1:** Young woman sharecropper worms tobacco, Wales County, North Carolina, 1939.
**2:** German-American farm, near Windsor Locks, Connecticut, 1942.
**3:** Tobacco sharecropper near Douglas, Georgia, 1938.
**4:** Tobacco tenants, Granville County, North Carolina, 1939.
**5:** Child working in fields, Aroostook County, Maine.

For Farm Security Administration: photos 1, 3, 4 by Dorothea Lange; photos 2, 5 by John Collier.

# Sweet Mother of Our Food

**1:** Setting out garden cabbage plants, Pie Town, New Mexico, 1940.
**2:** Migrants sewing onion bags near Cedarville, New Jersey, 1940.
**3:** Day laborers pick beans, Bridgeton, New Jersey, 1941.
**4:** Japanese-American women washing celery sprouts for transplanting, Malheur County, Oregon, 1942.

For Farm Security Administration: photos 1, 4 by Russell Lee; photo 2 by Jack Delano; photo 3 by Marion Post Wolcott.

2

4

# We Shall Not Be Moved

**1:** Native American sugarbeet worker, Adams County, Colorado, 1939. Today, in a resurgent tradition of militancy, Native American women are struggling to reassert control over their lands.

**2:** Twin Oaks Community, Louisa, Virginia, 1978. This young woman works in one of the few successful back-to-the-land efforts.

**3:** Migrants picking beans, Bridgeton, New Jersey, 1942. Predominantly urban now, some Black women are attempting to halt the loss of land remaining in Black hands.

**4:** Polish-American woman at farmers' market, Ann Arbor, Michigan, 1967. Some women, grown old on the land, believe that children will return.

For Farm Security Administration: photo 1 by Arthur Rothstein; photo 3 by John Collier.

2

4

# About the Author

JOAN M. JENSEN is an associate professor of history at New Mexico State University, Las Cruces, where she teaches women's history and special courses on women and work. She received her Ph.D. in history from the University of California, Los Angeles. After a number of years of teaching, she moved to Colorado to farm, learning to plow and to irrigate, to raise animals, to make butter and cheese, to cook on a wood stove, and to spin and weave, before she returned to teaching and writing. A pioneer in researching the history of women and agriculture, she has published numerous articles on this subject, and has been the recipient of a grant from the Regional Economic Historical Center at the Eleutherian Mills-Hagley Foundation, for research on mid-Atlantic farm women, 1750–1850. She is the author of *The Price of Vigilance*, a study of civil liberties during World War I, and co-editor of a forthcoming anthology on the history of the feminist movement between the two world wars.

# A Note on Language

IN EDITING BOOKS, The Feminist Press attempts to eliminate harmful sex and race bias inherent in the language. In order to retain the authenticity of historical and literary documents, however, our policy is to leave their original language unaltered. We recognize that the task of changing language usage is extremely complex and that it will not be easily accomplished. The process is an ongoing one that we share with many others concerned with the relationship between a humane language and a more humane world.

# Notes

### Introduction

1. Maris A. Vinovskis and Richard M. Bernard, "Beyond Catharine Beecher: Female Education in the Antebellum Period," *Signs* 3 (Summer 1978): 863.

2. The Federal Writers' Project (1935-1943), a New Deal agency, paid unemployed white collar workers (lawyers, ministers, journalists, librarians, teachers, and professional writers) to produce a series of state and city guidebooks as well as to collect oral history. Most of the oral history remained in manuscript form until recently. For a history of the project see Monty Noam Penkower. *The Federal Writers' Project: A Study in Government Patronage of the Arts* (Urbana: University of Illinois Press, 1977).

3. See pages 285-288 for sources of the selections.

4. Historians have had difficulty in measuring the amount purchased by farm families termed "self-sufficient." In the past, it may have been as little as 10 percent of total consumption; today it may be almost 50 percent. Most farm families, from the mid-eighteenth century onward, sold some farm surplus on the market. See Rodney Loehr, "Self-Sufficiency on the Farm (1759-1819)," *Agricultural History* XXVI(1952): 37-42.

### In the Beginning: Native American Women

1. Carolyn Neithammer, *Daughters of Earth: The Lives and Legends of American Indian Women* (New York: Collier, 1977), contains additional information on the economic and political roles of women who lived in agricultural societies.

2. Joan M. Jensen, "Native American Women and Agriculture: A Seneca Case Study," *Sex Roles* V. 3 (1977): 423-441.

3. See the Introduction to David M. Schneider and Kathleen Gough, eds., *Matrilineal Kinship* (Berkeley: University of California Press, 1961).

4. Quoted in Sophie Drinker, *Music and Women: The Story of Women in Their Relation to Music* (New York: Coward-McCann, 1948). 8. Readers who wish to explore theories about the relationship of work to status in preindustrial societies should look at Michelle Zimbalist Rosaldo and Louise Lamphere, eds., *Women, Culture and Society* (Stanford: Stanford University Press, 1974).

5. See Dale Van Every, *Disinheritied: The Lost Birthright of the American Indian* (New York: Morrow, 1966).

### Staying Put, Moving On: Women East and West

1. Darrett Rutman, *Husbandmen of Plymouth: Farms and Villages in the Old Colony, 1620-1692* (Boston: Beacon, 1967).

2. Mary Alice Feldblum, "The Formation of the First Factory Labor Force in the New England Cotton Textile Industry, 1800-1848," (unpublished PhD dissertation, New School for Social Research, 1977), has the best discussion of this early nineteenth century farm transition. Easier to obtain are John Donald Black, *The Rural Economy of New England* (Cambridge: Harvard University Press, 1950), Catherine Fennelly, *Life in an Old New*

*England Country Village* (New York: Crowell, 1969), and Nancy F. Cott, *The Bonds of Womanhood: "Woman's Sphere" in New England, 1780-1835* (New Haven: Yale University Press, 1977), 19-62.

3. One frontier woman, for example, bought a Singer sewing machine in the 1860s from her washing earnings, and then she and her husband worked together, manufacturing leather gloves. Agnes Just Reid, *Letters of Long Ago* (Salt Lake City: University of Utah Library, 1973), 20.

4. Louisa May Alcott, *Work* (1873; reprinted, New York: Schocken, 1977) describes the types of work she later attempted in preference to remaining on the farm.

5. Charles Nordhoff, *The Communistic Societies of the United States* (1875; reprinted, New York: Schocken, 1965) contains many details on the work of the Shaker sisters.

6. For the lives of western women see Joan M. Jensen and Darlis Miller, "The Gentle Tamers Revisited: Viewing Women in the West," *Pacific Historical Review* (May 1980) and Lillian Schlissel, "Mothers and Daughters on the Western Frontier," *Frontiers* III (Summer 1978), 29-33.

### In Bondage to Cotton: Women in the South

1. Roger L. Ransom and Richard Sutch, *One Kind of Freedom: The Economic Consequences of Emancipation* (Cambridge: Cambridge University Press, 1977), 104-105.

2. *Ibid.*, 234.

3. Robert William Fogel and Stanley L. Engerman, *Time on the Cross: The Economics of American Negro Slavery* (Boston: Little, Brown, 1974), 68-82, gives numerous examples of the importance of women in the plantation economy.

4. Esther Boserup, *Woman's Role in Economic Development* (New York: St. Martin's, 1970), 18; and Schneider and Gough, eds., *Matrilineal Kinship* (Berkeley: University of California Press, 1961), 270-297.

5. Herbert G. Gutman, *The Black Family in Slavery and Freedom, 1750-1925* (New York: Pantheon, 1976).

6. Eugene D. Genovese, *Roll, Jordan, Roll: The World the Slaves Made* (New York: Pantheon, 1974).

7. Roger D. Abrahams, "Negotiating Respect: Patterns of Presentation Among Black Women," in *Women and Folklore*, edited by Claire R. Farrer (Austin: University of Texas Press, 1975), 58-80.

8. Gutman, *The Black Family*, 63.

9. Ransom and Sutch, *One Kind of Freedom*, 234.

10. Gutman, *The Black Family*, 89.

11. Anne Firor Scott, *The Southern Lady from Pedestal to Politics* (Chicago: University of Chicago Press, 1970) describes the work of plantation women in great detail.

12. Gutman, *The Black Family*, 402.

13. *Ibid.*, 226.

### On the Last Frontier: Women Together, Women Divided

1. See Wilcomb Washburn, *Red Man's Land: White Man's Law* (New York: Scribner's, 1971), 29-30, and Jane M. Smith and Robert M. Kvasnicka, eds., *Indian-White Relations: A Persistent Paradox* (Washington: Howard University Press, 1976).

2. E. Louise Peffer, *The Closing of*

the *Public Domain: Disposal and Reservation Policies 1900-1950* (Stanford: Stanford University Press, 1951), 137.

3. Wayne David Rasmussen, ed., *Agriculture in the United States: A Documentary History* (4 vols.; New York: Random, 1975), I, 540-542; II, 1022-1031; William T. Hagan, "Private Property: The Indian's Door to Civilization," *Ethnohistory* III (1956): 126-37.

4. Shu-Ching Lee, "The Theory of the Agricultural Ladder," *Agricultural History* XXI (Jan. 1947): 53-61.

5. Christie Farnham Pope, "Southern Homesteads for Negroes," *Agricultural History* XLIV (April 1970): 201-212 and Susan Armitage, Theresa Banfield, and Sarah Jacobus, "Black Women and their Communities in Colorado," *Frontiers* II (Summer 1977): 45-52.

6. Frances Leon Swadesh, *Los Primeros Pobladores: Hispanic Americans of the Ute Frontier* (Notre Dame: University of Notre Dame Press, 1974), 178-182.

7. Nadia Haggag Youssef, *Women and Work in Developing Societies* (1974; reprinted, Westport, Conn.: Greenwood, 1976).

8. Fred Bateman, "The 'Marketable Surplus' in Northern Dairy Farming: New Evidence by Size of Farm in 1860," *Agricultural History* LII (July 1978): 345-363 and Viola I. Paradise, *Maternity Care and the Welfare of Young Children in a Homesteading County in Montana,* Children's Bureau Bulletin No. 34 (Washington, D.C., 1919), 14. Butter was the ideal market product because it would keep better than milk, was easier to transport, would be taken in trade by country stores, and was easier to produce than cheese, which necessitated longer

and more elaborate preparations and greater control over temperature. Some women did sell milk and cheese as well as eggs and poultry, but most relied on butter for their main income.

9. Homer E. Socolofsky, "Success and Failure in Nebraskas Homesteading," *Agricultural History* XLII (April 1968): 103-107 and Sheryll Patterson-Black, "Women Homesteaders on the Great Plains Frontier," *Frontiers* I (Spring 1976): 67-88.

10. Christine Stansell, "Women on the Great Plains, 1865-1890," *Women's Studies* 4 (1976): 87-98 and Mary W.M. Hargreaves, "Women in the Agricultural Settlement of the Northern Plains," *Agricultural History* L (Jan. 1976): 179-189. For a delightful account of the expectations of a Croatian immigrant woman who left the farm see Anna Zellick, "Immigrant Homesteader in Montana, Anna Pipinich," *Environmental Review* 4 (1977): 2-16.

11. Leonard J. Arrington, "The Economic Role of Pioneer Mormon Women," *Western Humanities Review* IX (Spring 1955): 145-164 and Claudia L. Bushman, ed., *Mormon Sisters: Women in Early Utah* (Cambridge, Mass. Emmeline, 1976): 43-66, 89-112, 133-156, and 177-198.

12. Stephanie Smith Goodson, "Plural Wives," in Claudia L. Bushman, ed., *Moromon Sisters* (Cambridge, Mass.: Emmeline, 1976).

13. Beverly Beeton, "Woman Suffrage in Territorial Utah," *Utah Historical Quarterly* 46 (1978): 100-120.

14. Beverly P. Smaby, "The Mormons and the Indians: Conflicting Ecological Systems in

the Great Basin," *American Studies* XVI (Spring 1975): 35–48 and P. Holder, *The Hoe and the Horse on the Plains: A Study of Cultural Development Among North American Indians* (Lincoln: University of Nebraska Press, 1970).

15. Theodora Kroeber, *Ishi in Two Worlds: A Biography of the Last Wild Indian in America* (Berkeley: University of California Press, 1961).

### Less Corn, More Hell! Women and Rural Reform

1. See section 2, pp. 41–43.

2. The abolition movement was, of course, the great political movement of early nineteenth-century women. At least 20,000 women supported the movement by joining anti-slavery groups, signing petitions, and raising funds for abolition organizing. Only a small group of these women supported feminism and full equality with men organizationally. Those who did tended to support separation from all political institutions, like the government, that helped to sustain slavery. The more conservative faction of the anti-slavery movement that favored coalition tactics, including third parties, refused women equality within their groups. In contrast, late nineteenth-century farm groups supported greater participation by women within the traditional political party structures. See Blanche Glassman Hersh, *The Slavery of Sex: Feminist-Abolitionists in America* (Urbana: University of Illinois Press, 1978), 6–38.

3. Anne Mayhew, "A Reappraisal of the Causes of Farm Protest in the United States, 1870–1900," *Journal of Economic History* XXXII (June 1972): 464–75.

4. D. Sven Nordin, *Rich Harvest:*

*A History of the Grange, 1867–1900* (Jackson: University Press of MIssissippi, 1974) and Earl W. Hayter, *The Troubled Farmer, 1850–1900: Rural Adjustment to Industrialism* (DeKalb: Northern Illinois University Press, 1968).

5. Bettie Gay, "The Influence of Women in the Alliance," in Nelson A. Dunning, *The Farmer's Alliance History and Agricultural Digest* (1891; reprinted, New York: Arno, 1975); Julie Roy Jeffrey, "Women in the Southern Farmers' Alliance: A Reconsideration of the Role and Status of Women in the Late Nineteenth Century South," *Feminist Studies* 3 (Fall 1975): 72–91.

6. See the articles on Annie Diggs and Sarah Emory as well as Lease in Edward T. James, ed., *Notable American Women*, 3 vols., (Cambridge: Harvard University Press, 1971).

7. So little research has been done on Blacks in the farm reform movements that it is difficult to judge how many Black women participated in the organizations.

8. Lawrence C. Goodwyn, "Populist Dreams and Negro Rights: East Texas as a Case Study," *American Historical Review* 76 (1971): 1135–71 and *Democratic Promise: The Populist Moment in America* (New York: Oxford University Press, 1976); and Peter H. Argersinger, *Populism and Politics: William Alfred Peffer and the People's Party* (Lexington: University Press of Kentucky, 1974), 159–172.

9. William L. Bowers, *The Country Life Movement in America, 1900–1920* (Port Washington, N.Y.: Kennikat, 1974).

10. Lance G.E. Jones, *The Jeanes Teacher in the United States, 1908–1923* (Chapel Hill: University of North Carolina Press, 1937).

11. Joan M. Jensen, "Politics and the American Midwife Controversy," *Frontiers*, 1 (Spring 1976): 19–33; N.L. Sims, *Elements of Rural Sociology* (New York: Crowell, 1928), 263.

12. Mary Meek Atkeson, "Women in Farm Life and Rural Economy," *Annals of the American Academy of Political and Social Science* 143 (May 1929): 188–194.

13. Merwin Swanson, "Professional Rural Social Work in America," *Agricultural History* XLVI (Oct. 1972): 515–526. For further material on the Depression and the New Deal, see section 6, "The Uncertain Harvest," and "Documentary Photography during the Depression," pp. 249–251.

14. James H. Shideler, "Flappers and Philosophers, and Farmers: Rural-Urban Tensions of the 20s," *Agricultural History* LII (1978): 238–299.

15. Robert L. Tontz, "Memberships of General Farmers' Organizations, United States, 1874–1960," *Agricultural History* XXXVIII (July 1964): 148.

**The Uncertain Harvest: Women Who Don't Give Up**

1. John L. Shover, *First Majority— Last Minority: The Transforming of Rural Life In America* (DeKalb: Northern Illinois University Press, 1976).

2. Cornelia Butler Flora, "Rural Women," *Associates NAL Today* 2 (Sept. 1977): 16–21.

3. For other women landowners see Ruth Gallaher, *Legal and Political Status of Women in Iowa* (Iowa City: State Historical Society of Iowa, 1918), 92–93 and Margaret Beattie Bogue, "The Scott Farms in a New Agriculture, 1900–1919," in David M. Ellis, ed., *The Frontier in American Development: Essays in Honor of Paul Wallace Gates* (Ithaca: Cornell University Press, 1969), 217–245 and Robert Diller, *Farm Ownership, Tenancy, and Land Use in a Nebraska Community* (Chicago: University of Chicago Press, 1941), 48.

4. Edgar A. Schuler and Carl C. Taylor, "Farm People's Attitudes and Opinions," in Carl C. Taylor, et al., *Rural Life in the United States* (New York: Knopf, 1949), 502 and JoAnn Vanek, "Time Spent in Housework," *Scientific American* 231 (Nov. 1974): 116–120.

5. Rena B. Maycock, "Home Economics Work in the Resettlement Administration," *Journal of Home Economics* 28 (Oct. 1936): 560–62.

6. Walter J. Stein, *California and the Dust Bowl Migration* (Westport, Conn.: Greenwood, 1973).

7. Arthur F. Raper, *Preface to Peasantry: A Tale of Two Black Belt Counties* (1936; reprinted, New York: Arno, 1971).

8. For rural schools and schoolteachers see "I Expect I'll Get a Plaque," *Southern Exposure* VII (Summer 1979): 74–77. For the interplay of Black reformers and the Black rural community see Alice Walker's novel *Meridian* (New York: HarBraceJ, 1976).

9. The best analysis of Black farm holdings is in a special issue on land use by *Southern Exposure* II (Fall 1974).

10. Mark Reisler, *By the Sweat of Their Brow: Mexican Immigrant Labor in the United States, 1900–1940* (New York: Greenwood, 1976), 228–246.

11. Paul S. Taylor, "Mexican Labor in the United States, Imperial Valley," in Paul S. Taylor, *Mexican Labor in the United States* (1930;

reprinted, New York: Arno, 1970) and my personal observations in the San Luis Valley of Colorado.

12. For the United Farm Workers see Jerald Brown, *The United Farm Workers Grape Strike and Boycott, 1965-1970* (Ithaca: Cornell University, Latin American Studies Program, 1972).

13. On Asian women see Emma Gee, ed., *Counterpoints* (Los Angeles: University of California, Asian-American Studies Center, 1978) and "Asian American Women," in *The Bridge* 6 (Winter 1978-79): 16-53 and 7 (Spring-Summer 1979): 9-49. For World War II experiences see Audrie Girdner and Anne Loftis, *The Great Betrayal* (New York: Macmillan, 1969) and Maisie and Richard Conrat, *Executive Order 9066: The Internment of 100,000 Japanese Americans* (San Francisco: California Historical Society, 1972).

14. Wallace E. Huffman, "The Value of Productive Time of Farm Wives: Iowa, North Carolina and Oklahoma," *American Journal of Agricultural Economics* 58 (Dec. 1976): 836-841, documented the continuing economic importance of farm women on family farms. See also Harold D. Guither, *Heritage of Plenty: A Guide to the Economic History and Development of U.S. Agriculture* (Danville, Illinois: Interstate, 1972).

15. *Agricultural Education*, 47 (June 1975) includes a number of articles on women's agricultural education. Between 1973 and 1978, women's enrollment in schools of agriculture rose 90 percent.

16. The best introduction to land issues on reservations is *Economic Development in American Indian Reservations* (Native American Studies, University of New Mexico, Development Series, No. 1, 1979). For women's activities see Jane B.

Katz, *I Am the Fire of Time: The Voices of Native American Women* (New York: Dutton, 1977), especially Ada Deer's speech 148-151.

17. Margaret Bouvard, *The International Community Movement* (Port Washington, N. Y.: Kennikat, 1975) is the best introduction to this movement.

18. See individual issues of *Country Women* (Albion, California).

19. For Twin Oaks see Kathleen Kinkade, *A Walden Two Experiment: The First Five Years of Twin Oaks Community* (New York: Morrow, 1973).

## A Photo Essay:
## Documentary Photography
## During the Depression

1. Material quoted in this essay is drawn from F. Jack Hurley, *Portrait of a Decade: Roy Stryker and the Development of Documentary Photography in the Thirties* (Baton Rouge: Louisiana State University Press, 1972).

2. Collections of Lange's photographs were published in Dorothea Lange and Paul Schuster Taylor, *An American Exodus: A Record of Human Erosion* (New York: Reynal and Hitchcock, 1939), *Dorothea Lange* (New York: Museum of Modern Art, 1966), and *Dorothea Lange Looks at the American Country Woman* (Fort Worth, Amon Carter Museum of Western Art, 1967). See also accounts and photographs in Milton Meltzer, *Dorothea Lange: A Photographer's Life* (New York: Farrar, Straus and Giroux, 1978). James Agee and Walker Evans, *Let Us Now Praise Famous Men* (Boston: Houghton Mifflin, 1941) has become a classic account of the Depression.

3. Stein, *California and the Dust Bowl Migration*, contains descriptions of the FSA camps.

# Sources

### In the Beginning:
### Native American Women

"Sky Woman." Ella Elizabeth Clark, *Indian Legends of Canada* (Toronto: McClelland and Stewart, 1960), 1-2.

"Corn Woman." Alice Marriott and Carol K. Rachlin, *American Indian Mythology* (New York: Crowell, 1968), 106-11.

"Seneca Corn Rite." William N. Fenton, ed., *Parker on the Iroquois* (Syracuse: Syracuse University Press, 1968), 26-27.

"Pueblo Grinding Tools." Katherine Bartlett, *Pueblo Milling Stones of the Flagstaff Region and Their Relation to Others in the Southwest: A Study in Progressive Efficiency*, Museum of Northern Arizona, Bulletin No. 3 (Flagstaff: Northern Arizona Society of Science and Art, 1933), 27-29.

"Zuni Grinding Song." Natalie Curtis, *The Indian's Book: Songs and Legends of the American Indians* (1923; reprinted New York: Dover, 1968), 429-30.

"Buffalo Bird Woman." James E. Sperry, ed., "Waheenee: An Indian Girl's Story Told by Herself to Gilbert L. Wilson," *North Dakota History*, 38 (Winter-Spring, 1971), 92-98.

"Mary Jemison." James Everett Seaver, *A Narrative of the Life of Mary Jemison* (1824; reprinted New York: Garland, 1977), 46-48.

"Pima Past." Anna Moore Shaw, *A Pima Past* (Tucson: University of Arizona Press, 1974), 5, 70, 72-74.

"Speech of the Cherokee Women." Archives of the American Board of Commissioners for Foreign Missions, 18.3.1., Vol. 2, No. 113, Houghton Library, Harvard University.

### Staying Put, Moving On:
### Women East and West

"New England Farm Woman." Eva Mariotti, "The Diary of Mary Poor of Indian Hills Farm," *New England Magazine*, 13 (Nov. 1895), 319-320.

"Susan B. Anthony Talks to the Farmers." Susan B. Anthony Papers, Library of Congress.

"Pioneering in the Northwest." Abigail Scott Duniway, *Pathbreaking: An Autobiographical History of the Equal Suffrage Movement in Pacific Coast States* (1914; reprinted New York: Kraus, 1971), 9-10, 13-15.

"Keeper of the Keys." Eulalia Perez, "Una vieja y sus recuerdos dictados," translated by Erlinda Gonzales-Berry. Original in the Bancroft Library, University of California, Berkeley.

"Transcendental Wild Oats." Ednah D. Cheney, ed., *Louisa May Alcott: Her Life, Letters, and Journals* (Boston: LIttle, Brown, 1899), 35, 36, 37. Louisa May Alcott, "Transcendental Wild Oats," in *Bronson Alcott's Fruitlands* (Philadelphia: Porcupine Press, 1975), 147-148, 149-150, 151-154, 156-158, 166-168, 173.

"Shaker Sisters." Marcia Bullard, "Shaker Industries," *Good Housekeeping*, 43 (July 1906), 37.

"I Have Plowed and Planted and Gathered." *Narrative of Sojourner Truth* (1878; reprinted New York: Arno, 1968), 134.

"A Norwegian Farm Woman."

Theodore C. Blegen, "Immigrant Women and the American Frontier," Norwegian-American Historical Association, *Norwegian-American Studies and Records*, 5 (1930), 26–29.

"Iron Teeth." Thomas B. Marquis, "Red Ripe's Squaw: Recollections of a Long Life," *Century Magazine*, 118 (June 1929), 201–202, 206–207.

## In Bondage to Cotton: Women of the South

"Overthrow the System." Angelina Emily Grimké, "Appeal to the Christian Women of the South," *The Anti-Slavery Examiner*, Vol. 1, No. 2 (Sept. 1836), 17–18, 19, 23, 28.

"The Slaves'New Year's Day." Linda Brent, *Incidents in the Life of a Slave Girl* (1861; reprinted New York: Harcourt Brace Javanovich, 1973), 13–14.

"A Louisiana Plantation." David Weeks and Family Papers, Archives and Manuscripts Department, Louisiana State University, Baton Rouge.

"A Texas Farm Woman." Charles Goodnight, Emanuel Dubbs, John A. Hart, *et al.*, contributors, *Pioneer Days in the Southwest from 1859 to 1879* (Guthrie, Oklahoma, State Capital, 1909), 246–248, 250–251.

"Hoeing Cotton." Benjamin Drew, *The Refugee: or the Narratives of Fugitive Slaves in Canada* (1865; reprinted New York: Negro Universities Press, 1968), 224–225.

"A North Carolina Plantation." James C. Bonner, ed., "Plantation Experiences of a New York Woman," *North Carolina Historical Review*, 33 (July 1956), 391–392, 399–400, 402, 410–411.

"Never Did Hev No More Overseers." Narrative of Annie Coley, ex-slave, WPA Collection, Mississippi Department of Archives and History.

"Diary from Dixie." Ben Ames Williams, ed., *A Diary from Dixie by Mary Boykin Chestnut* (Boston: Houghton Mifflin, 1949), 142–143, 593, 527.

"Farm Women Refugees." John F. Bayliss, compiler, *Black Slave Narratives* (New York: Macmillian, 1970), 125–126.

"Freedom's here and Slavery's Past." Federal Writers Project Papers, Southern Historical Collection, University of North Carolina Library, Chapel Hill.

"I'd Rather Belong Somewhur." Federal Writers Project Papers, Southern Historical Collection, University of North Carolina Library, Chapel Hill.

## On the Last Frontier: Women Together, Women Divided

"Jubilee." Margaret Walker, *Jubilee* (Boston: Hougton Mifflin, 1966), 315–316, 327, 330.

"A Woman Works Everywhere." Dearfield Oral History Project. Interview by Theresa Banfield.

"Women of the Llano." Fabiola Cabeza de Baca, *We Fed Them Cactus* (Albuquerque: University of New Mexico, 1954), 59–61.

"North from Mexico." Working lives of New Mexico Women Project, New Mexico State University, Las Cruces, New Mexico. Interviewed and transcribed by Aracelli Pando.

"Memories of the Plains." Eva Hendrickson Klepper, "Memories of Pioneer Days," in the May Avery Papers, Nebraska State Historical Society, Lincoln.

"My Ántonia." Willa Cather, *My*

*Ántonia* (Boston: Houghton Mifflin, 1954), 122-124, 125-126, 197-198, 199-200, 201-202.

"Homesteading in Wyoming." Elinore Pruitt Stewart, *Letters of a Woman Homesteader* (1942; reprinted Lincoln: University of Nebraska Press, 1961), 213-217, 279-282.

"Homesteading in New Mexico." Emma Marble Muir, "Pioneer Ranch," *New Mexico Magazine,* 36 (June 1958), 62-63.

"I will Just Write My Morning Chores." Diary of Lucy Hannah White Flake, Harold B. Lee Library, Brigham Young University, Provo, Utah.

"When You Come, We Die." Natalie Curtis, *The Indian's Book: Songs and Legends of the American Indians* (1923; reprinted New York: Dover, 1968), 569.

2 (Sept./Oct. 1977), 48-49.

"A Jury of Her Peers," Susan Keating Glaspell, "A Jury of Her Peers," in *American Voices, American Women,* edited by Lee R. Edwards and Arlyn Diamond (New York: Avon, 1973), 370-376, 379-381.

"The Rural Social Worker." Josephine C. Brown, *The Rural Community and Social Case Work* (New York: Family Welfare Association of America, 1933), 67-68, 69-71, 108.

"I Just Up and Bashed Him Good." Federal Writers Project Papers, Southern Historical Collection, University of North Carolina Library, Chapel Hill.

"The Misses Hodges." Federal Writers Project Papers, Southern Historical Collection, University of North Carolina Library, Chapel Hill.

## Less Corn, More Hell! Women and Rural Reform

"Mary Elizabeth Lease." *Journal of the Kinghts of Labor* (April 2, 1891), 2.

"A Strike for Farm Housewives." *The Literary Digest,* 63 (Dec. 20, 1919), 74, 78.

"Country Life and the Country School." Mabel Carney, *Country Life and the Country School: A Study of Agencies of Rural Progress and of the Social Relationship of the School and the Community* (Chicago: Row, Peterson, 1912), 188-190, 192, 194.

"The Jeanes Teachers." Lance G.E.Jones, *The Jeanes Teacher in the United States, 1908-1923* (Chapel Hill: University of North Carolina Press, 1937), 127-132.

"I am Quarlsome When Tired and Fatigued." Joyce Antler, "Letters on Maternity," *Women & Health,*

## The Uncertain Harvest: Women Who Don't Give Up

"Brown Hills." Judy Van Der Veer, *Brown Hills* (New York: Longmans, Green, 1938), 8, 69-73.

"Mothers of the South." Margaret Jarman Hagood, *Mothers of the South: Portraiture of the White Tenant Farm Woman* (1939; reprinted New York: Norton, 1977), 77-79, 79-80, 83-84, 89.

"Gertie." Harriette Arnow, *The Dollmaker* (New York: Macmillan, 1954), 186, 188, 189, 383

"Coming of Age in Mississippi." Anne Moody, *Coming of Age in Mississippi* (New York: Dial, 1968), 68, 71-73.

"Una Campesina de Texas." Maria Salas, "Entrevista con una Campesina de Texas," *Hembra* (Spring 1976), 7. Translated by Charles Tatum.

"Dolores Huerta: Un Soldado del

Movimiento." *La Voz del Pueblo* (Nov./Dec. 1972).

"We Got through Together." *Third World Women, Third World Communications* (1972), 58–59.

"I Remember." Isabel Flores, "I Remember," *Chicanas en la Literature y El Arte* (Berkeley: Quinto Sol, 1973), 80.

"Obāchan." Gail Miyasaki, "Obāchan," Asian American Studies at the University of California, Berkeley, *Asian Women* (1971), 16–17.

"Mita y Yo." Rosa Gonzalez, "Mita y Yo," *Imagenes de la Chicana* (Stanford: Chicano Press, n.d.), 13.

"Ranch Widow." Blanche Irving, "Ranoh Widow," *The American Mentor Magazine,* 16 (Winter 1978), 54.

"The Militant Middle." Michigan State Horticultural Society, *Annual Report,* 102 (1973), 65–70, 72–74.

"A Woman Who Won't." Beth Wood, *Rio Grande Weekly,* 6 (March 4–11, 1977), 2.

"The Next Step: Women-Identified Collectives." Jeanne Tetrault, "The Next Step: Women Identified Collectives," *Country Women,* 6 (June 1973), 29–31, 34.

"Twin Oaks." Richard Fairfield, *Communes USA: A Personal Tour* (Baltimore: Penguin, 1972), 62–68.

"Kneeling Here, I Feel Good," Marge Piercy, *Living in the Open* (New York: Knopf, 1976), 16.

# Index

This book was composed in Trump and Olive Antique by Weinglas Typography Company, Port Washington, New York. It was printed and bound by R.R. Donnelley & Sons Company, Chicago, Illinois. The covers were printed by Algen Press, Queens, New York.

*(acknowledgments continued from page vi)*

Fabiola Cabeza de Baca, "Women of the Llano." Excerpted from *We Fed Them Cactus* by Fabiola Cabeza de Baca. Copyright © 1954 by The University of New Mexico Press, Reprinted by permission of the publisher.

Willa Cather, "My Ántonia." From *My Ántonia* by Willa Cather. Copyright © renewed 1954 by Edith Lewis. Reprinted by permission of Houghton Mifflin Company.

Mary Boykin Chestnut, "Diary from Dixie." From *A Diary from Dixie by Mary Boykin Chestnut* edited by Ben Ames Williams. Copyright © 1949 by Houghton Mifflin Company. Reprinted by permission of Houghton Mifflin Company.

Ella Elizabeth Clark, "Sky Woman." From *Indian Legends of Canada* by Ella Elizabeth Clark. Copyright © 1960 by McClelland and Stewart, Limited. Reprinted by permission of the Canadian Publishers, McClelland and Stewart Limited, Toronto.

Natalie Curtis, "When You Come, We Die." From *The Indian's Book: Songs and Legends of the American Indians* by Natalie Curtis, copyright © 1968 by Dover Publications. Reprinted by permission of the publisher.

Natalie Curtis, "Zuni Grinding Song." From *The Indian's Book: Songs and Legends of the American Indians* by Natalie Curtis, copyright © 1968 by Dover Publications. Reprinted by permission of the publisher.

Richard Fairfield, "Twin Oaks." From *Communes USA: A Personal Tour* by Richard Fairfield. Copyright © 1971 by Alternatives Foundation. Reprinted by permission of Penguin Books.

William N. Fenton, ed., "Seneca Corn Rite." From *Parker on the Iroquois* edited by William N. Fenton. Copyright © 1968 by Syracuse University Press. Reprinted by permission of Syracuse University Press.

Lucy Hannah White Flake, "I Will Just Write My Morning Chores." From Diary of Lucy Hannah White Flake. Used by permission of Harold B. Lee Library, Archives and Manuscripts, Brigham Young University.

Margaret Jarman Hagood, "Mothers of the South." From *Mothers of the South: Portraiture of the White Tenant Farm Woman* by Margaret Jarmon Hagood. Copyright © 1939 by The University of North Carolina Press. Copyright renewed 1967 by Margaret Benaya. Reprinted by permission of The University of North Carolina Press.

Blanche Irving, "Ranch Widow." Copyright © 1978 by Blanche Irving. Reprinted by permission of John Westburg, editor, *The North American Mentor Magazine*, Fennimore, Wisconsin 53809.

Eva Hendrickson Klepper, "Memories of the Plains." From "Memories of Pioneer Days" by Eva Hendrickson Klepper. Used by permission of the Manuscripts Division of the State Archives, Nebraska State Historical Society.

Emma Marble Muir, "Homesteading in New Mexico." Excerpted from "Pioneer Ranch" by Emma Marble Muir, originally published in *New Mexico Magazine*. Copyright © 1958 by Emma Marble Muir. Reprinted by permission of William Marble Kipp.

Alice Marriott and Carol K. Rachlin, "Corn Woman." From *American Indian Mythology* by Alice Marriott and Carol K. Rachlin. Copyright © 1968 by Alice Marriott and Carol K. Rachlin. Used by permission of T.Y. Crowell.

Gail Miyasaki, "Obāchan." Originally published in *Asian Women*, copyright © 1971 by *Asian Women*. Reprinted by permission of *Asian Women*.

Anne Moody, "Coming of Age in Mississippi." Excerpted from the book *Coming of Age in Mississippi* by Anne Moody. Copyright © 1968 by Anne Moody. Reprinted by permission of The Dial Press.

Rachel Swayze O'Connor, "A Louisiana Plantation." From David Weeks and Family Papers. Used by permission of the Department of Archives and Manuscripts, Louisiana State University.

Guri Olsdatter, "A Norwegian Farm Woman." From "Immigrant Women and the American Frontier" by Theodore C. Blegen, originally published in *Norwegian-American Studies and Records*. Reprinted by permission of the Norwegian-American Historical Association.

Aracelli Pando, interviewer, "North from Mexico." Used by permission of Working Lives of New Mexico Women Project, New Mexico State University.

Eulalia Perez, "Keeper of the Keys." From "Una vieja y sus recuerdos dictados" by Eulalia Perez, translated by Erlinda Gonzales-Berry. Original in the Bancroft Library, University of California, Berkeley. Used by permission.

Marge Piercy, "Kneeling Here, I Feel Good." Copyright © 1975 by Marge Piercy. Reprinted from *Living in the Open*, by Marge Piercy, by permission of Alfred A. Knopf, Inc.

Virginia Estelle Randolph, "The Jeanes Teachers." Excerpted from *The Jeanes Teacher in the United States, 1908-1923* by Lance G.E. Jones. Copyright © 1937 by The University of North Carolina Press. Used by permission of the publisher.

Anna Moore Shaw, "Pima Past." From *A Pima Past* by Anna Moore Shaw. Copyright © 1974 by University of Arizona Press, Tucson. Reprinted by permission of the publisher.

James E. Sperry, ed., "Buffalo Bird Woman." From "Waheenee: An Indian Girl's Story Told by Herself to Gilbert L. Wilson." Originally published in *North Dakota History*. Copyright © 1971 by State Historical Society of North Dakota. Reprinted with permission.

Elinore Pruitt Stewart, "Homesteading in Wyoming." From *Letters of a Woman Homesteader* by Elinore Pruitt Stewart. Copyright © 1942 by Elinore Pruitt Stewart. Reprinted by permission of Houghton Mifflin Company.

Jeanne Tetrault, "The Next Step: Women-Identified Collectives." Excerpted from an article originally published in *Country Women*. Copyright © 1973 by *Country Women*. Used by permission.

Margaret Walker, "Jubilee." From *Jubilee* by Margaret Walker. Copyright © 1966 by Margaret Walker Alexander. Reprinted by permission of Houghton Mifflin Company.

## Photograph Acknowledgments

**Cover:** Russell Lee, FSA, Library of Congress. **Frontispiece:** Arthur Rothstein, FSA, Library of Congress. **Pages 2-3, 30-31, 64-65:** Library of Congress. **Pages 100-101:** Solomon D. Butcher Collection, Nebraska State Historical Society, Lincoln. **Pages 142-143:** FSA, Library of Congress. **Pages 188-189:** Arthur Rothstein, FSA, Library of Congress. **Pages 248-249:** Dorothea Lange, FSA, Library of Congress. **Pages 252-253:** 1—B.W. Kilburn, Library of Congress. 2—Library of Congress. 3—J.W. Dunn, Library of Congress. 4—Solomon D. Butcher Collection, Nebraska State Historical Society, Lincoln. **Pages 254-255:** 1—Strohmeyer & Wyman. 2—Kauai Museum, Lihue, Hawaii. 3—Nebraska State Historical Society, Lincoln. 4—Harold B. Lee Library, Brigham Young University. **Pages 256-257:** 1, 2, 3—Dorothea Lange, FSA, Library of Congress. 4—Russell Lee, FSA, Library of Congress. 5—Library of Congress. **Pages 258-259:** 1,5—Women's Bureau, U.S. Department of Labor. 2—Library of Congress. 3—Russell Lee, FSA, Library of Congress. 4—Dorothea Lange, FSA, Library of Congress. **Pages 260-261:** 1, 2, 4—Dorothea Lange, FSA, Library of Congress. 3—Jack Delano, FSA, Library of Congress. **Pages 262-263:** 1—Russell Lee, FSA, Library of Congress. 2, 4—Dorothea Lange, FSA, Library of Congress. 3—Arthur Rothstein, FSA, Library of Congress. **Pages 264-265:** 1, 3,—Russell Lee, FSA, Library of Congress. 2—Dorothea Lange, FSA, Library of Congress. 4—Arthur Rothstein, FSA, Library of Congress. **Pages 266-267:** 1, 3—Arthur Rothstein, FSA, Library of Congress. 2—Jack Delano, FSA, Library of Congress 4—Russell Lee, FSA, Library of Congress. **Pages 268-269:** 1—Arthur Rothstein, FSA, Library of Congress. 2, 3—Russell Lee, FSA, Library of Congress. 4—Dorothea Lange, FSA, Library of Congress. **Pages 270-271:** 1—Arthur Rothstein, FSA, Library of Congress. 2—John Collier, FSA, Library of Congress. 3—Sheldon Dick, FSA, Library of Congress. 4—Dorothea Lange, FSA, Library of Congress. **Pages 272-273:** 1, 3, 4—Dorothea Lange, FSA, Library of Congress. 2, 5—John Collier, FSA, Library of Congress. **Pages 274-275:** 1, 4—Russell Lee, FSA, Library of Congress. 2—Jack Delano, FSA, Library of Congress. 3—Marion Wolcott, FSA, Library of Congress. **Pages 276-277:** 1—Arthur Rothstein, FSA, Library of Congress. 2—Twin Oaks Community, Louisa, Virginia. 3—John Collier, FSA, Library of Congress. 4—© 1967 by Susan B. Trowbridge .